Sacred Transgression

Other Works of Interest from St. Augustine's Press

Sacred Transgressions
A Reading of Sophocles' *Antigone*

Seth Benardete

ST. AUGUSTINE'S PRESS
SOUTH BEND, INDIANA

Manufactured in the United States of America.

1 2 3 4 5   21 20 19 18 17 16 15

Library of Congress Cataloging in Publication Data
Benardete, Seth.
Sacred transgressions: a reading of Sophocles' Antigone /
Seth Benardete
p.   cm.
Originally published in three essays in *Interpretation*
Includes bibliographical references.
ISBN: 1-890318-77-9 (cloth: alk. paper)
1. Sophocles. Antigone. 2. Antigone (Greek mythology) in literarture.
3. Tragedy. I. Title
PA4413.A7B46   1998
882'.01–dc21   98-6761
Paper edition: ISBN: 978-1-58731-763-7

∞ The paper used in this publication meets the minimum reqirements of the American National Standard for Information Sciences—Permanence of Paper for Printed Materials, ANSI Z39.48-1984.

ST. AUGUSTINE'S PRESS
www.staugustine.net

CONTENTS

A READING OF SOPHOCLES' *ANTIGONE:* I

1 (1). 1.1.[1] Antigone meets Ismene outside the gates of the royal palace. She usurps for the planning of her crime the place Creon had designated for his own meeting with the elders (33). As they converse without any chance of being overheard (19), they must be imagined to meet in semidarkness, before anyone has set out for work (cf. 253). The Chorus, at any rate, will greet the sun as though it has just come up (100); and it is still early enough for them to convene at the palace without attracting undue notice (164). In this semidarkness Antigone introduces the theme of the play with her manner of addressing Ismene. "Oh my very own sister's common head of Ismene." The "head of Ismene," which "common" characterizes, is not held in common.[2] Antigone appeals to that part of Ismene that most distinguishes her from everyone else (cf. *OC* 320-1, 555-6), and which makes her individually lovable (cf. 764), at the same time that she insists on the togetherness of Ismene and herself. The

---

[1]The text used is Pearson's OCT except where otherwise indicated. I have myself, however, not always accepted his readings wherever I am silent, for if I did not see any connection between the reading chosen and my interpretation of the passage, I have passed over my own preference.

Each line or group of lines interpreted is given a section number, with the line numbers in parentheses after it. Each paragraph of every section is numbered as well for ease of cross-reference.

[2]Nauck recognized the peculiarity of κοινόν but not its significance: only if Ἰσμήνης κάρα were the same as Οἰδίπου τέκνον would κοινόν be in order. In κοινόν lurks the incest of Oedipus; cf. *OT* 261-2, *OC* 533, 535. It is no doubt accidental that the periphrasis 'head of X' occurs only in Sophocles' Oedipus plays (Euripides has it only thrice: *Tr* 661, *Hc* 676-7, *Cy* 438), but it seems more significant that in the vocative the phrase is restricted in classical poetry to *Ant* 1 and *OT* 40 (Oedipus), 950 (Jocasta), 1207 (Oedipus). Eur. *Or* 476 is very different: Ζηνὸς ὁμόλεκτρον κάρα (Tyndarus); cf. *Or* 1380. The normal usage is either the person's name in the vocative followed by "head" with a qualifying adjective or an adjective plus "head" by itself.

link between "head of Ismene" and "common" is supplied by αὐτάδελφον. Antigone recognizes Ismene's head as a sister's head, and not just because she loves some girl called Ismene, no matter what her genealogy, does she address her in this way. Antigone's love for Ismene as a person is mediated through Ismene's kinship with herself; and not only mediated through, but identified with, that kinship; for Ismene's head is αὐτάδελφον, nothing but a sister's. Ismene is herself in being a sister. Only if Ismene acknowledges herself to be nothing but a sister to Antigone and Polynices will Antigone continue to love her. Ismene the individual, with such and such bodily characteristics, is loved because she belongs to the same family as Antigone. Her distinctiveness merely signifies for Antigone her membership in the family that Antigone loves unreservedly. Ismene can, therefore, be readily sacrificed for the sake of her family, particularly as the semidarkness in which she and Antigone meet partly conceals her distinctiveness along with the reasons for it.

1.2. One cannot help wondering, in light of the body, the soul, and the self that necessarily are of importance in a play about burial, whether Antigone's virtual identification of Ismene as her self with Ismene as a relation does not foreshadow Antigone's understanding of what is involved in her burying Polynices.

1.3. Antigone refers twice more to someone's head: Eteocles' and Polynices' (899, 915), each of whom she calls κασίγνητον κάρα. That Eteocles and Polynices are dead in no way changes Antigone's manner of address. Her brothers keep in death their individual lovableness.

1.4. αὐτάδελφος also occurs twice more, once by Antigone (503), and once by Haemon (696), and both times of Antigone's burying of Polynices. The substantival use of αὐτάδελφος indicates that Antigone dared to bury Polynices solely because he was her brother, and that Polynices the enemy of Thebes had no part in her daring (cf. 15.3).

1.5. Words compounded with αὐτ—are particularly frequent in this play:[3] αὐθαδία (1028), αὐτάδελφος, αὐτογέννητος (864), αὐτόγνωτος (875), αὐτοκτονέω (56), αὐτόνομος (821), αὐτόπρεμνος (714), αὐτουργός (52), αὐτόφωρος (51), αὐτόχειρ (306, 900, 1315). Of these Antigone uses three: αὐτάδελφος of her three siblings, αὐτογέννητος of the incest of her mother, and αὐτόχειρ of her performing the funeral rites for her parents and brothers with her own hand.

2 (2-10). 2.1. Antigone's use of a verb of awareness (ὄπωπα) in talking about herself reveals her kinship with her father. She says that there is nothing painful, shameful, or dishonorable that she has not seen. She does not say, as

---

[3]For the meaning of such compounds see F. Sommer, *Zur Geschichte der griechischen Nominalkomposita*, 83–6.

Ismene's phrase (16–7) suggests that she could have, that she has full knowledge of every possible evil and suffers accordingly. She does not speak of suffering (*οὐ πέπονθ'* instead of *οὐκ ὄπωπ'*),[4] If she had, she would have admitted that she shares in Ismene's sorrows, and that her suffering is not just her own. But in spite of *κοινόν* in the first line and her use of the dual for Ismene and herself (*νῷν*), she nevertheless distinguishes between Ismene's evils and her own (*τῶν σῶν τε κἀμῶν*). Their evils are distinct from the start (cf. 31–2).

2.2. Antigone distinguishes between the evils from Oedipus that Zeus has fully brought to completion for Ismene and herself,[5] and those evils set in motion by their enemies (Creon) that are approaching their friends (Polynices).[6] The evils that await Polynices do not belong to Antigone and Ismene, nor is Zeus the cause of them. There cannot be anything painful or disgraceful in Creon's decree, since Zeus failed to inflict no evil that could possibly arise from Oedipus, and Antigone has seen every disgrace and pain there could be as already among the evils that are Ismene's and her own. Antigone's actions, however, evidently belie any separation between Polynices' evils and her own (cf. 48); but she has to admit, even if only tacitly, that there is a difference between them, and that to count Polynices' evils as her own is to enlarge the domain of her own (cf. 238, 437–9).

2.3. Antigone moves in this speech from the evils that because of their single origin in Oedipus belong jointly to Ismene and herself, the still living offspring of Oedipus, to the two sets of evils that she observes as belonging severally to Ismene and herself, and from these to evils (the only *κακά* without

---

[4]Cf. the imitation in Dio Cassius 62.3.2 (cited by Bruhn): *τί μὲν γὰρ οὐ τῶν αἰσχίστων, τί δ' οὐ τῶν ἀλγίστων πεπόνθαμεν*; and *El* 761–3 (*ὧν ὄπωπ' ἐγὼ κακῶν*), where seeing is opposed to hearing.

[5]Boeckh's reason for taking *νῷν ἔτι ζώσαιν* as genitive rather than dative convinces me that it is dative: "denn der Zusatz *ἔτι ζώσαιν* wäre nichtig, weil ihren, waren sie todt, nicht leicht Uebel begegnen konnten" (209); cf. 925–6.

[6]So the scholium; Schneidewin-Nauck, Wolff-Bellermann, Mü(ller; Jebb's interpretation—the enemies are all the Argives left unburied—rests on a misunderstanding of 1080–3 (cf. 55.5). The apparent redundancy of *τῶν ἐχθρῶν κακά*, to which J. H. Kells objects (*BICS* 1963, 40–53), if Antigone means that their enemies inflict evils, is only apparent: Ismene does not know that Creon is their enemy, and Antigone would hardly admit that Zeus is their enemy, despite his having inflicted evils on them. In light, however, of 23 and 79 *τῶν ἐχθρῶν* should not be taken as a generalizing plural, any more than *τοὺς φίλους* in light of 75 and 89 should be taken as referring exclusively to Polynices.

the article) that threaten Polynices. The central κακά, in separating Antigone's and Ismene's evils, points to Antigone's subsequent shaking off of her living connection with Ismene and her joining her fate with the dead Polynices.[7]

2.4. Antigone does not consider Creon's decree as one of the evils that are from Oedipus. (She never again refers to Oedipus by name.) She is not aware of any connection between Polynices' being deprived of burial and his being the son of Oedipus. She is able to keep them apart because she altogether disregards here and throughout the play the war that has just occurred. Her only reference to it is oblique: she calls Creon the general (8). By suppressing any direct mention of the war, she suppresses as well the rivalry of Eteocles and Polynices for the throne of Oedipus. Her silence about the war and the cause of the war thus leads to her silence about three things: that Polynices was killed in the war and did not just die in some miserable way (26); that Polynices attacked and Eteocles defended Thebes; and that Eteocles and Polynices killed one another. We learn of all this from Ismene, the Chorus, or Creon but never from Antigone. Antigone abstracts from everything except the fact that Polynices lies unburied.[8]

3 (11–17). 3.1. Ismene at once thinks of pleasure and happiness as well as of pain and disaster (13, 17). She does not speak of dishonor and shame. Creon, who thinks solely of honor and dishonor (cf. 4.5)—he never uses ἄλγος or any of its derivatives—stands at one extreme, and Ismene, who speaks solely of pleasure and pain, stands at the other, while Antigone, who speaks of and acts on both principles, occupies the center, where pain and pleasure, honor and dishonor, meet.

3.2. In spite of what Antigone says, Ismene does not preclude the possibility of a change for the better in her circumstances. But Antigone cannot conceive, especially with her knowledge of Creon's decree, of an open future. That Ismene and herself are still alive (ἔτι ζώσαιν) does not carry with it any hope.

3.3. Ismene says that she and Antigone have been deprived of their two brothers. They are from now on without any brother (58). To have a brother means to have a living brother (cf. 48.7). Death puts an end to any relationship that obtains on earth.[9] Ismene can only refer to her brothers in the past tense

---

[7]The importance of triads of every kind in Sophocles was cursorily treated by H. St. John Thackeray (*Proc. British Academy* XVI, 1931).

[8]Antigone reports that Creon intends to announce his decree to those who have no knowledge of it (33); she, no more perhaps than those from whom she heard it, has any suspicion of, or any interest in, the political reasons for Creon's convocation of the Chorus.

[9]Cf. Pl. *Lgs.* 959c2–dl.

(55; cf. 1.3). Antigone must remind her that the corpse she is asked to help bury is her brother (not just her brother's), even if she does not wish it to be (43–6).[10]

3.4. στερέω occurs twice more. The Chorus ask Creon whether he will deprive his son of Antigone (574); and Creon says that Antigone will be deprived of her sojourn on earth (890). Death, then, in all three cases, seems to entail an unqualified loss (cf. 575). But Haemon is not totally deprived of his bride; the messenger, at any rate, says that he obtained in Hades' house the marriage rites (1240–1). Haemon's loss is thus (at least metaphorically) qualified. Ismene then might be mistaken as to whether she ceases to have her brothers with their death. The question of body, soul, and self would once again be decisive (cf. 1.2). Antigone's loss, however, of a sojourn on earth is absolute and does not admit of any qualifications (cf. 46.6; 47.4).

4 (21–36). 4.1. Antigone's presentation of Creon's decree must be compared with Creon's own presentation to the Chorus (194–201). Both begin the same way (Ἐτεοκλέα μέν), but after that they diverge. Antigone replaces Creon's explanation for his honoring Eteocles—he died fighting on behalf of his country and proved to be the best warrior—with what she ironically calls Creon's just use of law and justice.[11] She thereby suppresses any mention of the war and the city, about which it would have been difficult to be ironical. Antigone never casts doubt on patriotism. Creon hid Eteocles, she then says, below the earth endowed with honor among the dead below. Creon, however, says that he had ordered Eteocles to be hidden in a grave and sanctified with everything that goes below for the best dead. Antigone disregards all the rites that accord honor to Eteocles among the dead; but Creon connects or confuses, through his mention of the rites, the excellence of Eteocles in war with the excellence of Eteocles among the dead. Antigone must separate the honor of Eteocles among the dead from whatever honor he would have obtained if he had lived; but Creon must hold them together (cf. 209–10). The city must for him keep itself intact below. "Below" therefore cannot be more exactly determined; it is only an extension in depth of Thebes. For Antigone, however, who with Ismene (65) alone specifies that below means below the earth (cf. 26.2), burial means a removal from Thebes and its concerns. The city is restricted to the surface of the earth.

---

[10]Cf. schol. 45: κἂν μὴ προσποιῇ αὐτὸν εἶναι σὸν ἀδελφὸν ἀλλ' ἀλλοτρίοις σαυτὴν τῆς συγγενείας ἐγὼ θάψω τὸν ἐμὸν καὶ σὸν ἀδελφόν.

[11]Line 24 seems to be hopeless; but I should suggest, in light of Thucydides 5.18.4 (δικαίῳ χρῆσθων καὶ ὅρκοις):—χρῆσθων δικαίῳ καὶ νόμῳ— as Antigone's parenthetical comment on ὡς λέγουσι σὺν δίκῃ. For the coordination of δίκαιον (δίκη) and νόμος see the passages collected by R. Hirzel, *Themis, Dike und Verwandtes*, 164 n.1

4.2. The word for the dead below is the plural of the word for corpse, so much is it taken for granted that corpses are buried and so little does the language itself indicate what the condition might be of the buried dead.

4.3. Antigone says that Creon forbade the burial of Polynices' corpse; Creon says that the burial of Polynices is forbidden. Antigone seems to separate Polynices from his corpse; Creon, in order to justify his vindictiveness, seems to identify them; but Antigone speaks of the haplessly dead corpse of Polynices, as though his corpse and not Polynices had suffered and died. It is not enough to say that she speaks by enallage, or that there is a reminiscence of the Homeric expression νεκύων κατατεθνηώτων. If one unscrambles the phrase, the pathos and the point both equally disappear. She does not mean "the corpse of the haplessly killed Polynices," for she is not out to vindicate Polynices' death. Jebb's translation, "the hapless corpse of Polynices" is right, but only if one adds that "hapless" properly refers to the living. Antigone must speak catachrestically, for neither she nor anyone else in the play ever explains why, apart from the law, a corpse must be buried. No one says that there are living souls in Hades (cf. *El* 841, 1418-9), whose admittance there depends on the burial of corpses here.[12] No one speaks of this kind of separation of body and soul (cf. *El.* 245-50). In the absence of any such account, Antigone attributes everything that belongs to Polynices to his corpse. His corpse is in and of itself the object of her care.

4.4. Antigone says καλύψαι, as she had said ἔκρυψε before, and Creon says κτερίζειν, as he had said ἀφαγνίσαι before. Antigone is vague where Creon is precise about the rites to be denied Polynices. She omits those aspects of ritual that are not connected with the mourner's sorrow (cf. 3.1). Both say μήδε (τε) κωκῦσαί τιν α, but whereas Creon says Polynices is to be left unburied, Antigone adds that he is to go unwept. Perhaps Creon omits the prohibition against weeping because, unlike ritual lamentation (κωκῦσαι), it is almost impossible to regulate (cf. H 427; Pl. *Lgs.* 959e7-960a2; Cicero *in Pisonem* 8.18).

4.5. Antigone says the proclamation was made to the townspeople, Creon to this city (cf. 7). It seems to mark a great change in Antigone when she finally calls the Thebans citizens (806, cf. 79, 907, 30.2).

4.6. Antigone says Polynices is to be left for the birds, Creon says for the birds and dogs; and according to the messenger, who is altogether truthful

---

[12]Cf. M. Pohlenz, *Die Griechische Tragödie,* 195. Aeschines, in commenting on the law that absolves a son whose father has sold him for purposes of prostitution from taking care of his father but still enjoins him to bury him with the customary rites, says that this prevents the father from profiting while alive, and when dead, ἡνίκα ὁ μὲν εὐεργετούμενος οὐκ αἰσθάνεται ὧν εὖ πάσχει, τιμᾶται δὲ ὁ νόμος καὶ τὸ θεῖον (1.14).

(1192–3), he was torn apart by dogs alone (1198, cf. 1017, 17.3). Antigone says that Polynices' corpse has been left to be for the birds as a sweet treasure-trove whenever they descry him to feed on at their pleasure.[13] Creon says that the body is to be left to be eaten by birds and dogs and seen disgraced in its mangling. For Creon the seeing is done by men, for Antigone by birds; hence Creon considers the disgrace and Antigone the pleasure. For Creon the eating of Polynices is like the burying of Eteocles: a manner of showing honor or dishonor for what the dead stood for. But for Antigone, who sympathetically enters into the birds' perspective, the eating like the burying is a trait that belongs to the corpse itself. The sweet treasure-trove that is Polynices indicates the preciousness of Polynices even though dead.[14] Antigone can maintain his preciousness because she does not contemplate his consumption. He is an inexhaustible find for the birds. The corpse as corpse does not disgust her (cf. Pl. *Rep.* 439e7–440a, Xen. *Cyrop.* 1.4.24). On her second visit to the putrescent corpse, when the guards have retired to a hilltop to avoid its stench (411–2), she pays no attention to it.

4.7. Nonadverbial χάρις occurs twice more: the guard says he owes much gratitude to the gods for saving his life (331), and Creon asks Antigone how she can honor Polynices with a grace that his brother finds impious (514). The guard's χάρις is in exchange for a favor received, and the favor Antigone renders Polynices is at least partly in exchange for the loving reception she will receive after her death (cf. 9.4); but the favor Polynices' corpse renders the birds is without reciprocity. Perhaps this selfless generosity of Polynices makes Antigone dwell so lovingly upon it, for in revealing a preciousness in his corpse that seems not to be in its nature to have, it cancels out any defects Polynices might have had when alive (cf. 15.3). Antigone might thus regard the burial of Polynices as a way of showing favor to what in itself, even apart from the law, deserves to be favored. She might then come a second time in

---

[13]For the feeling expressed in θησαυρός see Eur. *El.* 565; Pl. *Lgs.* 931a4–5: πατὴρ οὖν ὅτῳ καὶ μήτηρ ἢ τούτων πατέρες ἢ μητέρες ἐν οἰκίᾳ κεῖνται κειμήλιοι ἀπειρηκότες γήρᾳ.

[14]Compare Philoctetes' address to the birds no longer afraid of his bow: ἕρπετε, νῦν καλὸν ἀντίφονον κορέσαι πρὸς χάριν ἐμᾶς αἰόλας (1155–7). καλόν shows that Philoctetes does not wholly regard his own consumption with horror. σαρκὸς αἰόλας is not "discolored flesh" (for which, see E 354) but "gleaming/brilliant flesh"; one is to think of Patroclus' ἀργέτι δημῷ (Λ 818) and Homer's own στήθεσι παμφαίνοντας (Λ 100; cf. E 295; Soph. *Tr* 94–5), which is not merely sardonic (cf. X 73; Tyrt. fr. 7, 21–8). Andromache's lament for Hector—αἰόλοι εὐλαὶ ἔδονται (X 509; cf. M 208)—also contributed to Philoctetes' expression.

order to feed her eyes on the corpse that she thinks of as full of grace (cf. 28.1).

4.8. For Antigone's calling Creon the good Creon, see 17.5.

4.9. Antigone says that the punishment for disobedience is death by public stoning. Creon does not mention the punishment; and indeed Antigone is not punished in that way (cf. 14.1, 43.1).

5 (37–8). 5.1. Antigone lays down a challenge for Ismene, who is to show whether she was born noble or base from noble parents. Antigone disregards the incestuous marriage of her parents. They were noble, and nothing prevents their offspring from being noble; rather, it is to be expected that blood will tell.[15] Not until her own death is very near does Antigone admit that the incest of her parents has been the source of the most painful concern for her (857–66).

6 (39–40). 6.1. Ismene calls Antigone daring (cf. 42, 47). ταλαίφρων occurs twice more, both times in Antigone's mouth of herself (866, 876). She first calls herself ταλαίφρων because she was born from incestuous parents, and then because she is going to her death unwept for, without friends, and unmarried. Her origin and her fate equally constitute her wretchedness. Ismene calls Antigone ταλαίφρων apparently because Antigone seems to believe that in the circumstances there is somehow room for their doing something that would reveal their nobility or baseness. Perhaps she implies as well that there is something strange for the offspring of an incestuous marriage to talk of nobility at all. Whom Antigone came from, what she dares to do, and what she suffers might be all of a piece. Her daring might have the same source as her wretchedness. She might be both daring and wretched by birth.

7 (41–8). 7.1. Antigone asks whether Ismene would help her in lifting up the corpse, plainly to wash and dress it, as would be customary (cf. 1201); but Ismene's refusal to help compels her to abandon the thought of giving Polynices all the rites she gave Eteocles and her parents (901). Her failure, then, to stress the rites in reporting Creon's decree seems to anticipate her failure to perform them.

7.2. Antigone tells Ismene that no prohibition can alter the fact that the corpse is their brother; and that as the corpse does not belong to the city, it cannot be concerned with the prohibition. Despite the special care Creon is taking, so that no one will be uninformed about his decree (31–5), only Antigone and Ismene willy-nilly are involved. If Antigone acts so as not to be convicted of treachery to her own, that cannot make her a traitor to the city.

---

[15]Cf. Xen. *Mem.* 4.4.23: πῶς οὖν, ἔφη ['Ιππίας], κακῶς οὗτοι [γονεῖς καὶ παῖδες] τεκνοποιοῦνται, οὕς γε οὐδὲν κωλύει ἀγαθοὺς αὐτοὺς ὄντας ἐξ ἀγαθῶν τεκνοποιεῖσθαι.;

7.3. Ismene asks Antigone whether Creon's prohibition does not daunt her; and Antigone replies that as Creon has no share in her own, he cannot keep her from her own (cf. 2.2). If Ismene had said, as she does later, that it is a prohibition of the citizens (79), would Antigone have given the same answer? She does not in the dispute that follows argue against Ismene's identification of Creon and the citizens; indeed, she later accepts it (907). Whether the city is competent or not to determine who should receive burial proves not to be the issue between the two sisters.

8 (49-68). 8.1. Ismene's speech is in three parts. The first gives an account of the fate of their father, mother, and brothers (49-57); the second matches that triad with three reasons for certain failure if they go against Creon's decree (58-64); and the third gives the conclusion that Ismene has drawn for herself (65-8). What holds the three parts together is Ismene's triple appeal to reasonableness and prudence: φρόνησον (49), ἐννοεῖν χρή (61), οὐκ ἔχει νοῦν οὐδένα (68). Her central thought, and what occupies the center of her speech, is that she and Antigone are the sole survivors of their family (cf. 548, 566). They alone can continue it. Antigone starts from the same premise but concludes differently. As they are the only living members of their family (3, cf. 3.2), they must join them. Ismene sees the family as a succession of generations—it is she who first mentions Haemon (568). Antigone sees their copresence in Hades (73-76; cf. 892-94, 897-99). Oedipus' confusion of generations (53), so that succession is replaced by togetherness, finds its proper extension in Antigone's refusal to think of any future apart from the dead. Her name, whose meaning—"generated in place of another"—bears witness to succession,[16] proves to mean antigeneration.

8.2. Oedipus' self-discovery of, and self-punishment for, his crimes, Jocasta's suicide by hanging, and their sons' mutual fratricide are balanced in the play by Creon's acknowledgment of his crime, Eurydice's suicide, and Haemon's. The figure that links the two groups is Antigone, whose suicide by hanging recalls her mother's, occasions those of Haemon and Eurydice, and brings home to Creon his crime.

8.3. The only historical present Ismene employs in this speech is to describe Jocasta's suicide: Jocasta "treats life in a despiteful way." Her outrage against life was due perhaps to a revulsion against generation. Her daughter, at any rate, embodies such a revulsion (cf. 50.3).

8.4. Ismene gives a threefold account of what their transgression would consist in if they buried Polynices: "if we despite the law shall transgress the decree or powerful authority of tyrants."[17] Law, decree, and power seem to

---

[16]Cf. Wilamowitz, *Aischylos Interpretationem*, 92 n.3.

[17]Schneidewin as an alternative gives the correct interpretation of the ἤ: "Doch kann Ismene auch meinen, nenn du es ψῆφος oder κράτη,

be identified. The confusion of law and decree tends to be a democratic assumption (cf. Th. 3.37.3–4; Arist. *Pol.* 1292a4–37);[18] but the confusion of law and power is tyrannical. If, however, one follows Plato's Thrasymachus, the identification of all three is a necessary consequence of asserting that justice is the advantage of the stronger. That Ismene is indifferent to the differences among them shows that she has no illusions about the foundations of the city.

8.5. There are two other reasons that, according to Ismene, should give Antigone pause. The first is that they were born women and hence are not fit to fight men; and the second is that they are ruled by those who are stronger, who may cause them to submit to still more painful things. Ismene does not reckon Creon's decree as the most painful thing. Exile, slavery, or death, if imposed without their committing any crime, might be more painful. Their future can be better or worse (cf. 3.2).

8.6. Antigone sets herself in opposition to Ismene's understanding of law, nature, and strength. Against the city's law she pleads a higher law; she shows herself, though not perhaps in Ismene's sense, as strong as or stronger than Creon; and as to her being by nature a woman she is eloquently silent. She never uses the word γυνή, though it occurs eighteen times in the play, nor any of the following cognate words (whose frequencies are shown in parenthesis): γένος (7), γίγνομαι (6), γενεά (3), γονή (3), γέννημα (2), γόνος (2), γένεθλον (1). Only thrice does she use words compounded with the root γεν-- εὐγενής—the nobility to be tested of Ismene (38), αὐτογέννητος—the incest of her mother (864), and προγενής—the gods who are her ancestors (938). Between divine birth in the distant past and possible proof of being well-born in the immediate future lies the marriage of her mother with him to whom she had given birth. The suppression of that link between the future and the past is Antigone's own name and nature as antigeneration, out of which comes the paradoxical ground of her actions. She as fully acknowledges consanguinity as she denies generation (cf. 1.1).[19]

8.7. Ismene is not impressed by the need to bury Polynices; for she believes that those beneath the earth will grant her pardon if, when she asks them, she cites the triple constraint of law, nature, and strength (cf. Th.

---

gesetzmässige Verordnung oder Gebot des Machthabers."

[18]Cf. K. J. Dover, *JHS* 1955, 17–20.

[19]The strongest evidence of the genuineness of the ending of Aeschylus' *Septem* (at least most of it) is the contrast between the Chorus of maidens and Antigone and Ismene as mature women; for Sophocles' invention mainly consists in unsexing Antigone and giving her the attributes of Aeschylus' Eteocles; see pp. 144–151 S. Benardete, *Wiener Studien* 1967, 22–30.

4.98.6). Ismene does not expect her argument to soften Antigone, but she does expect it to soften τοὺς ὑπὸ χθονός. Her appeal over the head of Antigone's intransigence to Polynices and the nether gods forces Antigone to give the first of her three major defenses (69–77, 450–70, 905–15). If the obligation to bury one's own is not absolute, Antigone is planning to do what is superfluous (περισσὰ πράσσειν).

9 (69–77). 9.1. Antigone begins very severely. She will no longer accept Ismene's help should Ismene later change her mind. If remorse overtakes her, Antigone will not grant her pardon. We do not know as yet whether Antigone's denial of repentance has the gods' sanction; but that Creon's remorse, which follows so quickly on his reiteration of his intransigence, does not alter the truth of Tiresias' prophecy, would seem to confirm Antigone's rejection of Ismene. One apparent defect in the plot of *Antigone,* that if Creon had submitted at once to Tiresias, the suicides of Antigone, Haemon, and Eurydice would have been averted, seems in fact to argue for the gods' agreement with Antigone. As soon as Creon issues his decree he already is too late. The irrelevance of time makes known the eternal presence of the gods.

9.2. A story in Herodotus illustrates this (6.86). A Milesian who had heard of the justice of a Spartan and knew the stability of his country requested that he hold in safekeeping one-half of his wealth; but when the Milesians' sons came much later to ask for the sum deposited, the Spartan denied that he had it; he decided, however, to ask the Delphic oracle what he should do, and the oracle threatened the complete disappearance of his race; whereupon the Spartan begged the god for pardon, to which the oracle replied: "To make trial of the god and to act are equivalent" (ἡ δὲ Πυθίη ἔφη τὸ πειραθῆναι τοῦ θεοῦ καὶ τὸ ποιῆσαι ἴσον δύνασθαι). If the story seems to explain the inevitability of Creon's punishment, it still remains doubtful whether Antigone justly extends the principle to include Ismene, whose constrained failure to comply with divine law is not the same as Creon's willful obstruction of it. This doubt is the first indication we have that Ismene stands next to Antigone as the most important figure in the play. That Antigone in her last speech tacitly denies her very existence only stresses her importance (941, cf. 599–600).

9.3. Antigone invokes the noble (καλόν), the dear (φίλον) and the holy (ὅσιον) in her defense. Antigone does not say that once she has buried Polynices it is fair and noble for her to die or be killed, but that it is fair or noble in doing it (τοῦτο ποιούσῃ) to die. Antigone borrows the language appropriate to the patriotic soldier whose dying on behalf of his country coincides with his fighting (cf. 194–5; *Ai.* 1310–12). With her task accomplished, it may be good, or as she later says, gainful, for her to die (461–4); but for it to be noble, there must be a necessary connection between the burial of one's own and one's own death. Antigone must imagine her act of burying as an act of fighting. What shows that she does so is her saying ὅσια πανουργήσασα.

To do the holy things (ὅσια δρᾶν) means to avoid committing any offense against the holy things—not to profane a holy place, for example; it does not mean to go out of one's way to perform some pious deed (cf. 256, 1349).[20] It is not enough, then, to translate Antigone's phrase paradoxically as "by my criminal piety," but one must be even more literal: "having stopped at nothing in the performance of holy things" (cf. 300-1). Antigone thus transforms the ordinariness of burying into something much more akin to the risking of one's life in battle. Creon surely makes that transformation possible; but one wonders whether Antigone does not need Creon in order to be what she is.

9.4. It is not easy to say how Antigone understands the connection between her saying that it is noble to die in this way and that she will lie dear with him who is dear. Does this mutual dearness follow from the nobility of her death, her death simply, or her piety? Antigone seems to supply the missing connection herself: "since it is for a longer time that I must please those below than those here, for there I shall always lie." The supposed connection, however, makes for a new perplexity.[21] Antigone does not say that she must please those below because her act of piety will please them forever, but because she will lie with them forever. She combines the pious proposition that she please those below more because what they demand is holy with the hope that she will be in loving communion with them for a longer time. She omits from the pious proposition "more because what they demand is holy," and replaces it by "for a longer time" that properly belongs to her hope. The holy thus turns into a means for making herself dear; but it can only be such a means through Creon's decree. Creon is essential to Antigone's obtaining something for herself in nobly devoting herself to another. The holy entirely resolves the usual tension between the noble and the dear.

9.5. The word φίλος is ambiguous.[22] It can mean dear as a friend is dear, or it can mean dear as one's own is dear. Antigone seems here to use the word in both meanings at once. She will lie with those who love her through what she does for them, and she will lie with those who already love her. She must first, to rejoin her own, acquire them as friends. Antigone proves her

---

[20]Cf. E. Fraenkel, *Ag.*, vol. 2, 355; K. Latte, *Kleine Schriften*, 337. For the difference between Antigone's phrase and ὅσια δρᾶν, see Thucydides 1.71.1, where the Corinthians distinguish the performance of justice from the abstention from hurting others; such a distinction does not normally exist in sacred matters; cf. Xen. *Mem.* 4.4.11.

[21]Cf. R. E. Wycherly, *CP* 1947, 51-2.

[22]On its Homeric usage see E. Benveniste, *Le vocabulaire des institutions i-e,* vol. I, 335-53; but his assertion that φίλος never means one's own cannot be taken as certain: πάτερ is modified by φίλε but μῆτερ by ἐμή.

right to be by deed what she already is by birth. She reconstitutes the family as something into which one freely enters. The love of her own almost becomes a matter of choice. It is this to which Antigone partly owes her awesome uncanniness (376).

9.6. Antigone's κείσομαι is as extraordinary as her ὅσια πανουργήσασα. She will not live but lie with Polynices; and "lie" suggests "lie dead and buried." Antigone's imagination does not go beyond the grave (cf. 4.2). She does not animate the dead, but thinks of their state as no different from corpses (cf. 4.3). If, however, one transposes the relation between Antigone and Polynices into a living one, Antigone then seems to be speaking the language of lovers: "I shall lie asleep, dear as I shall be, with him who is dear to me" (cf. Aesch. *Ch.* 894–5). Perhaps neither of these extremes exactly defines the way in which Antigone herself understands what she says, but it cannot be accidental that in her case the language of incest should coincide with the language of the grave.

9.7. Antigone mentions the gods last (Ismene never does) and the things they hold in honor. The noble, the dear, and the holy probably make up together τὰ τῶν θεῶν ἔντιμα; but if they are severally assigned to men, the dead, and the gods, one could say that Antigone's nobility draws the eyes of men (cf. 502–4), her dearness elicits the love of the dead, and her piety is confirmed by the gods' refusal to accept Creon's remorse. Punishment of the impious is the gods' reward for piety (cf. 927–8).

9.8. In Plato's *Euthyphro,* Socrates forced Euthyphro to choose between saying that the holy is holy because the gods love it, with the consequence that the holy loses its unity in the gods' contradictory affections, or that the gods love the holy because it is holy, with the consequence that the gods are dispensable guides for understanding what it is. Now in trying to understand Antigone we seem to be caught in a similar perplexity. Is it because the holy is holy that Antigone does what it commands, or because the holy just happens to be in accordance with what she wants to do that it looks as if she is obeying what it commands? We surely are not now in a position to justify our choosing either answer; but the parallel with *Euthyphro* indicates why in part Socrates and Euthyphro cannot arrive at a satisfactory definition of the holy. The dialogue wholly fails to consider the relation of the holy to the soul: ψυχή never occurs.[23] *Antigone,* on the other hand, is concerned with almost no other question. *Antigone* supplies what Plato thought it best to omit, and even perhaps in a way that Plato did mostly approve. Plato, indeed, may have omitted what he recognized the tragic poet alone could supply.

9.9. In the *Philebus,* Socrates lists seven occasions on which the soul by itself experiences a mixture of pleasure and pain: ὀργή, φόβος, πόθος, θρῆνος,

---

[23]I owe this insight to Professor Leo Strauss.

ἔρως, ζῆλος, φθόνος (47e1-2). Were it not for the central *thrēnos* we should be inclined to call them all passions or affections of the soul. *Thrēnos,* however, is not an affection but the expression of an affection of the soul. It is, strictly speaking, the Greek equivalent to a dirge and, more generally, any kind of lamentation.[24] In its general sense it can accompany any of the affections that Socrates lists; indeed, according to Socrates, comedy too is a kind of *thrēnos* (50b1-3, c5). In its strict sense, however, a *thrēnos* is the artful and conventional expression in song of the sorrow one has at a funeral; but no word in Greek or any other language that I know of names the unexpressed sorrow one has in the presence of death. That mourning for the dead is primarily the expression of that mourning (πένθος), that its expression is primarily artful and conventional,[25] and that the occasion of its expression is primarily at a funeral all point to the possibility that certain aspects of the soul are necessarily and essentially linked with poetry and convention. As these aspects only come to light in poetry and convention, to divorce them from poetry and convention is to destroy them. And yet to leave them in (and to) poetry and convention veils the seeing of them as they are in themselves. Only a very artful poet could, without destroying them, reveal them as they are in themselves.[26]

10 (78-99). 10.1. The thirteen speeches that follow are mainly concerned with the feasibility of Antigone's plan. Ismene says that she is by nature incapable of acting against the citizens, but that this does not imply that she holds in contempt τὰ τῶν θεῶν ἔντιμα. Her submission to Creon is not based on any agreement with Creon; as far as her intention goes, she is on Antigone's side. According to Antigone, however, Ismene puts forward her natural inability in order to conceal her contempt for what the gods hold honorable. She herself will proceed to heap up a tomb for her dearest brother. Antigone's language far outpaces her ability. The guard reports that the ground around Polynices' corpse was unbroken (249-50); and the tumulus that Creon later has raised for Polynices is the work of many men (1203-4). Antigone might then be using loosely one of the many ways of saying that she will bury Polynices; but the intensity of her desire to carry out her conventional duty tends to restore to the casual usage of everyday its full meaning (cf. 9.6). If she cannot in fact do what she plans to do, her ability is no greater than Ismene's, and she must be judged solely on intention. It is unclear, moreover, whether she succeeds in

---

[24]Cf. E. Reiner, *Die Rituelle Totenklage der Griechen,* 4-5.

[25]Cf., e.g., Aeschines 3.77: πρὶν πενθῆσαι καὶ τὰ νομιζόμενα ποιῆσαι.

[26]It is revealing that Plato has his Athenian Stranger use the example of burial in order to illustrate the advantage a poet claims to have over a legislator in contradicting himself (cf. *Lgs.* 719b12-e5).

even a minimal way in burying Polynices. If she did not finish the rites on her first attempt, she is prevented by the guards from doing so on the second; and if she did finish them on her first attempt, it is hard to understand why she returned (cf. 25.4). There is a further difficulty. If the guards in sweeping away the dust she had sprinkled on Polynices' corpse nullify her act of burial, as the need to bury him again implies, one must strictly say that Antigone's plan fails. Ismene, then, would rightly insist on their own weakness. If those below look to intention and not to accomplishment (cf. 9.1, 9.2), Ismene would be guaranteed as loving a reception as Antigone. Only if they demand that one attempt to do the impossible would she be inferior in their eyes to Antigone.

10.2. There is a still more terrible possibility: that those below will not even take into account Antigone's daring but will condemn her along with Ismene for her failure. This possibility depends on how one understands the Athenians' condemnation of their generals for failing to pick up the corpses after the battle of Arginusae. Although the Athenians later repented of their decision, one wonders why the generals' defense did not at once convince them: that the onset of a storm foiled their attempt; or, as their advocate puts it, incapacity does not argue for treachery (Xen. *Hell.* 1.7.33). What made them go against their own law, which laid it down that the accused should be tried individually? If intention, then, does not suffice, and incapacity is not a plausible excuse when one is dealing with holy things, but only the strictest conformity to the law is innocence, Antigone's superiority to Ismene would lack divine sanction. It would be closer to madness.

10.3. In *Oedipus at Colonus,* Oedipus profanes the sanctuary of the Eumenides; and after Theseus grants him Athens' protection, the Chorus ask that Oedipus purify himself for his violation. When the Chorus have carefully explained the ceremony, Oedipus turns to his two daughters and asks one of them to do it for him, since his lameness and blindness prevent him: "For I believe one soul is enough, if it be gracious there, to pay this debt even for ten thousand" (498–9). Ismene assumes the task and leaves; and the next thing we hear about her is that Creon's men have captured her (818–9). One may wonder then whether Ismene ever did get to purify her father. If one grants that she may not have, and discards the possibility of Oedipus' remaining to the end unpurified, Oedipus' intention to be purified would be equivalent to his purification. If such be the case, Ismene again would merit as much praise for holiness as Antigone. The extremes of Arginusae and *Oedipus at Colonus* show, if nothing else, how hard it is to understand what holds together the nobility and the piety of Antigone.

10.4. Ismene is afraid for Antigone, a fear that Antigone takes to be Ismene's fear for herself and the truth of her natural inability to act despite the citizens. She bids Ismene to keep upright her own fate. πότμος is usually not thought of as something over which mortals have control (cf. fr. 871), nor is it usual for it, without a qualifying adjective (cf. *Tr.* 88), to lose its ordinary sense of evil destiny or death; indeed, neither usage seems to occur anywhere else in the tragedians.[27] Antigone uses πότμος twice more, once of the destiny that attends the house of Labdacus (860), and once of her own death for which no friend mourns (881). Antigone, then, might be doing more than taunting Ismene for her cowardice. Ismene need not fear for Antigone because her deed and its consequences are her fate and nothing can alter it (cf. 235-6); and Ismene is blind if she supposes that her fate is under her own control and not simply a part of the doom inherent in her family. If the first of these implications holds, Antigone would seemingly be choosing her own fate (cf. 9.5); and if the second holds, Antigone would here betray her awareness that what she plans, does, and suffers is bound up with who she is and whence she came (cf. 5.1).

10.5. Ismene begs Antigone not to tell anyone of her plan; and that she herself will do likewise, will show Antigone, she hopes, that she is willing to do as much as she can to further her plan; but Antigone scorns this counsel of prudence and bids her to denounce her to everyone. Antigone, then, does not have a plan; she only has an intention. Had Ismene taken her at her word, Antigone would have failed at her first attempt. She would not have done anything for Polynices. Antigone seems to regard it as essential that she be caught and as inessential that she succeed. One thus begins to understand what she meant by saying that for her to die in burying Polynices, or rather, as we must now translate, in trying to bury him, is noble (cf. 9.3). That she will stop at nothing does not entail for her the use of craft. Even so, Antigone easily gets away with it, which cannot but amaze us, especially after hearing of Creon's preparations and listening to Ismene's plausible demurral.

10.6. Antigone's indifference to getting caught provokes Ismene into saying that she has a hot heart for cold things. In the context of the play, and in light of Odysseus' pun on ψυχή and ψῦχος (κ 555), one cannot help but understand Ismene as saying that Antigone shows all the artless intensity of life itself in her devotion to the heartless coldness of the law about corpses and "dead souls" (cf. *OC* 621-2).[28] Ismene now realizes that Antigone is not just fulfilling the requirements of a law, compliance with which, she might well think, does not have to dispense with cunning (cf. Her. 2.121ε2). A cool head may strictly preclude a pious heart, but it surely does not check one from the performance of a holy rite. Antigone's reply as much as admits (ἀλλ') the dis-

---

[27] Pindar, however, has several instances of neutral πότμος, but none where it is even remotely under one's own control.

[28] On the ellipse with ψυχροῖσι, see A. D. Knox, *CQ* 1931, 208.

crepancy between the subjective heat in her concern and its objective coldness; but she reconciles them by saying that she knows she is pleasing to those whom she most of all must please. Her gratifying of the dead mediates between the law and her passion, for the law seems to be the formulation of the duties of familial love. If one looks to the beneficiaries of the law, its coldness vanishes in their warmth.

10.7. Antigone says that she knows she is pleasing, not that she will be pleasing, to the dead. For the first time she uses the present tense in speaking of how the dead will regard her. Her use of the present tense can be understood in two ways: either her intention by itself, regardless of its accomplishment, is enough to please the dead, or, as Ismene takes it, the present tense reflects the vividness of Antigone's desire, for, as nothing can possibly frustrate her (πανουργήσασα), she imagines the deed already done. Ismene now thinks that the accomplishment alone can warrant Antigone's confidence in her pleasing the dead; and that depends on her ability, which is so much less than what is needed that only Antigone's love of the impossible can explain her readiness to try at all. Antigone does not deny the charge; she merely says that her efforts will come to an end whenever she loses her strength. Antigone seems to maintain that the attempt is all-important, and that she does not expect to succeed. Ismene then points to the utter unseemliness of hunting out the impossible; and at this suggestion that what she is doing is ignoble, Antigone turns vindictive: Ismene is certain to earn the immediate hatred of Antigone and the lasting hatred of Polynices. The reward for Antigone's attempt and the punishment for Ismene's abstention equally depend on the same principle: those below love or hate in accordance with one's willingness to go after the impossible. In loving those who try and fail, they love those who deliberately seek their own death. Ismene's natural inability to commit suicide justifies her punishment.

10.8. Words with the stem μηχαν- occur seven times, used thrice by Ismene, thrice by the Chorus, and once, between the two triads, by Creon. Ismene says that (1) she is naturally without a μηχανή to act despite the citizens (79), (2) Antigone is in love with things that have no μηχανή (92), (3) it is unseemly to hunt out things that have no μηχανή (92); the Chorus say that (1) man prevails over the mountain-ranging beast by μηχαναί (349), (2) man contrives his escape from diseases that have no μηχανή (363), (3) man has in the μηχαναί of his art something wise beyond hope (365); and Creon says that there is no μηχανή for knowing a man's ψυχή, φρόνημα, and γνώμη before he is tested in public affairs (175). Ismene's triad of impossibles is matched by the Chorus' triad of possibles, for their "device-less diseases" means "seemingly device-less diseases." The one strictly device-less occasion that confronts man is death (361–2). Antigone's love, then, of the impossible is her love of death (cf. 220). Her hot heart for cold things is precisely this ἔρως τοῦ θανεῖν; and this ἔρως, in turn, spells out one consequence of the antigeneration of her name.

10.9. Antigone in her love of the impossible and man in his overcoming of the impossible seem to refute Creon's assertion of the impossibility of knowing a man's soul, temper, and judgment apart from the exercise of political rule; but if one takes him to mean by extension that only in confrontation with the city can man be known, Antigone's artless defiance of the city and artful man's neutrality to the city (365–70) suggest that Creon correctly understands the city as the indispensable touchstone of man. The city somehow stands between the daring for which only death is a limit and the daring for which only death is its goal. If, moreover, Antigone's love of the impossible does not just accidentally express itself in an unrealizable attempt to obey the divine law, but there is some connection between them, the city would stand between the human that defies the impossible in one sense and the divine that demands the impossible in another. The city would owe both its existence and the precariousness of its existence to the impossible demanded by the gods and the impossible defied by man as man. As the city cannot be without both of these impossibles, so it cannot submit itself entirely to either of them. Antigone thus seems to be defending unreservedly one basis of the city that the city itself cannot afford to defend unreservedly.

10.10. In saying that she will not suffer anything as terrible as an ignoble death, Antigone comes close to forgetting her intention, for she implies without knowing it that the most terrible thing she could suffer would not be Polynices' lack of burial (cf. 2.2, 8.5). She transfers the nobility of her action to the nobility of her death, as if only her death could testify to the nobility of her action (cf. 9.3). By ignoring Ismene's suggestion that she practice a minimum of guile (if guile is not too strong a word for it), Antigone blurs the issue between them. The alternative to a noble death is not an ignoble death but life (cf. 555); and life in one of two ways: either to abandon her intention entirely and ignobly live on, or make an attempt in such a way as not to get caught. Antigone rejects both ways, but she ironically calls the rejection of the first way her δυσβουλία when it applies without any irony to her rejection of the second. Her lack of any plan guarantees her death even if it also guarantees her failure to carry out her intention.

10.11. Of the seven occurrences of πάσχειν, five are in the mouth of Antigone (96 bis, 236 [guard], 926, 928, 942, 995 [Creon]). She begins by ordering Ismene to let her suffer "this terrible thing," and she ends by ordering the Chorus to see what she, who reverenced piety, suffers at the hands of what sort of men. Her scorn of suffering finally gives way to her indignation at her suffering. With παθεῖν τὸ δεινὸν τοῦτο she ironically refers to her noble death (καλῶς παθεῖν); but if she can later be indignant at her suffering, its literal meaning must be the truth. καλῶς θανεῖν is not the equivalent of παθεῖν τὸ δεινὸν τοῦτο, for death in itself does not admit of nobility, any more than nobility can be of any account (as Antigone knows and Creon does not) when one is dead (cf. 4.1). One can show nobility in the action that precipitates one's death, or if the action accompanies it, even in the dying itself (cf. 9.3), but not otherwise (cf. Plato *Phaedo* 118a6–12). Because Antigone pretends that her action and her death will be simultaneous, she can now hide from herself the knowledge of what it means for her to die (cf. 36). Her passionate obedience to the law about burial, which is in keeping with her vivid awareness of what it means to be dead (cf. 4.5), perhaps even thrives on this self-delusion.

10.12. Ismene ends the stichomythia in the same way that Antigone had introduced it. Her ἀλλ᾽ εἰ δοκεῖ σοι echoes Antigone's σοὶ δ᾽ εἰ δοκεῖ (76); but whereas Antigone's apodosis accused Ismene of dishonoring what the gods hold in honor, Ismene's apodosis tells Antigone to proceed, secure in the knowledge that she is dear to her friends (Polynices, herself, and their whole family). Ismene thus separates what Antigone must hold together. Ismene sees no connection between the dearness and the piety of Antigone (cf. 10.3), for she does not think that madness can fit with piety, however painfully it can with dearness. She seems to forget that there is such a thing as divine madness.

11 (100–61). 11.1. The old men who make up the Chorus are the measure of Antigone's peculiar greatness, for she is the only suffering heroine in extant Greek tragedy who does not have a Chorus of women to console her. Ismene is a token of what such a Chorus would be like; hence it is plain before the Chorus enter that Antigone does not need the kind of consolation that only women could give. *Antigone* alone of Sophocles' extant plays lacks the vocative plural of φίλος (cf. 45.1).

11.2. As a hymn of patriotic thanksgiving the parodos could not be bettered; and the same appropriateness holds true for all that the Chorus sing. Man's skillful daring, Antigone's fatal madness, Love's power, Antigone's predecessors in suffering, Dionysus' invocation, to each of these themes the Chorus give the perfect expression. Their individual perfection is partly due to the Chorus' refusal to compromise with each theme. Each is in turn the whole truth; none is put within a horizon larger than itself. While the Chorus are thus as extreme in each case as Antigone or Creon consistently is, their continual shift in perspective makes them far more moderate than either can be. Their moderation does not arise from the steadiness with which they adhere to sober views, but exactly the contrary. The Chorus effortlessly move from the unlimited power to man (first stasimon) to the unlimited power of Eros (third stasimon), for they are totally persuaded of each at the moment, and they never give any thought to their reconciliation. Adaptability, in which moderation to a large extent consists, has never perhaps been so brilliantly parodied. The last words of the play, that moderation is the major component in happiness, are as true as they are empty in the mouth of the Chorus (cf. 65.1). The Chorus' lack of solidity, then, which paradoxically allows them to speak profoundly but thoughtlessly, makes it the right Chorus for Antigone, whose speeches accurately reflect her soul. The law Antigone obeys shines through Antigone. That her hot heart for cold things is not an accidental conjunction, the Chorus can never understand.

11.3. The threefold mention of Thebes (compare the threefold mention of her gates and of γῆ) holds the parodos together: Thebes for which the sun has never shone more beautifully (102), Thebes joyous in answer to the joyful presence of Victory (149), and Thebes the all-night celebrant whose ruler will be Dionysus (153). The parodos moves from the night whose terrors the sun (note the threefold φανέν, φάος, ἐφάνθης) has dispelled to the night that promises forgetfulness of them. As the first strophe thus corresponds to the last antistrophe, so the first of the anapaestic systems, which refers to Polynices, his quarrel with Eteocles, and his marshaled army, corresponds to the third, which describes the Argive panoplies left behind and the death of the two brothers; and the first antistrophe, which mentions Hephaestus and Ares, corresponds to the second strophe, which describes πυρφόρος Capaneus and Ares. The second anapaestic system, which is the center of the parodos' seven parts, is devoted to Zeus, whose lightning punishes the overboastful (cf. 1350–3). Within this "ring-composition" the parodos also moves from the war itself, over which the gods Hephaestus, Ares, and Zeus preside, to the victory and its aftermath, which the gods Zeus, Nike, and Bacchios determine, with Ἄρης δεξιόσειρος effecting the transition from the first triad to the second. The first triad of Hephaestus, the fire of the enemy's torches, Ares, the clatter of the enemy's army in retreat, and Zeus the hurler of lightning against Capaneus, seems to receive in the second triad their equivalents for triumphant Thebes. The dancing Bacchios ἐλελίχθων is to lead replaces the thud of βακχεύων Capaneus' fall (ἀντιτύπᾳ γᾷ); the renown Victory μεγαλώνυμος brings replaces the πάταγος Ἄρεος, and the trophy of brazen armor dedicated to Zeus the god of rout replaces the fire of Hephaestus, who is now to be thought of as χαλκεύς (cf. 52.4).

11.4. The parodos' movement from ἀκτὶς ἀελίου to χοροῖς παννυχίοις and ἐλελίχθων Βάκχιος parallels the movement of the play as a whole: from the time just before dawn to dawn (cf. 1.1), to high noon, when a sudden dust storm heralds Antigone's return to Polynices' corpse (416), to Antigone's departure from the light of the sun (808, 879),[29] to the Chorus' invocation of Dionysus as choregus of the fire-breathing stars, in whose honor the frenzied Thyiads dance all night (1146–54). The Chorus seem to sense from the start

---

[29]FThe metrical shape of 808–9 is the same as 100–2.

the way in which the day will unfold; but they owe this prescience entirely to their absorption in the demands of the moment and not to any insight into the nature of things. They say everything in one way or another that has to be said about *Antigone,* even to the point of duplicating here the rhythm of the play, but they never understand anything of what they say. They are the mouthpiece of wisdom without being wise themselves. They thus allow Sophocles to be always invisible while being always present. If Antigone finally becomes entirely transparent, so that she can be read off as easily from her surface as from her depths (the first indication of which is the meaning of her name), Sophocles, on the other hand, remains throughout opaque, since every manifestation of his wisdom is cut off from its source. Perhaps, then, the ultimate conflict does not consist in that between Antigone and Creon, or even between the family and the city, but between Antigone and Sophocles, of whom one is always what she shows herself to be, and the other is never what he shows himself to be (cf. 37.5).

11.5 The parodos has one trait of the kind one usually calls poetic that shows the Chorus' astonishing virtuosity. It characterizes in eleven different ways the eleven different beings to which a noncollective proper name is or can be given. It seems to display every possible degree or mode of animation. (1) The sun hovers between being a signal for the Argives' flight and the cause of their flight: it is seen, sees, moves, and sets in motion; (2) Polynices becomes so fused with the metaphor of an eagle that the same sentence attributes to him what can only belong to the eagle; (3) Hephaestus seems to be nothing but a name for fire (cf. 1007, 1126); (4) Ares, however, is slightly more than the clatter of war, for πάταγος Ἄρεος is in apposition to ἀντιπάλου δυςχείρωμα δράκοντος ("not an overcoming of its opponent the serpent"),[30] which through the story of the serpent's teeth (cf. 1124–5) galvanizes Ares into a higher degree of life than a personification can ever have; (5) Zeus is a fully living anthropomorphic god: he hates, hears, sees, and strikes down the wicked; (6) the anonymous Capaneus is something more than human: he is divinely inspired (βακχεύων) as he blows blasting winds of hatred against Thebes; (7) Ares like Polynices is fused with the metaphor of a trace horse, which in turn is fused with that of a charioteer and warrior, as though Ares were the moving spirit of πολυάρματος Thebes (149); (8) Zeus who turns the tide of battle is the god whom one honors with trophies; (9) the miserable Polynices and Eteocles are entirely human, born from the same father and mother and sharing a common death; (10) Nike brings, feels, and shows her feelings of joy; (11) Bacchios who shakes the earth is the god to whom one prays to be present at the night-long dances. It is extremely difficult

---

[30]On χείρωμα see E. Fraenkel, *Ag.* 1326; here, Müller.

to arrange this series on any scale of being, for one does not know on what principle the scale should be based. If, however, one dares to test them against the consistently literal, the degree, that is, to which the Chorus themselves might subscribe to a literal reading of their language, the Chorus would admit perhaps that Polynices and Eteocles (9) are farthest removed from Polynices the eagle (2); the clatter of Ares (4) from Ares the trace horse, warrior, and charioteer (7); Zeus the god of rout (8) from Zeus the god of just punishment (5); Bacchic Capaneus (6) from Bacchios himself (11); piney Hephaestus (3) from the eye of the golden day (1), and the victory Capaneus strives to announce (133) from Nike who rejoices in the joy of Thebes (10). Now in a play whose unstated issue turns on the being of a corpse (cf. 4.3, 9.6), it cannot but be relevant that we are presented at the start with such a variety of ways of being alive, from the poetic Polynices to the prosaic Polynices and Eteocles (with many shades between), especially if one recalls Antigone's ἡ δ' ἐμὴ ψυχὴ πάλαι τέθνηκεν (559–60), which plainly upsets any ordinary understanding of life and death (cf. 44.2).[31]

11.6. To the Chorus Eteocles is politically negligible, so much so that they only refer to him anonymously, without even etymologizing his name (cf. Aesch. *Septem* 829–31), and who along with his brother is pitiable (στυγεροῖν) and nothing more; he surely does not seem to be one who, as Creon thinks, deserved the *aristeia* (cf. 4.1). The Chorus, indeed, never allude to Eteocles again, any more then they do to Polynices, neither of whom holds any interest for them, once they cannot be the immediate cause of anything. Now that they are dead they are nothing (cf. 3.2). The Chorus therefore do not speak here of Eteocles as the former ruler of Thebes; Creon is now the king, and their concern is only for what he will devise for the new situation (155–61). That Creon deliberately convoked them because he knew of their loyalty to the house of Laius (164–9) makes their silence all the stranger. What, however, somewhat accounts for their silence about Eteocles' *aristeia,* if not for their silence about his rule, is that they ascribe the triumph of Thebes entirely to the gods.[32] Human excellence has no place where Zeus and Ares directly participate in battle. To infer, however, from this that the Chorus hold human effectiveness to be severely limited by the gods would be mistaken, for the first stasimon recognizes no limit to man but death. The Chorus, then, have merely fragments of convictions, each of which lasts just as long as the occasion that provokes it (cf. 11.2).

---

[31]There are several other passages that confirm the significance of the ways in which the Chorus sing here: 487 (29.3); 658–9 (39.3); 854 (46.7); 1007 (52.4).

[32]Cf. A. Maddalena, *Sofocle,* vol. I, 55.

11.7. If the Chorus treat Polynices more fully than Eteocles, it is not out of any indignation at his treachery to his country, his impiety to the gods, or deliberate intent to commit fratricide (cf. 199–202), for they make all of the Argive army indiscriminately guilty of *hubris,* and only single out Capaneus for particular obloquy. The lacuna at 112 makes it uncertain, but it would seem that they do not regard Polynices with hatred. Polynices is simply the leader of the Argives, whose description thus easily passes into that of the whole army. Only the etymologizing of his name particularizes him and makes him somewhat responsible for the war. The Chorus' mildness, then, about Polynices and their indifference to Eteocles together suggest that Creon has not chosen his supporters wisely. And if Creon cannot gauge correctly the temper of the Chorus, he seems bound to fall wildly short of the mark when he has to face Antigone.

12 (162–210). 12.1. Creon's speech falls into three main parts: the legitimacy of his rule (162–74), the principles of his rule (175–91), and the first act of his rule (192–206), to which he adds a restatement of his principles (207–10). Although the theme of the speech is the *polis,* which occurs seven times, twice in each main part and once in the restatement (162, 167, 178, 191, 194, 203, 209), each part has its own triad on which it turns: the first part turns on the rule of Laius, Oedipus, and his two sons; the second on man's ψυχή, φρόνημα, and γνώμη which only the exercise of political rule can reveal; and the third on Polynices' triple crime, against his country, its gods, and his brother (cf. 27.1).

12.2. Jebb's mistranslation of the opening of Creon's speech brings out what one might otherwise have missed: "Sirs, the vessel of our State, after being tossed on wild waves, hath once more been safely steadied by the gods." Creon, however, says that the gods shook τὰ πόλεος and then righted them (cf. *OC* 394). He thus seems at once to absolve Polynices of any guilt for the war and deprive Eteocles of any credit for the victory. He goes much further than the Chorus did, who only assigned the victory to the gods, but left the guilt of the Argives intact (cf. 11.6). Whatever reasoning led Creon to think that the gods were totally responsible (Oedipus' curse of his sons perhaps), his σείσαντες ὤρθωσαν compels one to reflect when he says four lines later, ἡνίκ' Οἰδίπους ὤρθου πόλιν. If Creon alludes to the plague, it would be equally true to say of Oedipus as of the gods that he shook the city and righted it again, for he both caused and removed the plague. If, as might seem more likely, Creon alludes to the Sphinx, one would have to say that the gods shook the city and Oedipus righted it. Creon, however, cannot be alluding to either possibility, for not only does the imperfect ὤρθου preclude them both but Creon does not recall Oedipus either because of his riddle solving or because of his discovery of his own crimes. Creon mentions Oedipus solely to establish the legitimacy of his own accession to the throne through his kinship with him, and hence his own right to demand the loyalty of the Chorus, who he knows were always loyal to the royal family. One now sees that Creon's temporal clause about Oedipus allows him to gloss over the irregularity of Oedipus' accession as well as the bearing of his crimes on his sons' succession. The balanced phrases τοῦτο μέν-τοῦτ' αὖθις suggest that one is to insert mentally some form of line 166 after ὤρθου πόλιν but, as Jebb remarks, this is impossible, as the καί of κἀπεί must link διώλετ' with ὤρθου. This grammatical peculiarity has the effect of suppressing any specific mention of the Chorus' loyalty to Oedipus; instead, Oedipus and his sons are lumped together in the phrase τοὺς κείνων παῖδας, where κείνων refers to Laius as the father of Oedipus and Oedipus as the father of Polynices and Eteocles. Oedipus, then, is used simply as an indispensable transition between Laius and Oedipus' sons (cf. 8.6). Creon is forced to adopt such involuted language because the Chorus could not have been loyal to Oedipus as the legitimate successor to Laius by birth, but only to Oedipus the solver of the riddle, whose reward was the throne of Laius and marriage to his own mother. One can easily imagine that as soon as Oedipus' crimes became known, and hence his legitimacy was ironically confirmed, the Chorus ceased to be loyal to him. κείνων should, but cannot, mean Oedipus and Jocasta, for only through his sister is Creon entitled to the kingship (cf. 486). Creon does everything he can to regularize the royal house without abandoning the truth entirely. He tries to pretend that succession is through the male line only, so that the Chorus will not remember, as if they could ever forget, that Polynices and Eteocles were the offspring of an incestuous marriage (cf. 5.1). He wants the Chorus to understand τοὺς κείνων παῖδας as meaning the descendants of Laius and Oedipus, but he cannot quite bring himself to say that the Chorus was loyal to Oedipus as Laius' son, which alone would have given to τ.κ.π. the meaning he needs; nor can he, on the other hand, suppress all mention of Oedipus, for he still needs him to maintain the fiction of legitimately normal succession through three generations.

12.3. As Creon must here misrepresent the line of succession, he must mistakenly describe the Chorus' loyalty to the successive occupants of the throne as loyalty to the royal family, which, as we saw, it could not have been. He takes their adaptability to circumstances for their firmness of principle (cf. 11.7). He further does not seem to be aware that this attempt to bind the Chorus to him does not jibe with his attempt to be the spokesman for the city as a whole. If he calls the Chorus together because of their past loyalty to the royal house, he implies that the city has and had discordant elements within it, some of which are not and never have been loyal to the Labdacids (cf. 289–92). His first mention of the city thus gains in significance. τὰ πόλεος might be just a periphrasis for the city itself; but, if the city is not a whole, with a single common interest, τὰ πόλεος is indistinguishable from the present monarchical regime, and merely a euphemism for τὰ Λαβδακιδῶν θρόνων κράτη. Later, in the anger of debate, Creon will have to admit as much and more (738), but now he cannot do so, for his title to rule must be unblemished; this, however, can be the case only if the royal house has consistently identified its interests with those of the city. Creon, then, has another reason for being so vague about Oedipus, as well as for implying Polynices' innocence. Polynices, no less than his brother, is needed for Creon's own succession. Their only crime is mutual fratricide, which, as Creon presents it, has nothing to do with the city and its troubles.

12.4. Creon distinguishes ψυχή, φρόνημα, and γνώμη from each other as follows: ψυχή is what one is most devoted to or loves, and how one ranks other things in relation to it;[33] φρόνημα is the temper of one's devotion, whether it shows itself as intense or lax, savage or mild, firm or weak; and γνώμη is the reasons one has for one's devotion and the consequences one draws from it. Creon illustrates this triad in two ways: first about any ruler, τῶν ἀρίστων βουλευμάτων takes up γνώμη; ὅστις...ἅπτεται...ἀλλ' ἔχει expands φρόνημα; and μεῖζον'...νομίζει explains ψυχή; and then again about himself, οὔτ' ἂν...σωτηρίας is his φρόνημα, οὔτ' ἂν...ἐμαυτῷ his ψυχή, and ἥδ'...ποιούμεθα his γνώμη. Creon does not see the problem for the ruler as a question of either ψυχή or γνώμη—they are self-evident—but of φρόνημα, the way one acts on one's judgment and on what one most loves. As the fatherland is to rank highest for both ruler and ruled and for the same reason, only the ruler has in addition to be courageous and speak out in warning against what threatens everyone's ψυχή and γνώμη. This is why Creon calls his decree his φρόνημα (207). His decree, which is the political formulation of his ψυχή, is such an example of courage, for the whole city never was particularly loyal to the Labdacids. It does not think so highly of Eteocles or so little of Polynices as Creon must.

12.5. Creon calls his ψυχή, φρόνημα, and γνώμη his νόμοι because for him they mean his ἔννομος ψυχή and ἔννομον φρόνημα. He therefore does not consider what relation obtains between the νόμοι of the soul and the νόμοι of the city, for he assumes that they are in perfect agreement. But such an agreement depends on the coincidence of the πόλις with the πάτρα and χθών, with which he replaces it in formulating his ψυχή (182, 187). The difference between city and fatherland most plainly appears in Creon's saying that Polynices wanted to destroy his fatherland (199), but Eteocles died on behalf of the city (194), though metrically he could have said *πάτρας ὑπερμαχῶν. The city is whatever its present regime is, but the fatherland is thought to be prior to any regime and that which persists through all changes of regime. (The Chorus in the parodos never mention πόλις.) Hatred of the fatherland is

---

[33]Cf. Dem. 18.280–1.

ipso nomine unpatriotic, but hatred of the regime is often thought to be the highest kind of patriotism. Now Creon is forced to identify the fatherland and the city because he employs two different arguments for establishing his right to rule, either one of which would suffice but which together are contradictory. Creon first proves the legality of his accession and then the probable excellence of his rule. The legality, however, turns on the regime, the house of the Labdacids, but the excellence turns on the fatherland. Creon wants the Chorus to remain loyal to the royal family and hence to himself, while he himself will show his perfect devotion to the city as fatherland. He thus appeals to the irrational loyalty of the Chorus, which he nevertheless must esteem, as he declares his own rational loyalty.[34] By failing to prove, which he could not if he wanted to, that the Labdacids were consistently patriotic, Creon asks the Chorus to love a family more than their country, and the very family, besides, that his decree is designed in part to dishonor. His own loyalty, on the other hand, to the fatherland is rational, for the love that attaches the Chorus to the Labdacids or one countryman to another depends for its possibility on the country's freedom from enslavement. Creon could have avoided this contradiction if he had said that the Chorus had shown exceptional patriotism through three generations of kings, and that he expects their allegiance to him because he will show himself as patriotic as they have done in the past. Not only does the need to prove the legality of his accession prevent him from taking this approach, but he somehow senses as well that the love of a fellow countryman grips everyone far more deeply than love of country: he speaks of the Chorus' reverence for the Labdacids, but not of his own reverence for Thebes. The $\psi v \chi \dot{\eta}$ that only the exercise of political rule reveals as undivided love of country is not the $\psi v \chi \dot{\eta}$ of those who do not rule, whose love is necessarily divided between their $\phi i \lambda o \iota$ and the country that makes that love possible. Perhaps Creon, then, does not avoid the contradiction between the first and second parts of his speech out of pride in his unique ability to sacrifice his deeper feelings for the sake of his country (cf. 38.1). His swearing of an oath here may indicate this pride (cf. 19.3).

12.6 The phrase $\tau o \dot{v} \varsigma \ \phi i \lambda o v \varsigma \ \pi o \iota o \dot{v} \mu \varepsilon \theta \alpha$ (instead of *$\tau . \phi . \ \kappa \varepsilon \kappa \tau \dot{\eta} \mu \varepsilon \theta \alpha$) assumes that all $\phi i \lambda o \iota$ are a matter of choice, and no one is $\phi i \lambda o \varsigma$ by necessity.

---

[34]Cf. Aristotle *Ath. Pol.* 28.5; L. Strauss, *City and Man*, 167. Creon's confusion of fatherland and regime is shared by the commentators: "*verissime Suevernius monuit Creontem non private in Polynicem odio haec imperare, sed quod boni civis et regis officium esse censeat iustum esse aeque adversus eos, qui ament patriam, atque qui ei se inimicos praebeant; neque in Antigonam severum esse odio quodam, sed quod sustinedum putat imperium suum*" (Wunder, on 198 sqq.).

One picks or drops a friend at will. One can therefore calculate whether such a friendship will come into conflict with love of country and act accordingly (cf. *OC* 607–15). Love of country, however, is far more deliberate, for it even begins in calculation. One has to figure out the need for it. Love of one's own, on the other hand, precedes all calculation and survives in spite of calculation (cf. 98–9): Antigone never speaks of her γνώμη (cf. 4.3). Creon's silence, then, about the possible conflict between the love of one's own and of one's country shows how unprepared he is to confront Antigone. That Antigone, too, somehow regards the love of her own as a matter of choice is part of her strangeness (cf. 9.5), and does not justify Creon's omission.

12.7. Creon's proclamation, which makes up the third part of his speech, is the brother (ἀδελφά) of the second part, in which he presented the laws by which he intends to magnify the city. It is a special case of the general laws of the country, which are in turn the laws that inform Creon's soul. Creon commits the democratic error of identifying decree and law on a completely non-democratic basis (cf. 8.4).[35] But in what way is his decree the brother of his laws? His laws stated that he counts as nothing anyone who puts a friend before his fatherland, and that he himself would make no one a friend who was an enemy of his land. To bury Eteocles, then, must be an act of friendship, and to deprive Polynices of burial an act of enmity. Creon thus seems to equate honor with love and dishonor with hatred. He knows nothing of honor given without love, or dishonor without hatred. He does not understand reverence and awe as distinct from love. He does not understand that one can honor but not love someone at a distance and without ever seeing him (cf. 1.1); and that contempt as easily squares with indifference—τοῦτον οὐδαμοῦ λέγω—as with hatred (cf. 35). For Creon, then, to let Polynices be seen disgraced, the prey of birds and dogs, would disclose more his hatred than his dishonor; but just to order Eteocles to be buried, without performing the rites with his own hand (cf. 900), would be a mark of honor and not of love (cf. 524–5). Creon could, after all, without violating his patriotism, have prohibited the burial of Polynices in Theban territory: the Athenian punishment for treachery and sacrilegious theft was the prohibition of burial in Attica (Xen. *Hell.* 1.7.22).[36] That he goes out of his way to express his hatred for Polynices but not his love of Eteocles shows how imperfectly Creon understands his own equation of honor and love; an equation that seems to have arisen from his taking the laws

---

[35]The Chorus characterize Creon's convocation of themselves with an expression that recalls the technical phrase at Athens for an extraordinary assembly (160–1).

[36]Cf. Eur. *Phoen.* 775–6, 1629–30; Wolff-Bellermann, Rückblick, 121–3.

of his soul for the laws of his country (cf. 9.4). Creon is in speech as passionate as Antigone when it comes to the law: but the laws he obeys do not shine through him, for he simply is not up to the degree of intensity needed to bring about such a transparency (cf. 10.6, 11.2). Perhaps, however, Creon's failure to represent the law perfectly is due no less to his own inability than to the recalcitrance in the law itself to being perfectly represented. Only Antigone can show up Creon.

12.8. For the interpretation of 194–206 see 4.6, and for 198–200, see 19.2. Despite the fact that κωκῦσαι strictly means the ritualistic lamentations of women, neither Creon nor anyone else suspects that Polynices' sisters might have tried to violate the prohibition. Creon seems to assume that women would perform their part in funeral rites only if there were men to prompt them. Precisely because it is ritualistic and therefore not a spontaneous expression of the heart, Creon regards it as inconceivable that any woman could be the originator of the plan to bury Polynices (cf. 22.10).

12.9. Of the seven occurrences of πόλις in Creon's speech, the first three concern, respectively, the gods, Oedipus, and any ruler (162, 167, 178), and the last three refer, respectively, to Eteocles, the whole city, and any loyal citizen (194, 203, 209); between the pair of triads stands Creon's reference to himself (191). The first triad has to do with ruling (ὤρθωσαν, ὤρθου, εὐθύνων), the second with obeying the city. Creon now sees no difficulty in his combining both. His enhancement (αὔξων) of the city is the same as his devotion to the city. In upholding the city, he is going to improve the city.[37]

13 (211–14). 13.1. The Chorus distinguish between Creon's pleasure (ἀρέσκει) with regard to Polynices and Eteocles and his power to make use of any and every law concerning the living and the dead. They barely suggest that his pleasure is not on the same level as law, and, even more tentatively, that there is a difference between the living and the dead. Creon has said that whoever is kindly disposed to Thebes will be honored alike alive or dead; the Chorus imply that personal pronouns in the nominative strictly apply to the living but not to the dead (cf. 35.1). The dead cannot be subjects of active verbs. It is doubtful, then, whether one can speak of either the benevolence or the malevolence of the dead. Creon surely does not believe that Polynices, if left unburied, will be powerless to injure Thebes, for he does not employ the magic of *maschalismos* to ensure Polynices' impotence; nor does he believe that Eteocles, if buried, will continue his support of Thebes. Eteocles, if publicly given a funeral and monument, can serve as a model of patriotism regardless of the city's opinion about burial; but Polynices' unburied corpse cannot serve as a warning against treachery unless the city supposes that burial

---

[37]Cf. Xen. *Mem.* 3.7.2; Lycurg. *c. Leocrat.*76–7.

is needed, and because a divine law commands it. Honor to the dead can share the same basis as honor to the living; but dishonor to the dead necessarily has a different basis from dishonor to the living. To bring dishonor into line with honor, Creon would have to prove that the gods have the same perspective as the city; and later he is forced to give such a proof (cf. 19.2), but now he is entirely unaware of the difficulty.

13.2. This difficulty can be more exactly defined as follows. μίασμα occurs three times in the play, all in the mouth of Creon: first, of the mutual fratricide of Polynices and Eteocles (172, cf. 12.3); next, of Antigone's punishment by starvation, which Creon has worked out in such a way that the whole city might avoid pollution (776); and third, of Polynices' corpse, whose devouring by the eagles of Zeus is not a pollution that he fears (1042). If fratricide makes the slayer unclean, the city should no more honor Eteocles than Polynices, unless one assumes that death automatically cleanses, an assumption that in turn would seem to weaken Creon's case against Polynices, for his crime would cease to be punishable with his death. In order, then, for Creon to make a distinction between Polynices and Eteocles, he must regard fratricidal pollution as politically irrelevant: the gods of the city are not the gods of the family. Antigone's punishment, however, is politically relevant, since failure to follow the proper rites would pollute the entire city. To avoid pollution, then, is not a matter of honor: Antigone as Antigone is not taken into account. Now in the case of Polynices Creon seems to have two ways open to him. If nonburial were a pollution like fratricide in being politically irrelevant, not to bury Polynices would not pollute the city but Antigone and Ismene only (cf. 7.2); but then to honor Eteocles could not solely consist in his burial, for that in itself would be politically irrelevant too. To honor Eteocles would need some special ceremonies (cf. 4.1), which would have nothing to do with burial as such, though they could accompany it, to distinguish him from Polynices. If, on the other hand, nonburial were a pollution like Antigone's punishment in being politically relevant, to allow Polynices' burial would not honor Polynices, any more than the burial of Eteocles would honor him. Creon chooses neither of these ways. He argues at once for the political relevance of burial, and hence to deprive Polynices of it is to dishonor him, and for the political irrelevance of nonburial, and hence the city cannot incur pollution if Polynices lies unburied. Creon tries to politicize burial, so that it is nothing but a question of honor or dishonor; but such a politicization requires that the gods be indistinguishable from the city, for if they are not, the gods could equally insist that the city bury Polynices to avoid pollution and honor Eteocles to glorify patriotism. Creon's politicization of burial will thus lead him to the divinization of the city.

14 (215–22). 14.1. Although Creon omitted from his formulation of the decree what the penalty is for its violation, the Chorus know that the penalty is

death (cf. 4.7). Do they assume that all crimes are capital crimes? Or that Creon would as a matter of course impose the death penalty? As they assume that the death penalty is an infallible deterrent, which automatically discharges them from the task Creon has asked them to perform, perhaps they imply that only such a penalty would prevent everyone from disobeying Creon's decree. They would thus agree with Ismene that suicide cannot be an obligation (cf. 10.7). That disobedience, however, is suicidal follows only if Creon's preventive measures are perfect; and they can be perfect only if those whom Creon has appointed to guard Polynices' corpse cannot be corrupted or overwhelmed by force or deceit. To rule out the possibility of corruption would imply that the guards are either fanatically loyal to Creon or mortally afraid of him; to rule out the possibility of superior force, that the disaffected elements in Thebes are weak; and to rule out the possibility of deceit, either that Creon's guards cannot be gulled or that no one would think of using deceit to bury Polynices (cf. 10.5). That nothing in the play contradicts the Chorus' assumptions shows again how easily their simplicity can pass for prescience (cf. 11.4). Without any awareness of the possibilities they reject, they pick the one possibility—only a fool has the *erōs* to die—that applies exclusively to Antigone (cf. 10.8).

14.2. Creon, unlike the Chorus, does not believe that the death penalty is an infallible deterrent, but he believes that, though the hope for gain can be stronger than the fear of death, no one can successfully commit a crime (cf. 313-4). Not the prevention but the detection of crime is infallible (cf. 494-5); and he too is not contradicted in the course of the play: Tiresias knows at once who is guilty of polluting the city's altars. Creon's first oath now yields its meaning: Ζεὺς ὁ πάνθ' ὁρῶν ἀεί (184) must hold if Creon can be certain that no crime goes undetected. That this should apply even to the present case shows the extent to which Creon relies on divine support for his decree. The gods must approve of his decree if it is guaranteed that whoever buries Polynices will come to light (cf. 327-8). Creon thus disregards the possibility that the gods could, in disapproving of his decree, still let its violator be known. His punishment could not have been what it was if Antigone had gone undetected. The gods, it seems, are at least as concerned with punishing Creon as with cleansing Thebes of pollution (cf. 9.1, 9.7).

15 (223-43). 15.1. The first speech of the guard is strange. The fact that he is now before Creon seems to make the need to justify his delay superfluous. Creon can know of his tardiness only through his own admission; and Creon is keener on learning the news than on blaming the guard, whose uncalled-for self-defense only serves to exasperate Creon. To the guard the most important thing is his own situation (τὰμαυτοῦ).[38] The crime in his eyes

---

[38]On the guard see F.W. Schneidewin, Einleitung, 12.

is scarcely a crime (247, 256), though he later expresses no repugnance at sacrilegiously sweeping off the dust from Polynices' corpse; indeed, he speaks of the good job he and his fellow guards did in laying the clammy body bare (409-10). If one supposes that those below pardoned him because he acted impiously under duress (cf. 1199-1200), Ismene's expectation of pardon for not helping Antigone seems to be reasonable (cf. 9.2). The guard, then, recognizes the sacredness of burial, but not its obligatory character. He is, moreover, wholly indifferent, as a slave, to the political purpose Creon affects to find in his decree. Unmoved by the religious or the political issue, he lives solely between fear and hopelessness; so fearful that he not only confesses without reason to the imaginary crime of tardiness (a curious confirmation of Creon's belief that no crime goes undetected), but continually increases the likelihood of his punishment by the very speeches supposedly designed to assuage Creon's anger; and so hopeless that he believes Creon's failure to punish him for his innocence can only be due to the gods (330-1).

15.2. The guard is the first person in the play to treat the soul as something separate, for the soul, in Creon's understanding, is nothing but what one loves and honors the most (cf. 12.4). If Creon had spoken of $\psi v \chi \dot{\eta}$, $\phi \rho \dot{\rho} v \eta \mu \alpha$ and $\gamma v \dot{\omega} \mu \eta$ as names for different aspects of men, nothing would have been lost of his meaning. With the guard, however, it is otherwise. He explains that his soul by much talking delayed his coming, for he always took as a command whatever it said. The Loeb translation of soul here is "conscience." He thus assigns to his soul his own desire for self-preservation. (The guard, like the Chorus, assumes that death is the penalty for any crime.) He separates himself from his soul in order to save his own skin (cf. Xen. *Cyrop.* 6.1.31-41). Were it not for his soul, nothing would have kept him from breathlessly reporting the crime. His soul is guilty, he is innocent. His soul gave him two pieces of contradictory advice, neither of which he could follow without being checked by the other. The soul is not a reliable guide, for it is dominated by the fear of punishment. Only hope can make the guard come forward. The soul in fear offers hope as the way out of the impasse it itself has made; but the hope it offers is in fact resignation to fate (cf. 274); the guard, if punished, will be unjustly punished. Fate thus seems to be the discovery of the soul confronted with the inevitability of unjust punishment; and the soul itself as something separate seems to be the discovery of the fear that such a confrontation arouses. However this may be, the first interpretation we are given of the soul is that it is separate and weak, guilty perhaps but unpunishable, and prone to paralyzing calculations.

15.3. If the soul, in being separate, is separate from the body, could not Antigone have resorted to an argument like the guard's to justify the burial of Polynices? Polynices is guilty, but the guilt is of his soul, and by losing it, what remains of Polynices is unpunishable. His body, it is true, obeyed his soul; but his soul, by balancing the injustice he suffers in being deprived of his throne against the injustice he will commit if he attacks his country, may have first brought him to a standstill; and then, in order to condone his initial indignation, held out the hope that he would if he failed only suffer what was fated (cf. 170). He is thus absolved from the crime his soul made inevitable. The debate between Antigone and Polynices in *Oedipus at Colonus*, which proceeds on not dissimilar lines, shows how Antigone here could have made a case (1416–44). Antigone, however, has barred herself from resorting to any such argument. As she does not mention the war or the reasons for it (cf. 2.4), she cannot make use of grounds that are in any way connected with it. She therefore cannot appeal to the innocence of Polynices' corpse, for its innocence would be bought at the price of her arguing on behalf of Polynices as individual, which she can never bring herself to do (cf. 1.1). Her own arguments turn at different times on different things, but they never touch the individual Polynices, with his distinct virtues or defects (cf. 4.1).[39] She argues on the basis of the Polynices whom she loves, of the law in its generality, and of the Polynices who is her brother (cf. 9, 27, 48), but never in a way that would ally her understanding with the guard's understanding of the soul (cf. 10.4).

16 (245–7). 16.1. The guard talks as if the corpse were properly buried, and no more needed to be done. If Antigone had poured libations (420–1), the thirstiness of the dust and the hardness of the soil (250) must have wiped out any trace of them. The guard, then, either is thinking in terms of a passer-by (256), who did all that a nonrelative should do, or he is not scrupulously exact in his report, and the possible omission of some part of the ritual does not concern him; but the rest of his report is so circumstantial—it reads like a detective story's presentation of a clueless crime—that one should rather conclude that the guard, no more than Creon or the Chorus, ever considers the possibility that Antigone and/or Ismene could be responsible.

16.2. As the guard says that someone sprinkled a light covering of dust on the corpse's skin (no one else in the play mentions its skin), we learn that Polynices before was lying naked in the plain (cf. 410); a fact we should not have inferred from the parodos, which excluded Polynices' armor from the panoplies dedicated to Zeus (141–3). The burial of a corpse, in any case, consists in the hiding from sight, not a body of flesh and bones, but its skin alone. Burial is, literally speaking, a superficial ceremony (cf. Her. 2.86.3–7). Nonburial, on the other hand, involves the entire body, all the boneless parts of which are liable to the devouring of dogs and birds. Burial does not avoid the

---

[39]Cf. *Ai.* 1342–5; H. Grotius, *de iure belli et pacis*, II.19.11.6: *hinc est quod officium sepeliendi, non tam homini, id est personae, quam humanitati, id est naturae humanae praestari dicitur.*

threat of being eaten, for no provision, however flimsy, has to be made against worms (cf. Her. 3.16.4), but the threat of being (seen) naked and torn apart (258, 1198, cf. 4.5). Burial conceals the looks and shape of man (255). It therefore poses at first, prior to the questions of body and soul, body and self, and self and soul, the question of skin and soul. It is a question that turns out only to look less profound than the others (cf. 25.3).

17 (249–77). 17.1. The guard's speech is in three parts: the discovery and description of the crime (249–58), the accusations of guilt and declarations of innocence among the guards (259–67), the casting of lots and the appointment of the guard (268–77). What holds the speech together are the three stages in the guards' reaction: disagreeable surprise (254), just indignation, and fear (270). One can wonder, however, whether their indignation differs from their fear.

17.2. The first part again is in three subsections, the first of which gives the setting (249–52), the second the discovery and the guards' reaction (253–54), and the last the state of the buried corpse (255–58). The impression of exactness that the guard conveys is primarily due to his dyadic phrasing: γενῆδος πλῆγμα-δικέλλης ἐκβολή, στυφλός-χέρσος, ἄρρωξ-ἐπημαξευνένη, ἠφάνιστο-τυμβήρης, θηρός-κυνῶν, ἐλθόντος-σπάσαντος. The first subsection shows how surprising it is that no one thinks at once of Polynices' sisters, for the absence of carts and pickaxes suggests that men of the city were not involved. But its true significance emerges only in light of the first stasimon: there is no trace of human skill (cf. 23). The guard's own inference, on the other hand, that the casual means of burial is explicable in terms of someone who just passed by points to the difficulty in Creon's attempt to politicize burial (cf. 13). If some non-Theban with no intention of violating Creon's decree—that no animal had yet discovered the corpse implies that it was buried soon after the Argives' rout, and perhaps even before the promulgation of the decree—felt obliged to bury the corpse, perhaps without even knowing whose it was, Creon has a much harder task than he imagines to prove that the dead belong exclusively to the city. In order to rule out the guard's inference, as he silently does, Creon has to suppose that the gods guarantee the prevention of the unintentional crime. As soon as Polynices fell, the gods must have erected a barrier of some sort around the corpse to forestall such a chance occurrence (cf. 26.1). To eliminate chance and yet not invoke fate requires a belief in the unfailing agreement between what law prohibits and what cannot happen accidentally. Creon must partially adopt a belief of the Persians, who deny that any son ever killed his own mother or father, for one would always find on inquiry that the supposed son was either a bastard or supposititious (Her. 1.137.2). If Creon does subscribe to the Persians' belief, even after witnessing the suffering of Oedipus and Jocasta, his attempt to regularize the royal house would not, as it first appeared, have been prompted by self-interest alone (cf.

12.2). He simply does not believe that those unintentional crimes of incest and patricide occurred. Fratricide is another matter (cf. 170, 200–1). Creon, then, understands his decree as a law that can neither be unintentionally violated nor go undetected (cf. 14.2). It is almost a self-evident law, which scarcely needs to be promulgated (it is the brother of his soul's laws); and if promulgated, does not need to have the penalty for its transgression spelled out (cf. 14.1). Creon wants to believe that no one will violate it, not because the death penalty will deter everyone, nor even because its violator will be caught, but because it cannot be done. He cannot, however, quite bring himself to believe it. His low estimate of men prevents him (221–2).

17.3. The guard opposes the wild beast to dogs (cf. 1081–2). Dogs, then, are domesticated animals, which belong to men living in cities. Antigone's failure to mention dogs as a possible threat to Polynices' corpse (cf. 4.6) might imply that she cannot admit that man's friend could thus betray him. It might be a sign of how necessary and self-evident it is for her that the dear and the holy coincide (cf. 9.4, 9.8). The corpse must be as precious as the man to those who love (cf. 4.7).

17.4. Each guard grandly boasted to the others his own innocence and ignorance. They were all ready to lift up hot ingots in their hands, walk through fire, and swear by the gods. Of this triad, the play puts to the test only their swearing: the guard admits that his return belies his oath (388–94). However this may be, the guards' willingness to undergo two fiery ordeals gives us by implication the second interpretation of the soul (cf. 15.2). The guards separate themselves as subject to bodily pain from their souls, or whatever one should call the repository of their knowledge of their innocence; and their innocence is so powerful that it can preserve them from any possible punishment. The body, then, is inviolable as long as the soul is guiltless (cf. Antiphon 5.93). Each guard seemed to lay claim to this belief in an effort not to be outdone by what another might say. As his peers could not force him to submit to the ordeal, it was a safe kind of boasting. The guard, in any case, when alone with himself, abandons the view that his soul has no limits to its power—he does not offer to prove his innocence—and replaces it with an abject submission to fate, which is the only way he sees to maintain the innocence of the punishable body and the unpunishable guilt of the soul. Collective μεγαλοψυχία yields to individual ἀθυμία (237). Belief in the gods' providential care of innocence in this life turns into resignation in the face of an undeserved but fated death. The swearing of oaths turns into the soul's speaking to oneself. It is not easy to say whether hope of worldly vindication or hopeless submissiveness represents the greater piety. The guard never suggests, as Antigone does, that the gods will vindicate him after his death (925–8). Antigone's piety is not based on either worldly hope or fear (cf. 896–7).

17.5. The unlimited power of the soul puts all the guards into as much of an impasse as the vacillatory weakness of the soul later puts the guard (cf. 233,

268, 274). The soul then discovered fate as a way out; now the way out is through chance. The casting of lots condemns (καθαιρεῖ) the guard. It seems to be the collective way of finding a scapegoat when confronted with collective innocence. The scapegoat, however, prefers to understand his election otherwise. Fearful of punishment, the guard answers the question, "Why me?" with "It is my fate." Fate is more a comfort than involuntary self-sacrifice, which only ironically can be called good (275). Antigone's willingness, on the other hand, to sacrifice herself forbids her from so invoking fate. She cannot thus console herself for her unjust punishment. And yet Antigone never calls her sacrifice good; indeed, the only time she uses the word, she too means it ironically: she calls Creon the good Creon (31). Creon alone uses "good" in its only other occurrence, without irony: whoever subordinates his private interests to the city remains in the stress of war a just and good comrade-in-arms (671). Could it then be that neither Antigone nor her sacrifice can be called good? That the city (Creon) has made ἀγαθός so exclusively its own that not even Antigone can appropriate it?[40] It would be consistent with this that of the three occurrences of ἄριστος all are spoken by Creon (179, 197, 1114), and of the four of χρηστός, three are spoken by Creon, and Haemon uses the other to speak ungrudgingly of Creon's good sense (299, 520, 635, 662). "Good" may be too worldly a word for Antigone, whose noble sacrifice is "good for nothing." She surely does not help anyone or anything, for neither the law nor the dead has to be helped (cf. 4.3). The very superfluousness that makes Antigone splendid would thus prevent her from being or doing good (cf. 8.7). Only if Creon's punishment, for which Antigone's actions are indispensable (cf. 14.2), is to be considered just would one be compelled to revise this conclusion.

18 (278–9). 18.1. It is not just the absence of clues that makes the Chorus think that the gods might have buried Polynices, but rather that, on their assumption that the death penalty is an infallible deterrent (cf. 14.1), only immortal beings could have done it.

19 (280–314). 19.1. Creon's speech consists of three parts: the first proves that the gods could not have buried Polynices (280–9a), the second reveals those truly responsible and how they managed it (289b–301), and the third threatens the guards unless they find the one guilty (302–14). Creon is far more certain that the guards have been bribed than that they did it (294, 306). He prefers, in any case, to believe in their active or passive complicity rather than in their carelessness (cf. 14.1), which comes close to implying either the god's concern for Polynices or the gods' indifference to Creon's decree (cf. 17.2).

---

[40]Cf. Pl. *Ap.S.* 24b4–5: Μέλητον τὸν ἀγαθὸν καὶ φιλόπολιν, ὥς φησι; Dem. 24. 127.

19.2. In arguing that to prohibit Polynices' burial is the self-evident consequence of his soul's laws, Creon says that Polynices wanted to burn to the ground the land of his father(s) and the gods of his race (or country), taste of common blood, and lead the rest of his city into slavery (199–202); but now, in order to prove that the gods could not have buried Polynices, he says that Polynices came to set fire to the columned temples, the votive offerings, and the earth of the gods and to scatter their laws. Creon drops the arguments based on fratricide and slavery, for the first is too private, and the second too political, for either to justify the gods' horror at Polynices' crime (cf. 13.2). He replaces, moreover, γῆ πατρῴα with γῆ ἐκείνων, (i.e., θεῶν) and θεοὶ οἱ ἐγγενεῖς with ναοί and ἀναθήματα. He first argued for Polynices' treachery against his own, whether it be his own land, gods, or brother; but now, in arguing for Polynices' impiety, he consecrates the city and all that belongs to it to the gods. The first charge had Polynices firing the gods themselves, who, Creon pretended, do not differ from their statues; but the second has him firing what belongs to the gods, who are now wholly separate from the monuments of their worship. As one could readily think of the gods as willing to forgive their own, especially one who was unsuccessful, Creon has to heighten Polynices' impiety to the point that forgiveness would be inconceivable; but this heightening has the effect of making the attack on things a more serious crime than that on persons. The fact that the Chorus accept Creon's proof—the first stasimon presupposes it—gives us the first inkling that a corpse could be more sacred than a person (cf. 256). The Πολυνείκους νέκυς of Antigone (26) might differ as much from Creon's Πολυνείκης (198) as Creon's ναοί and ἀναθήματα do from his θεοὶ οἱ ἐγγενεῖς (cf. 4.3). Polynices' corpse might have its significance for Antigone not despite but because it is more alien to her than either Polynices her brother (cf. 3.3) or Polynices himself (cf. 15.3).

19.3. As the gods could not have buried Polynices, which Creon takes to be the same as saying that they could not have honored him (cf. 13.2), Creon declares that the true culprits are political enemies. Creon moves from the politicization of burial to the divinization of the city, and from there back to the purely political conflict, without indicating how Polynices' sacrilegiousness could ever be the rallying point of those who secretly murmur against him. To revolt against him is to revolt against the gods. Creon keeps his original identification of his regime with the fatherland (cf. 12.5) at the same time that he has been compelled to replace the land of the ancestors with the land of the gods. As he cannot assume that the gods are the ancestors (cf. 938), for he has to deny every possible basis for the gods' forgiveness of Polynices, Creon implies that not only is he the legitimate heir to the throne, which in turn truly expresses the fatherland, but that he is the present regent for the distant gods (cf. 304). What plainly links his political legitimacy with his divinely appointed role are the laws of his soul, which are at once the test of statesmanship, the ground of the city, and the will of the gods. It is no wonder, then, that Creon swears so freely (184, 305, 758) and never deigns to refute Antigone's contention that divine law sanctions Polynices' burial (cf. 29.1). He is the first to speak of mortals and human beings (295, 299).

19.4. Creon exemplifies the bad effect of money in three ways: it sacks cities, it expels men from their homes, and it perversely instructs the good wits of mortals in shameless deeds. The city and the family, Creon implies, are unqualifiedly good; only the wits (φρένες) can be either good or bad. Creon shows no awareness of an essential conflict between the city and the family (cf. 12.6). Were is not for money they would always be in harmony. He furthermore suggests that, though money necessarily belongs to the city, which in itself is good, the city does not need money, which in itself is the source of all impiety. Money is the worst convention (νόμισμα) that ever grew (ἔβλαστε) among human beings. It owes its quasi-natural status to its universality. It is entirely conventional and yet universal. It therefore reminds one of burial rites, which equally seem to be conventional and yet universal; indeed, they seem to be even more closely connected, for they both have to do with what is beneath the earth (cf. 22.8): another name for Hades is Plouton (1200).[41] In one decisive respect, however, Plouton the god of wealth and Plouton the god of the dead differ. The conventionality of coined money does not stand in the way of exchange between one currency and another; but the conventionality of burial rites forbids the discovery of equivalents between two different rites. Darius offered money to both Greeks and Indians if either were willing to follow the burial practices of the other (Her. 3.38.3-4). This difference has its ground in another difference. Any set of burial practices takes its character from what is held about the soul. No other practice, as far as I know, implies so much so directly. Coinage, on the other hand, carries with it no such implications. A god may be held to preside over the ways in which money is exchanged (cf. Od. 19. 395-8); but no god determines the values, let alone the use, of this or that piece of money. One can without sacrilege deface it, bury it, melt it, or even not use it; and when it is in use, it always remains neutral, whether the transaction be between one man and another, or even between man and god (Charon's obol). But the corpse is never neutral. The gods and the soul have stamped it indelibly with themselves. Creon, however, treats the corpses of Polynices and Eteocles as if they were pieces of metal that could be coined at will in any denomination: Polynices' corpse is in the old currency,

---

[41]For the connection between νόμισμα and νόμος see Dem. 24.212-4; esp. 213: εἰπεῖν [Σόλωνα λέγεται] ὅτι αὐτὸς ἡγεῖται ἀργύριον μὲν νόμισμ' εἶναι τῶν ἰδίων συναλλαγμάτων ἕνεκα τοῖς ἰδιώταις εὑρημένον, τοὺς δὲ νόμους νόμισμα τῆς πόλεως εἶναι.

which is now to be discontinued; Eteocles' is in the new, which gives it a higher valuation. But Creon issues his new currency without altering the beliefs that alone can validate the change. Creon does not pretend to understand either the gods or the soul differently. He believes that the price ($τιμή$) he puts on each corpse is independent of such beliefs. He does not realize that the neutrality he thus assigns the corpse in itself entails a reassessment of both the gods and the soul (cf. 13.2). His impiety is not a radical impiety.

19.5. Creon gives the third interpretation of the soul. He threatens the guards with torture leading to death, so that in the future they might know the limits of rightful gain and act accordingly. The torture is justified not so much as a punishment (for which death suffices) as an education. Creon is the first to mention Hades; and though it seems to be the equivalent of death, Creon must assume the existence of Hades as a place where the guards can practice the lesson they will have learned so painfully. The guards' future reformation presupposes that under torture they will blurt out that which they and Creon already know; for the pain inflicted on the body opens up the truth hidden within (the soul) but does not distort it.[42] The soul, then, which is too guileless to invent a plausible lie, is tightly bound to the body, which is too weak to resist and through which it learns. The soul when subordinate to the body lacks both nobility and $δεινότης$. Creon thus assumes the inverse of the second interpretation of the soul, which held the soul to be separate from the body and yet strong enough to protect it from pain (cf. 17.4). Both interpretations, however, share the view that bodily pain is the true touchstone of the soul, whether to prove its innocence or its guilty knowledge.

20 (315–22). 20.1. After Creon's threats of torture, the guard presents a topology of the nonbodily pain that accompanies indignation. Indignation is of two kinds. One resides in the ears and reacts only to speeches, the other resides in the soul, or $φρένες$ and reacts only to deeds (cf. Her. 7.39.1). Creon, however, is unaware of this difference. He has confused the pain he feels at the report of the crime with the pain he feels at the criminal; and as the criminal is unknown, his indignation discovers the criminal in the reporter of the crime, the only person available. Creon's instant suspicion that his political enemies bribed the guards is merely a gloss on this confusion. Indignation of the soul cannot be satisfied with the emptiness of "the criminal"; it must always vent itself on "this criminal"; but as it has no special sense by which it can detect him, it finds the guilty everywhere. The guard thus seems to give the obverse side of his interpretation of his own soul (cf. 15.2). That interpretation showed the soul in self-induced fear and guilt prostrate before fate;

---

[42]On the pros and cons of torture in the orators see Wyse's not on Isaeus 8.12.1.

this interpretation shows the soul in righteousness lashing out at everyone but itself. What holds the two together is the pain of frustration, whether born of its awareness of undeserved but unavoidable punishment, or born of its ignorance of those who deserve to be punished. The first kind of frustration reminds one of Odysseus confronted with Posidon's wrath; the second of Achilles slaying Hector for a crime that is his own. The guard would thus be an ignoble Odysseus, who as cleverly talks his way out of danger; and Creon would be an ignoble Achilles, who also is forced to allow the burial of his enemy. Creon's remorse, moreover, has as little effect on his subsequent punishment as Achilles' atonement has on his fate.

20.2. It would not suffice, if one wished to paraphrase what the guard says, to have him say, "The criminal really makes you indignant, I am just a superficial irritant"; for if the guard means only that, he would not have to assign separate regions to Creon's twofold pain, but merely discriminate between its two external sources. The guard, rather, means, "The criminal makes the real you indignant, I irritate your superficial self." The soul thus stands for the true self, which is separate from the rest of oneself and scarcely communicates with it. In this sense, the guard reverses his former view of the soul's paralyzing influence on the true self, which is subject to punishment for crimes it was wholly unwilling to commit. Creon accepts this identification of the soul and the self, but he denies that it is something separate: "Not only did you commit the crime," he tells the guard, "but what is worse you betrayed your soul for money." Money seduced the guard into giving up his true self. Here for the first time soul keeps its primary meaning of life, but at the same time it bears a trace of Creon's first interpretation, which made it the same as what one should most love and honor (cf. 12.4). Creon thus insists as much on the inseparability of body and soul—he alone uses $\sigma\tilde{\omega}\mu\alpha$ as the equivalent of $\psi\upsilon\chi\acute{\eta}$ (675)—as the guard does on their separateness; for the guard wants to deflect Creon's anger away from himself, but Creon wants to punish anyone who thwarts him in a way that leaves nothing of one's own unpunished or uncorrected.

20.3. The scene between Creon and the guard presents five interpretations of the soul. The soul is: (1) separate and weak (15.2), (2) separate and strong (17.4), (3) connected and weak (19.5), (4) separate and oneself (20.1), (5) connected and oneself (20.2). What no one maintains is that the soul is connected and strong. Such an interpretation would have the soul rely on the gods as much as 2, but, unlike 3, be resistant to all bodily pain and, unlike 5, be contemptuous of life. One is therefore tempted to conclude that, as these traits exactly characterize Antigone, the ground for her devotion to Polynices' corpse, which is so great that she unnecessarily returns to it (cf. 10.1), lies in her living this paradoxical interpretation of the soul (cf. 95). Whether this is the true ground of her actions, or at best only a fragment of the true ground, only Antigone's two remaining defenses can properly determine (cf. 27, 48).

21 (323–31). 21.1. The guard is no longer afraid. In spite of Creon's reiteration of his threats that, unless the guards discover the culprits, they will be punished, he does not take him seriously. Not his diligence, spurred on by fear, but pure chance will decide whether the culprit will be found. The guard thus moves from expressing his own resignation to fate, with which he had entered, to expressing the indifference of chance, with which he leaves (cf. 17.5). The guard, then, has exaggerated either his initial fearfulness or his final lack of concern; and as he later indicates that he did take Creon seriously (390–1, 408, 413–4, 437–40), one must say that his relief at not being punished at once makes him veer to the opposite extreme. He acknowledges that he neither hoped for his escape nor judged it probable; for it was ultimately due, not to his own verbal dexterity, but to the gods. The gods do not intervene on behalf of the innocent in the spectacular way of the ordeal (cf. 17.4), but in the way of events turning out better than one hopelessly feared they would. The providential gods thus seem to be the discovery of the soul cheated of the future its own fears had devised. The debt, at any rate, which the guard believes he owes to the gods opens the way to our understanding why the first stasimon's implicit assertion that the gods do not stand as a limit to man is necessarily connected with man's artfulness in overcoming the seemingly impossible, equipped as he is with a wisdom beyond hope (366; cf. 10.8). The first stasimon, however, shows man in his limitlessness only by suppressing any mention of his soul (cf. 11.2), the significance of which clearly emerges if one compares the first stasimon of Aeschylus' *Choephoroi*. The guard therefore is just as necessary as the first stasimon for the full understanding of man. That the soul comes to light in the element of the ridiculous, while art comes to light with the greatest solemnity, although art has seemingly nothing to do with the play's action and soul everything, illustrates the way in which man's competence always outstrips his self-knowledge. It is a great but almost unavoidable error for us to give more weight to the first stasimon than to the guard and his speeches.

22 (332–75). 22.1. The first stasimon presupposes the correctness of Creon's proof that the gods did not bury Polynices (cf. 19.2), from which the Chorus silently concluded that men of great daring and skill were involved in perpetrating so clueless a crime. Man's πανουργία, which according to Creon constitutes man's impiety and *hubris* (300–1, 309), is now given the morally neutral name of δεινότης, for which the Chorus, in charting the extent of man's stopping-at-nothing, do not try to account. Creon had given the love of base gain (money) as the cause of man's criminality; but the Chorus do not, as one might expect, replace that cause with the neutral love of gain. Neither some ulterior end nor a Prometheus explains man's inventive daring. It is an irreducible part of man.

22.2. The stasimon presents man's uncanny awesomeness as consisting of four aspects, to each of which it devotes a strophe: man's restlessness, man's superiority to, and mastery of, all other living beings, man's devising and understanding, and man's freedom, which leaves to him the choice of following the good or the bad. Each strophe thus has its own characteristic set of verbs. The first begins with πέλει, which retains its original sense of motion and is echoed at the strophe's end by the cognate πολεύων; and these two verbs frame the rest: χωρεῖ, περῶν, ἀποτρύεται, ἰλλομένων. The first antistrophe is likewise all of a piece: ἀμφιβαλών, ἀγρεῖ, κρατεῖ, and Schoene's plausible ὀχμάζεται. The second strophe in turn has: ἐδιδάξατο, ἄπορος ἐπ' οὐδὲν ἔρχεται, ξυμπέφρασται; and the second antistrophe contrasts man's freedom with his sociality: παρείρων, παρέστιος, γένοιτο, ἴσον φρονῶν. Throughout the stasimon the prepositions, compounded or uncompounded, carry the notion of man's confronting, outflanking, and rising above every challenge, even those that threaten to swamp him: πέραν, περι-, ὑπ', ὑπέρτατον, ἀπο- (first strophe), (ἀμφι-, περι- (first antistrophe), ὑπ', ἐπ', ξυμ- (second strophe), ὑπέρ, ἐπ' (second antistrophe).

22.3. The stasimon seems to progress from showing man's mastery of the inanimate sea and earth (first strophe), to his mastery of animals (first antistrophe), and from there to his relation to himself as one who contrives the means for his own self-preservation (second strophe), which then leads by contrast to his relation with others, the city and the gods (second antistrophe) This schematization is open to the difficulty, of which the Chorus are scarcely aware, that the unwearied earth, which man tries to wear out, is a goddess, and the highest of the gods besides; which should place her as such in the second antistrophe, where the Chorus speak of the earth's laws, and how the city stands high.[43] Man's violation of the highest god, which, the Chorus recognize, illustrates man's δεινότης, does not fit with their later assumption that the arts are only willfully but not essentially subversive of the city, its gods and laws. For all the narrowness of Creon's belief that money accounts for all of man's πανουργία, he understands better than the Chorus its essential impiety. The Chorus do not see that art, as the breaking of apparent limits, whether it be in allowing man's passage across the dividing sea (i.e., traveling to other cities) or in its ignoring the surface of the earth as man's proper place, points to the city not only as the unwilling harborer of crime but as itself founded on crime. The descendants of Cain, who offered God the first fruits of the land, which God did not find acceptable, discovered the arts and founded the first city. However unaware the Chorus are that the city can only be high at the expense of the highest of the gods, the Chorus do see that the city cannot be, as Creon assumes, unqualifiedly good (cf. 19.4); for man's δεινότης partly consists in his teaching himself ἀστυνόμοι ὀργαί, which are evidently not the

---

[43]For the meaning of ὑψίπολις, see F. Sommer, *op. cit.*, 174.

same as man's submission to the laws of the land. Although the city must rest on both the arts and the gods (their laws), its two supports are not in harmony with one another (cf. 10.9):[44] for the city, which serves through the arts man's need or desire to preserve himself, does not as such necessarily find the gods useful.

22.4. The Chorus list nine ways in which man's δεινότης is revealed: (1) sailing, (2) farming, (3) hunting, (4) taming, (5) speaking, (6) thinking, (7) ἀστυνόμοι ὀργαί (8) housing, (9) medicine. The first four have to do with man's relation to non-men, the last five with his relation to himself and other men. One is therefore inclined to say that self-taught speech is central because it separates men from non-men. And yet there are the gods and their ἔνορκος δίκα. Oaths and prayers prevent the limiting of speech to man's hearing, and divine laws prevent its limitation to man speaking with man. What, then, does the play itself teach us about them? Leaving aside Creon's three vain oaths (184, 305, 758), we have the testimony of the guard, who suggests that mortals should never swear, "for the afterthought belies one's judgment" (388–94). If a change in circumstances sanctions one's right to depart from what one has sworn to, oaths could not be a way of ensuring truthfulness, in which justice has so large a share (cf. Her. 1.138.1).[45] The guard would thus unwittingly confirm the Chorus' attribution of speech to man's own discovery (cf. 17.4), were it not that divine law, to which Antigone appeals, contradicts it. But even apart from the speech of the gods, which is divine law, one cannot forget that Tiresias first suspects that Creon has violated divine law through hearing the barbaric sound of birds (1001–2). The light-witted birds speak more wisely than men. The Chorus do not recognize ornithoscopy or any other kind of divination as showing the limits of man's unaided resourcefulness. The future is wholly open to man as man (360–1). If speech, then, is entirely a human invention, and oaths, prayers, and omens are not ways of communication between gods and men, it remains mysterious how the Chorus would unite man's inventiveness and divine law in the city. The Chorus seem to take their actual coexistence in the city as a proof of the moral neutrality of man's inventiveness, despite the implication in their own description of it that denies it any such neutrality. By starting from Creon's proof that the gods could not have buried Polynices, the Chorus have drifted into a view that completely cuts off the gods from men.

22.5. Aeschylus' Prometheus also lists nine discoveries as his own: (1) housing, (2) astronomy, (3) numbers, (4) letters, (5) taming, (6) sailing, (7) medicine, (8) divination, (9) metallurgy (PV 450–504).[46] The first stasimon

---

[44]Cf. Arist. *Politica* 1328b11–3.

[45]Cf. S. Benardete, *AGON* 1967, 160–1.

[46]Cf. S. Benardete, *RhM* 1964, 126–39.

most strikingly differs from this list by the absence in it of anything above or below the earth: neither astronomy nor metallurgy, neither divination nor numbers. Apart from the slight penetration of the earth that ploughing involves, the stasimon restricts man's δεινότης to the surface of the earth. The different ways in which Prometheus and the Chorus treat housing also point to the stasimon's deliberate exclusion of τὰ οὐράνια. Prometheus says that men first lived in sunless caves, and he taught them to build out in the open houses that face the sun; the Chorus imply that men first lived under the open sky, exposed to frost and rain, and men taught themselves how to avoid them, but whether by building houses or retiring to caves is unclear. No light, natural or artificial, illuminates the horizontal plane on which man lives and moves. Man's daring is exercised in a closed world. His daring is without aspiration. There is no sense here of man's openness to things beyond himself, only of the inability of things to resist man. One therefore suspects that what permits the Chorus to regard man's daring as morally neutral is, besides their silence about what motivates it, just this closedness of the human world. Man crosses the sea not to trade with, conquer, or look at other men (cf. α3, Her. 3.139.1); he merely outbraves it, as though he were at play with the elements. Like an engine idling, whose gears have to be engaged before it does any work, man's daring has to be seen in the perspective of the city and the gods before it moves toward a good or evil end. Its terribleness is partly due no doubt to this idling; but at the same time the Chorus have thereby drained it of its essential recalcitrance to being harmonized with the city and the gods. Man is more terrible than even the Chorus believe.

22.6. The stasimon directly refers to man thrice, twice by name, and once by the neuter demonstrative pronoun: as ἄνθρωπος there is nothing more uncanny, as ἀνήρ he is περιφραδής, and as τοῦτο he crosses the sea and wears out the earth.[47] Neuter man, which exactly characterizes man as artisan, stands furthest removed from man under the sway of Eros (cf. 21.1.).[48] Antigone, then, for all her artlessness, shares something in common with him (cf. 10.8). If the law that provokes her daring needs the antigeneration of her name and nature, it must somehow be related to the arts that make manifest man's daring, which equally rests on his unerotic nature. How they are related one cannot now say; but the Chorus are not as far off in their conjecture as to the character of the culprit as they later imagine (cf. 23.1). The stasimon is relevant to Antigone in more than a negative way.

22.7. The stasimon mentions gods thrice, twice by name, and once collectively and anonymously: Earth, Hades, θεῶν ἔνορκος δίκα. Earth is the

---

[47]On τοῦτο see Schneidewin: P. Friedlander, *Hermes* 1934, 59.
[48]Cf. L. Strauss, *The City and Man*, 95–6.

highest of the gods, Hades is the only god or thing from which man cannot escape (note the triplet (φεύγειν, φεῦξιν, φυγάς), and the gods are those whose justice men swear by as a guarantee of their own. Both men and gods in Homer swear by Earth, and men swear as well by the sun, rivers, and Zeus, and the gods by Ouranos, sea, and Styx (Γ 276–80, Ξ 271–4, Ο 36–8). For the Chorus the sea is not divine, but merely an obstacle to man. Earth, though divine, is continually outraged by man; and the sun and sky are conspicuous by their absence. Their absence, moreover, seems to be deliberately referred to, for Earth is called the highest of the gods. ὑπέρτατος first occurs in Hesiod: Ζεὺς ὑψιβρεμέτης, ὃς ὑπέρτατα δώματα ναίει (OD 8). Pindar invokes Zeus himself as the highest in connection with his thunderbolts (O. 4.1); Euripides has someone call Eros the highest of all gods (fr. 269.2); and Aristophanes has the birds call Pisthetairos, once he has usurped Zeus' throne, the highest of the gods (Av. 1765). It is not uncommon, however, for "highest" to have entirely lost its literal sense of above the earth;[49] but when combined with Earth this sense is incongruously restored to it. The Chorus call the Earth highest, perhaps, as a result of an impossible compromise between its true owner, Zeus, to whom the Chorus deny any limiting power over man, and its omission, the consequence of which would have been that man as man has nothing to reverence or look up to. As that is far too radical for the Chorus, they attribute the epithet to Earth, the only god whose presence in the midst of men they believe cannot be denied. Everything divine, which the stasimon's theme forbids the Chorus to mention (in accordance with their brand of moderation [cf. 11.2]), is compressed into the Earth. One has only to compare the second strophe of the second stasimon to see what is properly highest, unaging, and unwearied. Earth, in any case, is the only god who survives in the dominion of horizontal man (cf. 46.7).

22.8. Earth as a goddess has so far perplexed our understanding of the stasimon in two ways, both of which pertain to the difficulty of reconciling the violation of the earth with the city, its oaths, and laws. There is, moreover, a third difficulty around which the whole play revolves. The stasimon acknowledges Hades as the only limit man cannot by any means breach or bypass: immortality is not such a means. It cannot be accidental, therefore, that the stasimon suggests that we put together man's violation of the earth, to whose surface his daring is otherwise restricted, with man's only limitation, which as a place is somewhere below the earth (cf. 4.1). Its omission of mining now

---

[49]When ὑπέρτατος is not to be literally understood, the object it qualifies is something the gods have raised to the top (cf. 684, 1138; Ph 402, 1347; OC 105). Are we to understand that the gods hold Earth to be the highest?

seems to be of some importance (cf. 19.4).[50] The wholly inviolable part of the earth would thus be Hades, whose masters are Plouton and Hecate (1199–1200); and they in turn are the gods in whose custody the laws and customs of burial reside (451). Not death in itself but Hades and his laws would constitute the true limitation of man, for the death of individuals cannot prevent one generation of men from passing on the fruits of its δεινότης to the next. The human world is not as closed to the gods as the stasimon makes out. The Chorus, however, are no more aware of this than they are of the other difficulties Earth makes for them. They do not understand the import of calling man a neuter this. They confusedly move from a class-characteristic of man, limitlessness, to a limitation that though equally universal applies to each man in a way that does not interfere with man's limitlessness. The consequence of thus treating the class as an individual is that nothing then stands between and hence connects the city and man as man. The laws of the land (χθών) are not in the Chorus' understanding the laws of Earth (Γᾶ), i.e., the laws of burial (cf. 382). Antigone therefore is a necessary corrective to the stasimon itself, for she provides the sacred bond between the land and the earth. It is through Hades that the particular and the universal come together.

22.9. In a way reminiscent of the parodos, which displayed various degrees of personification (cf. 11.5), the play as a whole seems to give an exhaustive list of the ways in which the earth can be understood. Of the twenty-one occurrences of γῆ, χθών, χώρα, the first refers to the dead below the earth (24), the middle to earth as a goddess (338), and the last to the tumulus of native soil Creon's servants erected for Polynices' remains (1203). Burial rites, in allowing for the sense of earth as stuff to coincide with that of earth as country, appears to be the unifying core of earth's divergent meanings. Somewhere between the earth (24, 65) and the earth's hard and unyielding surface, which either the goddess Earth or the earth in itself comprehends, lies the city, whether it be identified with the regime, the fatherland (the place where one's ancestors are buried), or the possession of the gods (110, 113, 155, 187, 199, 287, 368, 518, 736, 739, 806, 937, 1162, 1163). As the surface of the earth, moreover, no less than its depths, is linked through dust with burial (247, 256, 409, 429, 602), the city and Hades are never far apart. The roots of the city, however, do not all reach to Hades, for it is also founded on the violation of the earth; and only this passage in the play alludes to earth as the mother of all growing things (cf. 419, 1201–2). That the dead Eurydice can be called παμμήτωρ of Haemon's corpse (1282), though παμμήτωρ suggests the earth (Aesch. *PV* 90), seems to point again to the same abstraction from what earth primarily connotes. It is this abstraction, which is of a piece

---

[50]For the impiety of mining see Pliny *NH* 33.1–3.

with the ignoring of Ismene's existence (cf. 9.2), that allows Antigone as anti-generation to represent the laws of earth and hence of the city.

22.10. Of the nine manifestations of man's δεινότης only the seventh, ἀστυνόμοι ὀργαί, is not at once intelligible. What further emphasizes its anomalousness is that all the rest seem to be paired: sailing-farming, hunting-taming, speaking-thinking, housing-medicine. A way to its meaning is given, however, if one contrasts speaking and wind-swift thinking with the dumb fishes (cf. *Aj.* 1297) and light-witted birds men capture. It would then stand opposed to the savagery of land animals (θηρῶν ἀγρίων ἔθνη) and would mean man's self-domestication, the training of his temper without the aid of the gods. Such a self-limitation for the sake of living together on the part of a being that otherwise recognizes no limits the Chorus regard as uncanny; but this very claim that civility or decency results from man's own laws makes one think of burial. The ἀστυνόμοι of Athens were charged with the task of seeing to it that all dung was dumped farther than ten stades from the city's wall; and they themselves picked up anyone who died in the streets (Arist. *Ath. Pol.* 50). One is thus reminded of Heraclitus' saying, νέκυες κοπρίων ἐκβλητότεροι (fr. 96)[51] Even if a Socrates can laughingly agree with this precept (cf. Pl. *Phaedo* 115a3–5), the city does not treat corpses as it treats dung; and the difference of treatment must lie in the fact that some laws and customs of decency are not self-taught. The Chorus have simply not reflected on the connection between domestication and piety, on the ἀστυνόμοι θεοί behind the ἀστυνόμοι ὀργαί, for they understand piety only when it has decayed into habit and "good form."[52] The original meaning of ὁσίας ἕνεκα altogether eludes them (cf. Eur. *IT* 1461, Eubulus fr. 110.2, Ephippus fr. 15.4, Wyse at Isae. 7.38). They therefore can call Antigone, just after she has defended the divine law of burial, savage and from a savage father (471–2).

22.11. The triad of φθέγμα, φρόνημα, and ἀστυνόμοι ὀργαί, which man has taught himself, remind one of Creon's triad of ψυχή, φρόνημα, and γνώμη, which only the exercise of political rule can reveal (cf. 12.4). The triads cannot be matched one-to-one, for Creon's γνώμη embraces the Chorus' φθέγμα and φρόνημα, while their ἀστυνόμοι ὀργαί is a partial combination of his ψυχή and φρόνημα . The Chorus thus expand what Creon regards as the easiest aspect of ruling, and they contract into ἀστυνόμοι ὀργαί what Creon

---

[51]Note the juxtaposition of a word for nothing but human corpses with a word for excrement, whether human or not.

[52]The guards' willingness to go through fire (πῦρ διέρπειν) as a proof of their innocence well illustrates (and perhaps is meant to illustrate) the original force of a custom that later decayed into a manner of expression, as in Xen. *Symp.* 4.16: διὰ πυρὸς ἰέναι (cf. K. Latte, *Heiliges Recht,* 5–6, n. 2).

analyzes more carefully. For the Chorus, man's boldness is extrapolitical and astonishingly sacrificed in town life; for Creon, the courage of the ruler in abiding by the best deliberations is the ultimate test of his excellence. Creon, then, would correctly assert that for knowing a man rule is indispensable, for man's ὀργαί cannot be as mild as the Chorus believe. His ὀργαί must still retain enough savagery to defend his country. He must value his country more than his life. Despite the war that Thebes has just endured, and perhaps even because of it, the Chorus do not reckon the πόλις-πατρίς, as opposed to the ἄστυ, as constituting a part of man's δεινότης. They place it aside as the haven of all that is good and noble because they fail to consider its connection with the soul, a connection that even Creon somewhat understands.

22.12. The ordinary punctuation of line 360 makes παντοπόρος no different from ἄπορος κτλ; but without the colon it says that man, resourcefully resourceless, comes to nothing in the future (cf. *El.* 1000, fr. 871,8).[53] This is surely not what the Chorus mean, but as an unwitting portrayal of Antigone it could not be bettered: completely artless, but infinitely resourceful, Antigone goes to death (cf. 9.3, 10.5). For the Chorus, man's δεινότης consists in the gap between his daring and his apparent limitations, before which daring these limitations collapse. The one limitation that is equally apparent and real is death; but Antigone shows her πανουργία within the area that death seems to circumscribe for itself. She does not show that it too is only apparent; she breaks only the limits that Ismene thinks are insuperable: law, nature, and power (cf. 8.6). Antigone does not get around death, she sides with it against life. Death is brought within the realm of the δυνατά, though it seems to be recalcitrant to exploitation, through the unwritten law. Antigone's devotion to the law leads to her accepting the conditions of death itself: ἐκεῖ γὰρ αἰεὶ κείσομαι. Death is not the limit but the goal. If one thus misreads the Chorus' meaning, one must face the question of why Antigone should lurk behind a colon. What is the Chorus looking at when they pause between παντοπόρος and ἄπορος? Man's flight from death results in his daring confrontation with everything that threatens death. With his infinite resources man expands the horizon of possibility. He thus pushes to the periphery what originally was at the center and puts off into the future what remains right in front of him. The colon, then, between παντοπόρος and ἄπορος is grounded in the displacement of the horizon that man's artfulness has brought about. The Chorus' silence

---

[53] ἐπ' οὐδὲν ἔρχεται could be distinguished from ἐπὶ μηδὲν ἐ. as meaning that man comes to nothing of any account for all his resourcefulness, resourceless as he ultimately is (cf. *El* 245, 1129); but it is not to be insisted upon (cf. *Ai.* 1231; *El* 1166): κατθανὼν δὲ πᾶς ἀνὴρ γῆ καὶ σκιά· τὸ μηδὲν εἰς οὐδὲν ῥέπει (Eur. fr. 536).

represents the barrier that man himself has made there, and before which the Chorus stand in awe. Man's artfulness, however, does not exhaust his daring, which necessarily precedes it, and which in itself does not have to issue in it. Man's daring is not just morally neutral when it is art; it is neutral to art as well. The Chorus' omission of the cause of man's daring points to what it is before it has committed itself to art. The alternative to such a commitment would be Antigone's to the divine law of burial, in which there is not a displacement but a rearticulation of man's original horizon, so that the domain of Hecate and Hades comes to occupy the place of death and nothingness. As Antigone recovers the horizon that the gods once imposed on man (cf. 456-7), man's daring as radical piety turns out to be not only neutral but hostile to art: art is the perversion of man's original daring. Art is not at first morally neutral and then free to choose the good or the bad; it is from the start unholy, and the difference between its subsequent morality and immorality is, strictly speaking, illusory. Creon's mistake of identifying decree with law reflects a necessary mistake of the city itself, for the city cannot dispense with art; and therefore it must condone its essential unholiness while it punishes the accidental manifestations of its misuse. The city must blink in the glare that Antigone casts on this original compromise of the city. Antigone, therefore, has to be replaced by Tiresias in order for the city to forget once again what Antigone reminds it of (cf. 51).

22.13. The Chorus seem to enforce their punctuation of line 360 through the corresponding line in the antistrophe, where ὑψίπολις stands to παντοπόρος as ἄπολις to ἄπορος. The city is high if man weaves into (παρείρων) his artfulness his country's laws and the sworn-by justice of the gods;[54] but there is no city for him if thanks to his daring he embraces the ignoble.[55] The misreading, however, of line 360 suggests that here too one should repunctuate the line to read that whoever out of daring allies himself with immorality, for him the city is high and there is no city. This two-edged

---

[54]This is the only possible meaning of the mss. reading, with τέχνη the easily supplied antecedent for the παρ- (cf. παραπλέκω), which is how Hermann understood it; but it is difficult. The closest parallel I could find is Pl. *Lgs.* 823a4-5: ὅσα καλὰ αὐτῷ δοκεῖ καὶ μὴ καλὰ εἶναι, νόμοις ἐμπεπλεγμένα γράφειν (cf. *Phdr.* 244c1-2). It would be in accordance with the δεινότης-theme that the Chorus stress man's interlacing of art and law rather than man's obedience to law (γεραίρων or the like).

[55]Böckh (237) does put ὑψίπολις together with ἄπολις ("Auf des Staates Höh' ist staatlos, wem das Edle fern wohnt"), but only by taking παρείρων as the equivalent of παραβαίνων; he therefore does not recognize that his interpretation is contrary to what the Chorus intend.

immorality looks like Antigone's. It would consist in her daringly reminding the city of one of its divine sanctions at the same time and for the same reason that the city is of no account to her (cf. 2.4). This characterization of Antigone remains true even if one agrees with Antigone that what she does is noble (cf. 9.4), for her morality undermines the city no less than her immorality. As the gods, moreover, are the source of Antigone's double relation to the city, one is reminded of Creon's saying that the gods shook and set upright again the city (cf. 12.2). The city uneasily exists between the gods who support it and the same gods who cannot sanction its unpurifiable impiety. Just as Antigone, then, in herself nullifies the Chorus' silence between παντοπόρος and ἄπορος, so Antigone and the gods nullify their silence between ὑψίπολις and ἄπολις. But if one asks what the Chorus think justifies their silence between these two words, the answer can only be a hope or prayer for man's submissiveness to the city: μήτ᾽ ἐμοὶ παρέστιος γένοιτο. When the Chorus call Earth the highest of the gods, it is not just a blunder but a necessary blunder, for the city must rest on something outside of man; and if the city alone determines the good and the noble, that something can only be Earth, whose ambiguity as itself or one's country conceals the violence it suffers in becoming one's own. The Chorus, then, are compelled to point to the crime of the city in praising the city; and this in turn necessarily arises from their mistake as to the character of the culprit. Their belief that only man's artfulness can account for the success with which Creon's decree was violated justifies the seeming irrelevance of the stasimon; but what justifies its relevance is that this mistake of the Chorus is the city's crime. Man's omnicompetence is man's criminality (πανουργία).

22.14. The Chorus end with the hope that the culprit not belong to their own hearth; but their hearth is each one's separate hearth and not some collective hearth of the city. The private measures the depth of their revulsion against a public crime. The culprit is automatically without a city, but he is not thereby automatically without a hearth shared with others. His isolation is only completed by a hope, a hope that the Chorus employ to slide over the difference between the family and the city. If servants, relations, or friends of Antigone had comprised the Chorus, the presence of the arrested Antigone, after the expression of such a hope, would be poignant; but as it is, Antigone and the Chorus have in common only their Theban citizenship (cf. 11.1). No one, however, mentions the πόλις in the whole of the following scene; indeed, not until Creon confronts Haemon does it recur (656).[56]

23 (376-83). 23.1. Prometheus' gifts of fire and the arts were accompanied by his settling blind hopes in men, which deprived them of

---

[56]Cf. S. Benardete, "Sophocles' *Oedipus Tyrannus*," in *Ancients and Moderns* (ed. J. Cropsey), 3.

seeing death as the fate in front of them (*PV* 248). The human being who has
no arts, is wholly without hope, and sees death before her is Antigone (cf. 3.2,
10.5, 10.8). Antigone is pre-Promethean man. She thus stands outside of
everything that the Chorus have just mentioned to illustrate man's δεινότης,
and the Chorus acknowledge this by calling her a δαιμόνιον τέρας (one must
reject Platt's τὸ δέ), where δαιμόνιον fully restores to τέρας the "religious
nuance" that all neuters in -ας originally had.[57] Antigone is a more than
human *monstrum*. Whenever τέρας refers to a living being and not an event,
either that being is monstrous in shape or origin (Io or Helen), i.e., composed
of parts that do not belong together, or the gods are its immediate source (cf.
Tr. 1098, Aesch. *Suppl.* 570, Eur. *Hel.* 255–60, *Hipp.* 1214, Pl. *Crat.*
394d5). Antigone is the only nonvisibly monstrous and wholly human being
that is ever called a τέρας. Why, then, do the Chorus do it? Their association
of daughter with father suggests that her incestuous origin partly accounts for
her monstrousness. She is, besides, δεινόν in herself, not through her success
but her failure in breaking any of the apparent limits set for man. Man's
φρόνημα was for the Chorus an aspect of his δεινότης, but now they are confronted with Antigone's ἀφροσύνη. It had not occurred to them that human
irrationality, which belongs to rationality as much as silence does to sound,
could also be terrible (cf. 10.12, 21.1). In the guise of irrationality the divine
makes known its intrusion into the unlimited world of the first stasimon. The
gods are not an outer limit that always recedes before man's daring; they are
within even from the start. Human transgression is as nothing compared with
divine possession. The particularizing τόδε is the gods' answer to the
generalizing τοῦτο of the Chorus. With her hot heart for cold things, her love
of death, and her antigeneration, Antigone shows that the union of the divine
and the human, which (the Chorus thought) the city harmonized, is essentially
monstrous.

---

[57]Cf. P. Chantraine, *Formation des noms grecs*, 422; E. Risch, *Wort-
bildung der homerisechen Sprache*, 80. δαιμόνιον τέρας occurs in Bacchylides
16.35 (Snell) of Nessus' gift to Deianeira.

A READING OF SOPHOCLES' *ANTIGONE:* II

24 (384–405). 24.1. The guard's answer to the Chorus' question proves that he can be brief and to the point; but in answering Creon he seems to be as garrulously impertinent as he had been on his first entrance (cf. 15.1). His chief concern is still himself: on each occasion he is the tenor of his first and last remarks to Creon. His joy now prompts him to as much self-justification as his fear had done before; but there are differences. He then spoke only of himself; he now begins with a generalization that he finds applicable to himself (ἀπώμοτον-ἀπώμοτος). He then explicitly distinguished between soul and self; he now implicitly distinguishes between gods and mortals. He then expressed his resignation to his fate; he now glories in his luck. His parting remark—οὐκ ἔσθ' ὅπως ὄψῃ σὺ δεῦρ ἐλθόντα με—did not suggest that he later would replace it with an oath. He must have thus bound himself while the Chorus were singing of the boundlessness of human daring. But the guard now admits that he could not maintain that self-imposed limitation. He accordingly brings out the difference between human and divine law. In ignorance of future circumstances mortals cannot obligate themselves; only the gods, it seems, could stipulate that some action be unqualifiedly binding on men. And yet one might ask whether men must acknowledge such an obligation; and if so, in what way. Does the divine command alone automatically establish the obligation? Or must each man swear to it before he can be punished for his failure to abide by it? Antigone, in her second self-justification, tries to account for the source of her obligation (cf. 27).

24.2. The guard speaks of hope and expectation three times, twice before and once after the first stasimon (235, 330, 392). When Creon frustrated the guard's expectation that he would meet his fate, the latter attributed to the gods the cause of his survival, so contrary to his expectation and judgment (330-1). The Chorus then sang of man's artfulness beyond expectation and its entire independence from the gods. The guard now speaks of his stroke of luck that set at naught his expectation, of which he had been so certain that he had confirmed it with an oath. But the guard does not now give thanks to the gods, perhaps because he thinks that the gods would not pardon even his trivial and harmless perjury. He now tells of his unexpected joy and boundless pleasure

(392–3); and he later asserts that the greatest pleasure lies in the escape from evils, and that for him everything else naturally (πεφύκει) takes second place to his own safety (436–40). He had not mentioned pleasure when he expressed his gratitude to the gods. Not the gods but chance is the author of his joy (cf. 328): he does not owe the gift of Hermes (θοὔρμαιον) to Hermes (cf. 274). He no longer needs either oaths or gods to prove his innocence. The movement from the guard's first entrance to his final departure seems to be from fate to art (the first stasimon) to chance. The movement reminds one of the argument of the tenth book of Plato's *Laws*. Three causes, according to the Athenian Stranger, are said by some to be the sole causes of everything: φύσις, τέχνη, τύχη (*Lgs.* 88e4–90a2). The Athenian Stranger then goes on to trace this understanding of nature to the supposed priority of body to soul, a priority that necessarily leads to the assertion that pleasure is the greatest good (886a9–b2). The Stranger himself, however, asserts the temporal and hierarchical priority of soul or mind to body, a priority that he links up with the existence of gods and the goodness of a providential order. Now the guard's understanding of fate is plainly not the same as this, for fate for him is no less unintelligible than it is unjust; but it is remarkable that he drops the soul and fate when he drops the gods, and that pleasure, chance, and nature take their place (cf. *OT* 977–83). The guard, who originally had spoken about what the first stasimon omitted, now speaks in accordance with the first stasimon. Antigone is entirely isolated.

24.3. The guard uses the verb θάπτω three times: "we caught her burying" (385), "she was burying the man" (402), "I saw her burying the corpse you had forbidden" (404–5). The guard offers the last of these as a plainer formulation of the second; and it is the only one that seems to be literally true (cf. 6.2); for the first fails to say what Antigone was burying (the only case out of seven where θάπτω lacks an object), and the second uniquely refers to Polynices' corpse as the man (τὸν ἄνδρα). Their inexactness, however, seems to catch Antigone's own understanding of what she is doing better than the literal third. If burial is not indispensable for conveying the soul to Hades, as the silence about it throughout the play implies (cf. 4.3), θάπτω would not be essentially a transitive verb, but would mean the whole set of rites that the mourner performs, regardless of whether any of them involves the corpse or not (cf. 395–6). Nothing, even if done to the corpse, would be done for the corpse. That the guard, moreover, when he does say what Antigone was burying, can call it "the man" suggests how readily Antigone can disregard the difference between Polynices' corpse and Polynices himself (cf. 4.3). The unity of body, soul, and self, which the guard's words convey, hardly squares with his former attempts to distinguish them. Now that the guard is not compelled through fear to disassociate himself from himself, he finds no difficulty in attributing a similar unity to the dead (cf. 20.3).

25 (406–40). 25.1. The guard's speech falls into four main parts, the first three of which describe in turn the waiting of the guards (407–21), the discovery of Antigone (422–31), and the arrest of Antigone (432–5), while the last part concerns the guard's own reaction to her arrest (436–40). One καί clearly marks off the second from the first part, and another the third from the second. The guard distinguishes between the time prior and subsequent to the dust storm (415–22), during which the guards had their eyes shut. Antigone thus approached the corpse undetected; she was able to move straight toward it despite the fact that she too must have shut her eyes against the dust that totally filled the air. She moved through the storm with the same assurance that the blind Oedipus displayed when he went unassisted to his sacred grave *(OC* 1541–6, 1588–9). Antigone is as irresistibly drawn to the corpse as any beast that feeds on carrion would be: the guard speaks of her capture as if she were a beast (432). There is no need, then, to assume that the gods directed Antigone's steps through the trackless plain (250–2). The most one could say, if one is too fastidious to attribute to her a canine sense of smell, would be that Antigone homes in on Polynices' corpse by "instinct." Polynices' corpse is her home.

25.2. The first stasimon implicitly denied that either the chthonic or the celestial imposed any limitation on man, and that man as man had any concern with understanding what manifestly stands above him or exploiting what lies hidden below him (cf. 22.5). The dust storm, then, seems at first to refute it; but the refutation lies wholly in the language in which the facts are couched, not in the facts themselves. The guard uses the words τυφώς, σκηπτός, and οὐράνιον metaphorically. τυφώς by itself, could mean a fireless thunderbolt, and σκηπτός any kind of lightning that strikes the earth [(Arist.) *de mundo* 395a21–5]; but as the ablative-genitive χθονός makes plain, the guard is describing a terrestrial phenomenon. "Heavenly harm" and "divine plague" are thus equally inexact (cf. Aesch. *Pers.* 573, 581); indeed, the guard, when he could have used οὐρανός in its precise sense, preferred to speak of the air (415–6). The dust storm, in any case, has only to be endured, and that is easy enough (cf. 356–60); it does not entail a response of reverence or of awe.[1] The dust storm, moreover, even if it does not hinder Antigone, does not help her. An eclipse of the sun would perhaps have let her get away undetected a second time; but the dust storm seems only to conceal Antigone when she does not have to be concealed, for the guards seize her only when she already has begun the rites of burial. In spite of Creon's prohibition against ritual lamentations (204), the guards choose to convict her for her deeds (strictly understood) and not for the sounds and curses that she utters, let alone for any intention to be

---

[1]Cf. Th. 2.64.2; L. Strauss, *The City and Man,* 161.

inferred from her presence with a pitcher of libations (cf. 384, 434–5; 4.4). The dust storm, then, is more indicative of Antigone's unerring sense of direction than of the gods' support. The dust storm also seems to fail her in another way: it does not re-cover Polynices' corpse. That moist and putrescent flesh should be as bare of dust after such a storm as before it looks like the single most uncanny event in the play. (But we must note that the guard never calls the storm a dust storm, and that this is directly due to his bringing down to earth a celestial vocabulary.) If the dust storm had continued for days on end, even Creon might have had to admit that the gods themselves buried Polynices; just as the Chorus of the first stasimon might then have had no less to acknowledge a limitation to man's power. But burial is something that men themselves must do; the simple vanishing of the body is not enough; for burial consists at least as much in the rites themselves as in whatever effects those rites might have (cf. 24.3). On this ground, then, it seems safer to say that Antigone sees the corpse as still unburied because she recognizes that the dust of the storm is not her own. What distinguishes the two dusts is this. What is unseemly for Polynices' unburied corpse to suffer from birds and dogs is the opposite of the unseemliness that the dust storm inflicted on the foliage in the plain (206, 419). The guard ascribes malicious intent to the storm; and this malice that blasted every vestige of life cannot be the same as the love that Antigone poured into the dust that covered Polynices' corpse. Furthermore, no matter how unelaborate her original arrangements might have been, they might yet have borne the marks of human artifice, which the haphazard swirling of the dust could not duplicate. Perhaps, however, Antigone's ritual dust and whatever dust clung to Polynices' corpse during the storm differ not so much (if at all) because artifice and chance differ as because Antigone had stamped that dust with herself. It carried in the eyes of the loving Antigone her own signature. No rule or law that governs a performance can be so strict as to exclude all variations (cf. Pl. *Rep.* 473a1–3); at best, it can only exclude those variations that would make a difference; and yet the indifference of the law to an indifferent difference would not make that difference irrelevant to Antigone. Antigone's recognition, then, that the storm's dust is not her dust perfectly agrees with the law's prescription that man must bury man. The law Antigone obeys shines through Antigone (cf. 1.2).

25.3. The guard likens Antigone to a bird that on seeing her bed bereft of its nestlings burst out with a piercing cry of lamentation. The guard is the first, except perhaps for the Chorus (113), to make use of a likeness. The strangeness of Antigone compels him to find in the familiar something comparable to her; but the differences between the image and the imaged seem to outweigh the similarities. The cries of a bird are not the same as ritual cries of mourning; Polynices is not Antigone's son; and while the bird grieves because she does not see her young, Antigone grieves because she does see Polynices. That a probable source for this simile (in Aeschylus' *Agamemnon*), which tries to compare vultures bewailing the loss of their young to Agamemnon and Menelaus setting out as plaintiffs in a legal action against Troy for the loss of Helen, should be equally inexact in its parallelism does not seem to be accidental (*Ag.* 40-67; see Fraenkel ad loc.); for beasts can no more unqualifiedly be called νεκροί or νέκυες than they can be subject to justice (cf. *Ag.* 308-9). What defeats the guard in his attempt to make Antigone intelligible is her humanity, for the purity of her devotion, which surpasses a mother's love for her children,[2] is due to the law. Antigone lives the law. She has nothing in common with beasts. The guard in borrowing the word λέχος from the human world only stresses its inapplicability to Antigone. She is the very opposite of generation. The guard succeeds in humanizing the likeness by being false to what he likens. And yet only if one takes the guard literally can one grasp the peculiarity of the bond that obtains between Antigone and Polynices. The likeness is revealing because it is misleading. Polynices' corpse stripped of its ritual dust affects Antigone in the way in which the loss of her brood affects the mother bird. The corpse is Antigone's nest, the dust her young. The corpse now stands tenantless; it was occupied when Antigone clothed it in dust. The corpse is lifeless now that it no longer houses the dust. The life of the corpse is the dust; it is the dust that is Antigone's own. The guard in sweeping away the dust swept away what Antigone looked on as strictly her own—not Polynices, not his corpse, not his head, and not his soul. Antigone's attachment is not just manifest in the dust; her attachment consists in the dust. The dust is as much the object as the means of her devotion, for it comprises the two sources of her devotion, the law and Polynices. The law makes the thirsty dust (246, 429) an essential property of Polynices' corpse, so that without it the corpse is ψιλός, i.e., deprived of what properly belongs to it; and Polynices turns the dust into his nourishment, so that Antigone is compelled to keep on returning with it like a mother bird who leaves her brood only in order to forage for them (cf. Luc. *de luctu* 19).[3]

25.4. The well-wrought brazen pitcher from which Antigone poured the libations does not seem to have been a sacred object, but merely a domestic instrument that could serve the purpose (cf. *OC* 472). The pitcher seems to illustrate that neutrality of art that was the burden of the first stasimon. Its use

---

[2]That Antigone speaks of burial as a "lightening" (κουφιεῖς, 43) indicates the extent to which she regards it as caring for the most helpless of beings; cf. *Tr.* 1025; *Or.* 218.

[3]One has to reckon with the possibility that εὐνή here bears the secondary and poetic meaning of tomb, and λέχος the meaning of bed on which a corpse is laid out (cf. 1224-5).

for libations rather than for washing or wine-pouring wholly depends on the user. In this case, moreover, its artfulness does not either add to its usefulness or give delight to Antigone and Polynices. The beautiful does not of itself belong to the sacred (cf. 32.11).[4] Yet it does not seem to be accidental that the pitcher is of bronze, for bronze often occurs in sacred contexts (cf. fr. 534,3 P; Her. 2.37.1, 147.4); and, according to a Theocritean scholium (2.36), bronze was thought to be pure, effective in averting pollution, and therefore employed for every kind of expiation and purification (cf. Macrob. *Sat.* 5.19.11). Antigone, then, seems to think herself polluted or liable to pollution, as if she were somehow at fault because Polynices now lies unburied. One can readily imagine such self-reproach in the case of a mother whose absence from her young leaves them defenseless before predators. But if Antigone thus comes prepared to make amends, she must have either guessed that the guards would sweep away the dust—Creon did not order it—or know by "instinct" of their desecration. In either case, Antigone's understanding of her obligation must have deepened. She now interprets the law as commanding her continual presence by the side of Polynices' corpse; and since his corpse is eternally helpless, she can never quit her vigil. The guards' naive way of trapping Antigone—it assumed that the criminal always returns to the scene of his crime—succeeded because Antigone accepted the trap as pointing to the true intention of the law. To bury the dead is not just "for form's sake" (cf. 22.10). Antigone's reinterpretation, however, exposes her to another difficulty. Is not Antigone now obliged to stay alive in order to preserve through the performance of yearly rites the tranquility of the dead (cf. Wyse ad Isae. 2.25.4)? Should she not thus have resorted to the utmost guile to escape detection? And is not Ismene's appeal to the perpetuation of the family as faithful to τὰ νομιζόμενα as Antigone's desire to die (cf. 8.1)? Only the union, it seems, of Antigone and Ismene could fulfill the law. But the guard, in passing over in silence one part of the burial rites, indicates how impossible that union is. A prayer to the dead that asked them to send up good things accompanied the pouring of funeral libations (Aristoph. fr. 488, 12–4 K; cf. Aesch. *Ch.* 147–9). Antigone utters evil curses against the guards and Creon; but one cannot conceive of what good things she could ask for (cf. 17.5). She rejects the very notion of worldly benefits; and for her to ask the dead to bring about her own death so that she can join them would make Creon's impiety serve a pious end (cf. 9.4). Antigone's unlimited devotion to the dead thus precludes her from praying to the dead. She can satisfy her desire to die only by failing to satisfy the letter of the law.

26 (441–8). 26.1. Creon does not dismiss the guard until Antigone confirms the guard's testimony—so reluctant is he to let the guard go free and con-

---

[4]Cf. Th. 2.34.5; Xen. *Mem.* 3.8.8–10.

vict his niece. He seems loath to have his suspicion falsified, that the burial of Polynices was a political crime, directed not at upholding the divine law but at upsetting his authority. It does not now occur to him that his enemies could have put Antigone up to it, for no one in his opinion would have done it except for worldly gain (221–2). Antigone's confession, however, does not suffice to make her punishable; she must have known that she was violating his proclamation (cf. Pl. *Plt.* 297e1–3). Creon thus acknowledges what he had before denied, that someone could have buried Polynices in perfect innocence, i.e., in accordance with the demands of custom (cf. 17.2).[5] It seems, then, to be a remarkable coincidence that Antigone, who knew of Creon's decree, should have tried to bury Polynices, while Ismene, who had not known of it (Antigone knew that she would not know, 18), should not have at once begun the rites of mourning, even if she just confined herself to ritual cries of lamentation, which Creon had no less prohibited. Ismene's grief—and Antigone never accuses her of being unfeeling—does not express itself of necessity in conventional ways. Creon's decree does not go against her grain. Antigone, on the other hand, is thwarted precisely along the lines of her nature. She was at once aware of Creon's prohibition, as later of the guards' desecration, because as the living embodiment of the law no violation of it could be unknown to her. In this sense, the Chorus correctly suspected that the first burial of Polynices was θεήλατον, i.e., the automatic consequence of the divine law (278);[6] for it is through Antigone that the law's execution follows at once on the law's existence.

26.2. Of the seven occurrences of κάρα, three are in similar forms of address (1, 899, 915, cf. 1.1), three in phrases describing some bodily movement (269, 291, 441), and one in a periphrasis for the personal pronoun (1272, cf. 764, 1345). In six of these cases κάρα is not the inevitably right word for a matter of fact: Antigone could have addressed her sister and brothers in a different way; the guard could have said that he and his colleagues were afraid without ever mentioning how they hung their heads; and Creon could have rephrased his suspicion that some Thebans were champing at his rule. κάρα seems to be an affective word: Creon enhances the pathos by saying that a god heavily struck his head. Only in Creon's address to Antigone—"You who bow your head to the ground"—does κάρα occur in a phrase that could not be

---

[5] Creon's question is even more damaging than in this regard to his own case; for, as Aristotle remarks (*EN* 1113b32–14a3), ignorance of a prohibition of positive law that one could only be ignorant of through negligence is punishable. So Creon tacitly admits that his decree is not a self-evident consequence of his soul's laws that everyone must acknowledge.

[6] Cf. Müller, 74

altered. The sameness of the guard's ἐς πέδον κάρα νεῦσαι and Creon's σὲ τὴν νεύουσαν ἐς πέδον κάρα is deceptive. Creon perhaps does not think, any more than we should if we were seeing Antigone for the first time, that her posture is compatible with defiance and contempt. But nothing suggests that Antigone now bows her head out of fear or shame; she is the same now as she was when she betrayed no emotion on her capture (433). Antigone, however, is not just meditating whether she will admit to Creon what she admitted to the guards; rather, she faces the ground because she believes that the dead are there (cf. 4.1). Her body follows her thoughts.[7] She is a "fundamentalist." It is more inevitable that Antigone look down than that the three-footed Oedipus did (cf. *OT* 795, Hes. *OD* 433–4). She is one step beyond her father. Oedipus spoke inexactly and metaphorically what was literally true;[8] Antigone acts out exactly and literally what law and convention may not have meant so strictly. Antigone cannot live the law unless she takes it literally.

27 (449–70). 27.1. Antigone's reply to Creon's question as to how she could bring herself to transgress his decree—Creon persists in speaking of it as a law—falls into three parts plus an epilogue of two lines (450–60 δώσειν, 460–4, 465–8). Each part contains its own key word, repeated three times (cf. 12.1). The first is "gods" (451, 454, 459), the second "die" (460, 462, 464), the third "pain" (466, 468bis), and the epilogue contains the triplet "foolishness," "folly," and "fool." Gods are understood as opposed to men, to whom Antigone refers three times as ἄνθρωπος, θνητός, and ἀνήρ (452, 456, 458);[9] death is understood as opposed to life (464); but pain is not understood as the opposite of pleasure and joy. The ordinary pleasures of human life are not considered, for the divine law that unconditionally commands burial is linked with Antigone's pain at Polynices' nonburial through the fact that she counts her own death as a gain. The link between gods and pain is death: θανουμένη γὰρ ἐξῄδη, τί δ' οὔ is the central line of the whole speech.

27.2. In each part of her speech Antigone suppresses something the seeming absence of which makes each part incoherent. Her enthymemes presuppose that Creon accepts her unstated major premises. Although she believes that Zeus failed to inflict no possible evil upon herself and Ismene (cf. 2.2), she

---

[7]Cf. Wolff-Bellermann; L. Campbell. On the form of Creon's address see T. Wendel, *Die Gesprachsanrede im griechischen Epos und Drama der Blutezeit*, 118.

[8]Cf. S. Benardete, "Sophocles' *Oedipus Tyrannus*," 5–6.

[9]K. Reinhardt rightly says that Antigone comprehends the uranian and chthonic gods with the "polar expression" Zeus and Dike (*Sophokles*, 85–6 with note on 86, 264); cf. 1075.

does not believe that he could have prohibited her from burying Polynices. Zeus is forever constrained by the laws that either he and Justice or the gods below have established among men.[10] Mortal Creon with all his proclamations is powerless to override the unwritten and unchanging νόμιμα of the gods, for these have eternal life, and no one knows when (or from what cause) they first came to light; and Antigone was not one, in fear of any man's pride, to face punishment before the gods' tribunal for violating them. Antigone opposes human to divine law, and human to divine punishment; but she inserts between these two arguments an argument of another kind, whose omission would apparently not have injured her case, or, if she had given it by herself, it would have been a sufficient defense. Aristotle, in order to illustrate the rhetorical use of natural right, quotes lines 456-7 alone (*Rhet.* 1373b6–13); for neither Antigone's assertion that Zeus (or the chthonic gods) established the law nor her appeal to divine punishment properly belongs to the argument from natural right.[11] If the gods have established these νόμιμα, they can be in accordance with human nature only if human beings cannot by themselves discover or are not immediately aware of what is in accordance with human nature; and if it is not known when these νόμιμα were first established (i.e., whether they are coeval with man), they are not self-evidently in accordance with human nature, for their antiquity, however remote, does not confirm their naturalness, though it may confirm their sanctity.[12] Antigone seems unable to square either their eternity with their antiquity, or their self-evident sanctity with the need for divine sanctions. Her argument would be in order if she supposes that the gods had to reveal the practice of burial in the past because of man's rude beginnings, which required that the gods thus supplement man's understanding; but now man has rediscovered for himself the eternal validity of these ancient practices. Antigone would thus point to man's moral progress and deny the separation between art and morality that the first stasimon had affirmed: ἀστυνόμοι ὀργαί would not be neutral to the difference between good and bad (cf. 22.10). Such a supposition, however, would not account for

---

[10] I am inclined to accept Earle's correction (also proposed by Bruhn), οἳ τοὺς...ὥρισαν.

[11] Cf. Cicero *de re publica* III.33.

[12] That the law is unwritten means that man cannot change it consciously; but since it also entails that if it changes one does not remember what it was before Antigone says ἀσφαλῆ (cf. 52.4). The addition of θεῶν to ἄγραπτα νόμιμα here seems to be unattested before Philo; νόμοι θεῶν ἄγραφοι occurs in a spurious fragment of Archytas (Stob. *flor.* IV.1, 132). Antigone does not want Creon to understand the unwritten laws as merely habits, the violation of which brings shame (Th. 2.27.3).

Antigone's fear of divine punishment unless she understands that punishment as the pain she would suffer if she allowed Polynices to lie unburied (cf. 94). Antigone does not have to learn the νόμιμα from another; she knows them because they live in her heart, and their violation affects her at once (cf. 25.1, 26.1). But this automatic self-punishment would be restricted to those who are, like Antigone but unlike Ismene, capable of experiencing such pain (cf. 8.5). The gods would still have to mete out another kind of punishment to those who are as insensitive as Creon. Of the thirteen occurrences of ἄλγος and its derivatives, six are in the mouth of Antigone, none in Creon's (4, 12, 64, 230, 436, 439, 466, 468 bis, 551, 630, 767, 857; cf. 316-9; *Ai.* 1332-3; 3.1, 10.11).

27.3. Antigone connects her knowledge of divine punishment if she violates the divine law with her knowledge of her own mortality that she possessed prior to Creon's decree. She did not need a proclamation in either case to know her obligations. Antigone does not distinguish between the lawful and the natural: her death is obligatory because she is mortal, her burying Polynices is obligatory because she is human. The one is certainly, the other may well be equally imposed on men by the gods. She is indifferent to the possibility that she may suffer a violent and painful death, for such suffering will be as nothing compared to that which would have awaited her if she had not observed the laws of burial. To this tacit argument Antigone adds another: death is in fact a gain for those as miserable as she is. Antigone, however, does not argue thus before she adds that she counts her death before her time as a gain. τοῦ χρόνου πρόσθεν is inconsequent, for it would seem to be her present misery and not her failure to live out her allotted span that turns her imminent death into gain (cf. 1326-7). We expect Antigone to say: (1) there is no hope that I could live forever; (2) death is a gain if one is miserable; and (3) since I am miserable, death is a gain for me. With her "before my time" Antigone makes a different point. There is no hope that she will ever cease to be miserable (cf. 3.2); and there is no such hope because man is born mortal. Man's mortality is either the necessary and sufficient condition for man's misery, or it itself constitutes man's misery. Antigone believes that the sooner she dies, the more she gains (cf. *OC* 1224-38), for the only eternity open to mortals is death (cf. 9.4). She seems to be as much oppressed as exhilarated by the eternal life of the law.

27.4. Antigone says that her death is a painless nothing, and disobedience to Creon equally unpainful, but her not burying Polynices would be painful. That not burying Polynices is painful does not seem to have anything to do with her death being painless; her death could be no less painful. If she had stopped at παρ' οὐδέν, everything, in thought as in language, would have been in order; but her thought, in racing on to what truly pains her, makes her cast her own death in its terms. Her death is both painless and gainful. It is gainful because she will then be with those she loves; it is painless because she regards it as a reward for obeying the divine law. Creon's decree is the unwitting instrument of divine benefaction. For Antigone, it is the indispensable coda to the divine law, without which the law carries in itself an automatic punishment only for its nonobservance, but no automatic reward for its observance. Death by public stoning, to which only Antigone refers as part of Creon's decree (cf. 4.9), is therefore a necessity for her; the punishment Creon later devises will not do, for if Creon has a change of heart, it allows for her being condemned to live. Antigone, accordingly, confers suicide upon herself as her reward. Only suicide can make her suicidal mission strictly suicidal (cf. 10.5) and extract from the divine law its hidden reward. The apparent defect in the plot of *Antigone,* that Creon seems to be just a little too late to save Antigone (cf. 9.1), and which was justified as revealing the way in which the gods punish intention no less severely than act, now turns out to be the same as the way in which the gods reward piety (cf. 14.2, 17.4). It is, however, of the utmost importance that Antigone does not here express the true content of her reward (cf. 48.9).

27.5 Antigone does not mention Polynices by name; instead, she so awkwardly refers to him—τὸν ἐξ ἐμῆς μητρὸς θανόντα—that she seems to make Polynices solely her mother's son and Jocasta her brother's murderer. Antigone never acknowledges that her brothers killed one another (cf. 2.4). Does she think that her mother killed them? She could think so if her abstraction from the war and its consequences led to a reflection on mortality: Jocasta by giving birth to Polynices assured his death (cf. Xen. *Ap.S.* 27). Life is a process of dying; the source of one is the source of the other; and pain for her consists solely in her mother giving birth to an unburied son.[13] As members of the family keep their relationships with one another regardless of whether they are alive or dead (cf. 3.4), Antigone is as indifferent to generation as to death. But she is antigeneration, the true offspring of an incestuous marriage. Only the abstraction from that which constitutes the family can normalize the family of Oedipus (cf. 12.2) and make Antigone a model of familial piety. Only in Hades can her family be at home, not just when it dies and goes there—"for with what eyes," says Oedipus, "if I went to Hades could I ever behold my father and wretched mother?" (*OT* 1371–3)—but only if it was formed and never left there. Antigone, then, must unsex her family and cleanse it of its origins; but she thereby removes the source of her own peculiar devotion to her family. She is made up out of the impossible demand that she combine the abstraction from the incest of her parents with the compulsion to fulfill a sacred duty that can come only from that incest (cf. 10.9). However

---

[13]Read εἰδόμην with H. D. Broadhead, *Tragica,* 73.

ironical σχεδόν τι may be in intention, with which Antigone seemingly qualifies her scorn for Creon, it indicates in fact that not only the fool would convict her of folly (cf. 10.12).

27.6 It is not accidental that Antigone's only defense of her actions in terms of the law should bring to light the relation in which she stands to her incestuous parents; for if they have caused her the most painful concern (857–68; cf. 10.4), they cannot be far from her consciousness when she speaks of the unwritten law. Lines 456–7 could equally serve to characterize the prohibition against incest. We do not know as yet whether *Antigone* reveals an essential bond between these two sacred injunctions. Must the unholiest of families breed the champion of all that is most holy in the family? Does Antigone embody the prohibition against incest as much as she embodies the law of burial? Her third defense suggests a way to answer these questions (cf. 48).

27.7. Agathias in his *Histories* (2.30–31) tells the following story. Seven Greek philosophers, dissatisfied with the prevailing opinion about God and falsely informed about the state of Persia, that its people were just and its ruler Plato's philosopher-king, decided to leave the place where the laws forbade them from living without fear and to settle in Persia, despite its alien and incompatible customs. Although they were royally entertained, they found that neither the Persians nor their king lived up to what they had heard; and on their journey back—the Persian king stipulating in his treaty with Byzantium that they were to be left alone regardless of their opinions—they came across the corpse of a man lately dead, tossed aside in accordance with Persian custom without burial. Out of compassion for the lawlessness of barbarian law and in the belief that it was not holy to allow, as far as it lay in their power, nature to be wronged, they had their attendants prepare the body for burial and then bury it in a mound of earth. That night one of the philosophers had a dream: a man whom he did not know and who bore no resemblance to anyone he knew, but for all of that with an august countenance and the beard and dress of a philosopher, seemed to address him with the following injunction: "Do not bury the unburiable; let him be prey to dogs. Earth, mother of all, does not accept the mother-corrupting man." Neither the dreamer nor his comrades could make anything of the dream; but on continuing their journey, and the lay of the land being such that they were compelled to retrace their steps, they came across the corpse they had buried the day before lying naked on the ground, "as though the earth of its own accord had cast it up and refused to save it from being eaten." Thunderstruck at the sight, the philosophers made no further attempt to perform any of the burial rites. They concluded that the Persians remain unburied as a punishment for their committing incest with their mothers and are justly torn apart by dogs.

28 (471–2). 28.1. It at first astonishes us that the Chorus seem to remark on the tone rather than on the content of Antigone's speech; they are as silent

about her argument from the divine law as Creon will be. But the Chorus do not speak of tone (note Moschopoulos' φώνημ'); they speak of a father's and a daughter's savagery. Their meaning is not plain, and even the way in which they phrase it seems strange: "It is plain: the offspring is savage from the savage father of the girl."[14] It is as though the Chorus wanted to separate Antigone the generated (τὸ γέννημα) from Antigone the daughter (τῆς παιδός). The hyperbaton, whether fully conscious or not, effects the same separation as Antigone desires: consanguinity without generation (cf. 8.6). The Chorus detect Antigone's secret while ignoring the plain meaning of her speech. Perhaps they noticed that her τὸν ἐξ ἐμῆς μητρός equally applies to Oedipus. In any case, their ὠμὸν ἐξ ὠμοῦ πατρός is too emphatic to be translated, with Jebb, "passionate child of a passionate sire"; nor does their own explanation, that Antigone does not know how to bend before evils, account for what they ascribe to Oedipus. Are they thinking of his blinding himself when he saw his mother dead (cf. *OC* 437)? But Antigone's dread of and Oedipus' horror at violating a divine law do not look the same, unless her glorying in the reward of death seems as brutal to them as his self-inflicted punishment. And yet why are they ὠμοί? The Chorus once thought that the love of death marked the fool (220). Now ὠμός occurs once more, in the compound ὠμηστής, of the flesh-eating dogs that Antigone tried to keep away from Polynices' corpse (697). Are Oedipus and Antigone raw like carrion? Or are they like dogs that become what they feed on? Are they cannibals? Are the violator of a most sacred law and the defender of a most sacred law united in their equal violation of a third unwritten law? Cannibalism and incest have one thing in common: both are extreme examples of the love of one's own. And some tribes bury their dead by eating them (Her. 3.38.4). Antigone was not disgusted by the corpse's stench (cf. 4.6), to which she found her way back in a blinding dust storm (cf. 25.1), and whose devouring by birds she thought would be a sweet treasure of delight (cf. 4.7). The Chorus, then, do comment on Antigone's argument. They sense that her devotion is incompatible with civility (cf. 22.10). The law, whose political effect is mansuetude, shows itself through Antigone as the instrument of bestialization. The Chorus shy away from attributing such opposite effects to the law; they prefer to charge Oedipus wholly with the responsibility for Antigone, which the law must share with him.

29 (473–96). 29.1. Creon picks up the Chorus' remark and directs his entire speech to them; not until Antigone claims that the Chorus side with her does Creon again speak to her (508). His speech falls into three part— Antigone (473–483), Antigone's and Ismene's punishment (484–9a), Ismene

---

[14]The repunctuation is due to J. Jackson, *Marginalia Scaenica,* 176 n.1.

and Antigone (489b-96—and eight smaller sections: (1) Antigone's twofold character (473-479), (2) her *hubris* of deed (480-1), (3) her *hubris* of boasting (482-3), (4) the necessity for her punishment (484-5), (5) the necessity for Antigone's and Ismene's punishment (486-489a), (6) Ismene's crime of plotting (489b-90), (7) her character (491-4), (8) Antigone's *hubris* of boasting (495-6). The lack of complete symmetry between the first and the last four sections—despite the balance between the *sententiae* οὐ γὰρ ἐκπέλει...πέλας (478-9) and φιλεῖ δ᾽ ὁ θυμός...τεχνώμενον (494-5)—indicates that Creon regards Ismene's as the lesser crime. Her punishment has only to exemplify Creon's impartiality when it comes to dealing with his own relations; Antigone's punishment has to be corrective as well, for she does not acknowledge that she has committed a crime (cf. 19.5). Yet Creon mistakes the meaning of Ismene's frenzy. It is not the sign of a guilty conscience but of sisterly concern; and when Creon learns this, he lets her off (at the Chorus' prompting), even though she had not told him of Antigone's intent. Creon does not hold her guilty knowledge to be punishable (cf. 266-7, 535). He allows her this measure of loyalty to her own, for he does not expect full devotion to the city of anyone except himself (cf. 12.5). But even if Ismene had conspired with Antigone, her frenzy would not necessarily have meant her acknowledgment that what she did was wrong; it could merely have signified her fear of punishment. Creon identifies the fear of punishment with remorse. To go in stealth against his decree, trying in every way to avoid detection, without thereby admitting that his decree is just, seems as impossible to Creon as to Antigone (cf. 10.5). They both deny that caution can be an ally of defiance. It is for this reason that Creon ignores almost everything except Antigone's stubbornness. Only punishment can teach her the error of her ways, so certain is he that his own case is irrefutable. Her arguments do not deserve an answer.

29.2. Creon assures the Chorus that excessive willfulness is particularly liable to collapse. He gives two examples: overtempered iron snaps and shivers of its own accord, and a small bridle disciplines the spirited horse. Creon suggests that Antigone's iron nature has been turned by the unskilled application of art into brittleness; she tried to be both uncompromising and resilient; but she failed, and the slightest resistance will destroy her. On the other hand, Antigone suffers from being nothing but untamed nature, easily brought into line with the slightest force and skill. She is both altogether artful and altogether artless (cf. 22.12). She has a nature that has been made over by art and a nature untouched by art. For art we must read law. Antigone is nothing but the law and nothing but her nature. Her nature has put on the law, but the law does not temper but exaggerate her nature. Creon understands Antigone's appeal to the law as the rationalization and not the expression of her natural willfulness. He thereby admits in a way the uncompromising character of the law; but he believes that Antigone is not tough enough to live up to it. She is principle without power, so that the very burden she has assumed will break her. Yet Creon is far more certain that he can subdue her than that he has correctly read her character: he replaces the πλεῖστ᾽ ἂν εἰσίδοις of his first example with οἶδα for the second. Creon must tame Antigone because it is out of the question, he says, for a slave to be proud. He takes her willfulness more seriously than her crime. If she goes unpunished, she derogates from his authority. He seems to see her as a possible rallying point of his political enemies, whom he had suspected of exploiting the issue of Polynices' burial (cf. 19.3). Creon thus offers three reasons in the course of his speech for punishing Antigone, only one of which applies to Ismene as well. Antigone must admit her crime—educative punishment, Antigone must have the humility proper to her position as a slave and as a woman—preventive punishment. And through Antigone and Ismene Creon must show his own willingness to punish all lawbreakers alike—exemplary punishment. We are reminded of Ismene's threefold attempt to dissuade Antigone: they would be violating the law, they are women, and they are ruled by those stronger than themselves (cf. 8.4–5). Ismene now proves to have predicted exactly Creon's response. His educative punishment assumes the weakness of Antigone; his preventive punishment is designed to keep Antigone in her place; and his exemplary punishment presupposes that his decree is a fundamental law, the violator of which must be punished if the city's fabric is not to be impaired. Exemplary punishment, however, counts far less with Creon than either preventive punishment, which occupies the two central lines of his speech, or educative punishment, with which he ends (and in a sense begins) his speech. He refers to the law, but he does not mention the city (cf. 22.14).

29.3. Creon says that Antigone and Ismene, regardless of their kinship with him, will not avoid the most miserable death; indeed, it seems to be because of their kinship that their death must be miserable (cf. 531–3). He thinks perhaps that they relied on kinship to save them from punishment. In order to indicate the norm of kinship Creon says, ὁ πᾶς ἡμῖν Ζεὺς ἑρκεῖος. The phrase means no more than "everyone who worships at our household altar of Zeus," i.e., Creon's immediate family. Creon, however, does not mention worship; Zeus merely stands in for the family. He therefore is unimpressed by Antigone's argument that she dared to transgress his decree because Zeus did not prohibit her. He took her οὐ γάρ τί μοι Ζεὺς ἦν ὁ κηρύξας τάδε as a specious periphrasis for "My family did not proclaim your laws" (cf. 658–9). The Zeus who should be fatal to his position is but part of a formula devoid of any sacred significance (cf. 192); and since this Zeus is his to do with as he likes, he prides himself on his willingness to sacrifice his own. In Plato's *Euthydemus,* one of the last arguments Socrates has with Euthydemus and Dionysodorus concerns the status of Socrates' own (301e10–

303a3). On Socrates' admission that his own consists in those things that he can use as he wants and, in the case of living beings, to sell, give, or sacrifice to any god, Dionysodorus forced Socrates to admit that, among other gods, Ζεὺς ἑρκεῖος is his. Creon accepts this argument. His ἡμῖν shows that he confuses the genitive of belonging with the dative of possession, a distinction of which he was aware when he spoke of the temples, dedications, and lands of the gods (ἐκείνων, cf. 19.2), but which, if he had admitted here, would have at once destroyed his case against Antigone. ἡμῶν Ζεὺς ἑρκεῖος is not subject to his will.

30 (497–507). 30.1. Creon says that his entire satisfaction consists in the killing of Antigone, and this in spite of his intention of converting Antigone. Her recantation, perhaps because he is so certain of it, is less important than her death (cf. 43.2). Antigone then says that the time for talking is over, and in a three-part speech—their mutual antipathy (499–501), her claim to the greatest glory (502–4a), the Chorus' silent approval of her deed (504b–7)—provokes Creon into talking to her (cf. 29.1). Of the eight occurrences of the notion "pleasing," seven are in the mouth of Antigone (75, 89bis, 500bis, 501, 504), of which the first three refer to her deed pleasing the dead (cf. 9.4.), the next three to the displeasure she takes (and always hopes to take) in Creon's words and the natural displeasure Creon takes in her (as a woman, as a slave, and in her pride), and the last to her deed pleasing the Chorus. Antigone here starts out with an opposition between Creon's deed and word, and in saying that nothing Creon says or (she hopes) will say in the future can make her recant, she implies that Creon's deed meets with her entire approval, an implication that checks her from saying "How else could I have more pleased the dead than by burying Polynices?" Her piety but not her fame is independent of her own death. Antigone, moreover, wants to show that though they cannot possibly agree on principles Creon must concede that only hers are compatible with fame. Creon is no less satisfied with his arguments than she with hers; and they will both find satisfaction in her death; but there the resemblance ends. Her glory, which derives from her piety, is the opposite of Creon's happiness that consists in his doing and saying whatever he wants. Nothing pleases her if it is not honorable; but Creon's self-gratification is at the expense of honor. He can through fear compel the acquiescence but not the admiration of the Chorus (cf. 13.1). One wonders whether Antigone understood the Chorus' remark, that she is no less savage than her father, as praise (cf. 38).

30.2. Creon is for Antigone a tyrant (cf. 8.4). He betrayed himself when he called her a slave (479). When it was open to him to say *δοῦλός ἐστι τῆς πόλεως or *τῶν νόμων he chose τῶν πέλας (cf. Pl. *Crito* 50e4). He thus revealed that he took the household as his model for ruling; and the punishment of Antigone, far from proving his impartiality, testifies to his understanding the citizen as his property. Creon never speaks of πολῖται (79, 806, 907) but only of ἀστοί (186, 193); nor does he ever mention Thebes by name (cf. 844, 937, 940). He calls the Chorus Cadmeans (508). Creon does not represent the city over against the family; he represents their identification, for which the loss of his family is the only fitting punishment. He is the direct opposite of Sophocles' Oedipus, who largely is the public man he thinks himself as being; but Creon is the private man who can only mimic his sister's son. It is Antigone who speaks of the πάνδημος πόλις and public punishment (7, 36).

31 (508–25). 31.1. The stichomythia falls into three parts, each of which presents in turn the Chorus (508–11), Eteocles (512–7), and Hades (518–25) as the proper judge of Antigone's deed. Antigone has implied that she does what she does because she is who she is; that Creon does what he does because he is now a tyrant; but that the Chorus do not say what they want to because fear constrains them. Creon ignores the first two and denies the last of Antigone's assertions (cf. 23). She is entirely alone in her vision; she does not see what is self-evident.[15] But Antigone's denial of her isolation compels Creon to phrase his point hypothetically: "Aren't you ashamed if you think apart from them [the Chorus]?" Antigone then drops the claim to glory: regardless of what they think, the reverent regard for one's flesh and blood can never be shameful (cf. 5). Her use of the plural τοὺς ὁμοσπλάγχνους lets Creon ask whether Eteocles is not equally her own brother. He is, Antigone replies, from one (mother) and the same father. Antigone again avoids saying mother and father in the same breath (cf. 27.5); when she later brings herself to do so, she bewails their incestuous marriage (865). Antigone, moreover, does not speak of one mother and one father—*ἐκ μιᾶς τε κἀξ ἑνὸς πατρός (cf. Pl. *Lgs.* 627c4). Their mother is one, but their father is the same; the same, we should otherwise suppose, for each of them; but, in light of Antigone's most painful concern, we are forced to remember that their father too is the same as themselves, their mother's son. Creon believes that Antigone has admitted what is fatal to her argument. Eteocles must regard her honor of Polynices as an impious favor. Antigone denies it, perhaps because Eteocles would neither think that private burial is an honor, nor hold himself to be the judge of what is impious (cf. 744–5). Antigone calls Eteocles "the dead corpse" (cf. 4.3). Creon never calls Eteocles a corpse; indeed, after the first scene (197, 217, 283), he never uses the word νεκρός again—he never uses

---

[15]For this meaning of ὁρῶ, cf. Pl. *Hipp. Mai.* 300c4–6: ἀλλὰ γὰρ ἐγὼ ἴσως κινδυνεύω δοκεῖν μέν τι ὁρᾶν οὕτως ἔχον ὡς σὺ φῂς ἀδύνατον εἶναι, ὁρῶ δ' οὐδέν.

νέκυς—until he sees the corpse of his wife in front of him (1299).[16] Antigone, on the other hand, does not hesitate to make a corpse bear witness—she could have said *ὁ κατθανὼν ἀνήρ (cf. 24.3)—so little does her imagination move beyond the grave (cf. 9.6). That Eteocles was patriotic and Polynices impious does not count beside their consanguinity. Polynices is Eteocles' equal by relation, and nothing that he did can affect what he is (cf. 15.3). He lived and died a brother. Neither the origin of their relationship nor its result is of any importance. Hades demands that she fulfill the law, even if the good Eteocles does not want to be treated like the bad Polynices (cf. Ai. 1344–5) The earth, in whose defense Eteocles perished, has no connection with what is below (cf. 4.1). "Who knows," Antigone says, "if this [the burial of Polynices] is free from pollution below?" Antigone pleads ignorance in the face of Creon's attributing his own opinion to Eteocles. She is as uncertain about the meaning as about the origin of the law (cf. 457). Her ultimate defense must therefore be that the law exactly coincides with her nature. Her nature validates the law. "It is not my nature to side with either of them in his enmity but to side with both of them in the kindness of their kind" (cf. 9.5).[17] To bury Polynices is an act of love, of compassion and tenderness, that unites her with her own (cf. 25.3). This is the essence of the law that enjoins the burial of one's own; and Antigone is that essence by nature. Creon understands and fails to understand when he scornfully says, "Go then below, and love them if love you must."

---

[16]There seems to be a recognizable difference in meaning between νεκρός and νέκυς as both Sophocles and Herodotus use them. In Herodotus, νέκυς only occurs in the first four books (always singular), νεκρός throughout. νεκρός is the corpse as something bodily, to which one can do things, while νέκυς, which often takes a defining genitive (rare for νεκρός), is the corpse in its relation to the living person, a being that can itself do something: Herodotus has νεκυομαντήιον, not νεκρο- (5.92η2; cf. Soph. fr. 399P). So the shepherd puts the νεκρός of his own son in the casket that carried the prince's but offers to show τοῦ παιδίου τὸν νέκυν to Harpagus (1.113.1–2); Tomyris seeks among the dead Persians for τὸν Κύρου νέκυν, but while abusing its head, she speaks over τῷ νεκρῷ (1.214.4); and most strikingly, in the story in 2.121, the corpse of the brother is always νέκυς, but the corpse whose arm is cut off to fool the king's daughter is νεκρός (121ε4,5); cf. 4.71.4. In Antigone, in those cases where the two are metrically equivalent, Antigone contrasts Eteocles τοῖς ἔνερθεν ἔντιμον νεκροῖς with τὸν Πολυνείκους νέκυν (26–6); Tiresias says, τῶν σῶν ἐκ σπλάγχνων ἕνα νέκυν νεκρῶν ἀμοιβόν (1066–7); cf. 515. νέκυς is surprisingly rare in the other plays of Sophocles as well as in the other playwrights; cf. El. 443; OC 621–2.

[17]Cf. Reinhardt, op. cit., 88.

His literalness shows how paradoxical is Antigone's living of the law. Burial for him is an honor and a reminder; it cannot be a way of life. In punishing Antigone, however, he will literalize her understanding of the law (cf. 47.3); and Antigone in a way cannot but be grateful for his easing the burden that nature and law have jointly imposed upon her (cf. 29.2).

31.2. Antigone hardly ever speaks to anyone in the expectation that she will be listened to. In her exchange with Creon (but never with Ismene or the Chorus) she twice drives home a point with τοι, once at the beginning in order to appeal to him on the only ground they could possibly share, the concern with reputation (502), and once at the end in order to define her nature (523). After that she does not use τοι again until in a single speech it occurs three times when she addresses the dead (897, 904, 913; cf. *Ai.* 854–5). They are her only friends (cf. 11.1).

32 (526–30). 32.1. The last word Creon utters before Ismene enters is γυνή. It applies far better to her than to Antigone, who hardly thinks of herself as a woman (cf. 8.5). Ismene sheds the tears of a loving sister; and if the tears fall down (κάτω), it is not because she has bowed her head to gaze at what lies below the earth (cf. 26.3). She shows a woman's way of expressing love and grief (cf. *Ai.* 579–80). But Antigone never weeps (cf. 831–2, 881–2), though even the Chorus are later moved to tears (802–3). Ismene's cloud of grief-laden tears makes her face ugly and wets her fair cheeks. Nothing is said of Antigone's beauty; all we know about her looks is that in death her cheek was white (1239). She does not become uglier in her grief: she is a τέρας (cf. 23.1). Nothing of Antigone's ever provokes the Chorus to such concentrated poetic expression as Ismene has done. Antigone is recalcitrant to poetry: the guard's attempt at a simile was most notable for its failure (cf. 25.3), Ismene's face is bloody, not from any blush of shame (cf. 540–1), but from raking her cheeks in accordance with a woman's way of mourning (cf. Aesch. *Ch.* 24; Soph. *El.* 90).[18] She has to mar herself in order to show to herself and to others how she has been affected. Creon saw her raving witlessly in the palace (492). Antigone has no need of such signs. If she had wished to go undetected, she would never have betrayed herself. She is thus the perfect vessel to be filled with the law's impersonality. Nothing of her own stands in the way of her observing the love of her own. In her passion she is neutral (cf. 34.2).

33 (531–7). 33.1. If one adopts Creon's triad of ψυχή, φρόνημα, and γνώμη (cf. 12.4), and Creon's first attack on Antigone (473–96) be regarded as mostly concerned with Antigone's φρόνημα, the kind of resolution she has brought to her action, and their exchange prior to Ismene's entrance (508–25)

---

[18]Heath, W. Schmid (*RhM* 57, 624–5), and G. H. Macurdy (*CP* 1946, 163–4) offered this interpretation; Bruhn did too but doubtfully.

as his attempt to discover Antigone's γνώμη, the reasons she may have for her action, then these lines between himself and Ismene prepare the way for Antigone's declaration of her ψυχή (538–60), what she is most devoted to or loves. Antigone's ψυχή, however, can be revealed only if Antigone confronts Ismene, for only her rejection of Ismene can show that that which distinguishes them in φρόνημα has its ground in the difference of their ψυχή. Up to then Creon cannot but suppose that Ismene's γνώμη would have been the same as Antigone's, which Creon mistook for a woman's reasons. Creon, moreover, primarily thinks of the soul as nothing more than an aspect of the self (cf. 15.2). When he likens Ismene to a viper lurking in his palace, he does not say, as Clytemestra says of Electra, that she drinks dry his pure life's blood (τοὐμὸν ἐκπίνουσ᾽ ἀεὶ ψυχῆς ἄκρατον αἷμα, *El.* 785–6), but merely that she drinks him dry. Creon cannot understand the soul as something distinct from the self or stronger than the body (cf. 20.2); the possibility, which Antigone in herself presents, that the soul in being what one most loves is the same as what one is, must look to him like madness (562).

33.2. Despite all the evidence to the contrary, Creon persists in the belief that Antigone and Ismene are part of a political conspiracy, directed to the overthrow of his rule (cf. 525), and which their punishment will prevent (cf. 29.2). Antigone was in a sense responsible for this error; by calling his rule a tyranny, she questioned his legitimacy, on which he had put such stress (cf. 12.2). He suspects that Antigone and Ismene have buried Polynices in order to embarrass him; for though Eteocles could be honored as his country's champion, Polynices contributed as much as Eteocles to Creon's right to succeed them (cf. 173–4). He cannot believe that Polynices was buried because he had to be buried. His first and last question is always, *cui bono*?

33.3. Creon asks Ismene whether she will swear to her ignorance of Polynices' burial; he did not ask Antigone whether she would swear that she did not do the deed (442). His estimate of Ismene's θυμός makes him suppose that only the fear of committing perjury would stop her from lying (493–4); he did not believe that Antigone's impudence would go as far as to deny, while not being under oath, what she had freely admitted to his servants. Creon thus acknowledges that her impudence has nothing to do with cleverness or impiety (cf. 300–1).

33.4. Ismene says that she did the deed; she does not admit her guilty knowledge, which not even Antigone could have denied her. Ismene exaggerates her culpability, on the assumption that intention counts as much as act. One cannot therefore help wondering whether Antigone's vehemence in insisting that act must be strictly understood does not arise from her fear that those below will hold her own act to be no more than an intention (cf. 10.1–3, 48.4).

34 (538–60). 34.1. There are seventeen exchanges between Antigone and Ismene, the same number as there were between Antigone and Creon. Their

exchange also falls into three parts (cf. 31.1), each of which in turn decides whose deed it was (538–45), whose death it should be (546–54), and whose choice it was (555–60). The "subjectivity" of its theme requires that Antigone use ἐγώ (five times), which she did not use once in talking with Creon. Parallel to Creon's assertion that Antigone's vision is her own stands Antigone's assertion that justice forbids Ismene from claiming Antigone's deed as her own; and just as then Antigone asserted that reverence for one's own cannot be shameful, regardless of human opinion, so she now makes Hades and those below bear witness to her deed being her own, regardless of what Ismene says. That the guards could testify on her behalf does not count. Yet she cannot bring herself to say that the nether world does not love her who loves in speech (*λόγοις φιλοῦσαν δ' οὐ φιλοῦσι τὴν φίλην). She cannot be certain of what holds there (cf. 521); nor can she be unaware that she too might have to plead intention. Ismene, at least, senses that Antigone's death is somehow the same as Antigone's sanctifying of the dead; for to share in one is to share in the other. If Creon understands the unsuccessful crime to be punishable, perhaps Hades will not determine too exactly the degree of failure on either's part. Punishment will validate the equation of act and intention. Antigone, however, decides, as Creon does later (771), that the actual touching of the corpse by hand makes all the difference (cf. 900). Perhaps she condemns Ismene in light of her own willingness (and more than willingness) to handle the rotting corpse, for which, she might suspect, Ismene had the same repugnance as the guards (cf. 28.1).

34.2. Creon had tried to argue that if Antigone granted that Eteocles was no less a brother than Polynices, she could not justify the burial of Polynices before his brother; but Antigone granted Creon's premise without drawing his conclusion, for their sameness of origin outweighed any subsequent difference. Now, however, Antigone has to distinguish between her sister and herself, while Ismene tries to die with her solely on the ground that they are sisters. She wants to die because her life without Antigone would cease to be φίλος. Life (βίος) for Ismene can be dear or hateful; life (ζωή) for Antigone is merely what she still lives (cf. 3.2). Ismene does not have the strength to live alone; Antigone has the strength to die alone. Antigone does not need to be helped; Ismene has Creon to care for. Ismene thinks that Antigone thus pains her gratuitously; Antigone replies that her mockery has its source in her pain.[19] Creon had said that Antigone's favor to Polynices was impious in the eyes of his brother; Antigone had replied that Eteocles could not, as a brother, object, and if he did, the laws of Hades took precedence. The mockery of Ismene matches the dishonor of Eteocles; and Antigone's pain excuses her mockery as

---

[19]Cf. J. H. Kells, *BICS* 1963, 53–5.

Hades' laws excuse the insult to Eteocles. Antigone can only live up to the law by putting aside the difference between her brothers; and she can only die in accordance with her choice if she puts aside the difference between βίος and ζωή. She can console Eteocles with the law; she cannot acknowledge his merits; and she can offer Ismene life; she cannot make her happy. Antigone consists of the choice of death and her obedience to Hades' laws; they are both necessarily painful; for the laws in their insistence on uniformity suppress the difference between goodness and badness that partly constitutes the ground for love and hatred, no less than the choice of death suppresses the difference between misery and happiness (cf. 27.3). Antigone can only live abstractly, i.e., piously. There are no words or even sounds for her pain (554, cf. 49, 82, 86).[20] She has a hot heart for cold things (cf. 10.6).

34.3. Antigone implies that Ismene's choice of life and her own choice of death are irrevocable; Ismene replies that as Antigone's choice was made in the face of her own warning, the choice was merely a lapse of judgment, and no more than a proof of her own inability to persuade Antigone. The arguments as arguments were sound. Antigone, however, denies that anyone else could have put a stronger case. Ismene's arguments met with the full approval of the living, she herself with the full approval of the dead. Ismene has no ground for self-reproach, for Antigone's choice was not based on argument, on reasons that someone could possibly refute. Ismene then tries one last time. As her warnings prove her guilty knowledge, their fault is equal. Antigone brushes this aside and continues her own line of thought. The fact that Ismene talks at all in terms of fault shows that she persists in accepting life. Ismene still believes that it could have been otherwise; but Antigone did not mean that either chose what she did among other possibilities. "My soul has long been dead, so as to be [exclusively] fit to help the dead." For Antigone, it is a "natural result," to use the language of the grammarians, that her soul in being dead helps the dead. ἡ δ᾽ ἐμὴ ψυχή —Antigone nowhere else speaks of ψυχή—

---

[20]It is remarkable to what an extent Antigone refrains from using the conventional interjections that express grief and other intense feelings. αἰαῖ occurs only in the mouth of Creon (1267, 1288, 1290, 1306); even Ajax uses it (370). ἰώ Antigone uses four times (844, 850, 862, 869), as does Creon (1261, 1266, 1284, 1320, cf. 1310 Erfurdt), the Chorus once (1146). Antigone never uses φεῦ, the guard and Tiresias each once (323, 1048), Creon five times (1276bis, 1300 ter, cf. 1310 codd). οἴμοι Antigone and Ismene each use thrice (86, 838, 933; 49, 82, 554), Creon five times (320, 1105, 1271, 1275, 1294), the Chorus once (1270). Other interjections are entirely absent: παπαί (Ph., OC, El.); ὀτοτοτοί (El.); ἔ (OC, Tr., El.); ἀπαππαπαῖ (Ph.); πόποι (OT, Tr.).

is not a periphrasis for ἐγώ: Philoctetes' τέθνηκ᾽ ὑμῖν πάλαι, as ὑμῖν shows, is not comparable (*Ph.* 1030).[21] Antigone's way of being alive has been to be in the state of death. Creon thought he was exposing Antigone's unconscious premise when he bid her in death love the dead below. Antigone now answers that she had been doing that all along. θάπτειν means συμφιλεῖν, and συμφιλεῖν means to be alive in death (cf. 31.1). Her choice of death has nothing to do with Creon's punishment; it is the same as her obedience to Hades' laws. Her performance of the rites of burial is her love of death (cf. 25.3). She is what she loves. Ismene cannot die with her because it would be only as punishment that it confirmed that Ismene buried Polynices; it would not be what it is for Antigone, the worldly equivalent to the truth of the unwritten law.

35 (561–73). 35.1. Creon again shows that his hatred of Antigone lets him see more deeply into Antigone than Ismene's love for her. Ismene's willingness to die is a momentary aberration; Antigone was senseless from birth. πάλαι in her ἡ δ᾽ ἐμὴ ψυχὴ πάλαι τέθνηκεν means, according to Creon, φύσει. Ismene, however, pleads—she hopes her deferential ὦναξ will have some effect—that no one in misery keeps a balanced mind. Creon concedes that that holds true for Ismene; but Antigone is not miserable (κακῶς πράσσει), she is bad and does bad things (πράσσειν κακά). It is part of Antigone's senseless nature to be bad; Ismene only made a bad and senseless choice. But Ismene says that she has no other choice; her life alone without Antigone is not worth living, for if Creon will kill the future wife of his own son, her own hopes for their family's survival collapse (cf. 8.1). Creon answers in such a way as to suggest that Ismene understands neither his own inflexibility nor her sister's nature; Antigone is not a ἥδε; she no longer is here among the living (cf. 13.1). Her life in death can therefore have no place for survival through generation. However crudely Creon expresses Antigone's ἡ δ᾽ ἐμὴ ψυχὴ πάλαι τέθνηκεν, he does not wholly mistake its meaning. Since Antigone is not a "this," to whom someone living can be attached, Creon can be crude: there are other fields for his son to plow. Antigone is particularly liable to others' abstraction: Ismene calls her "bridal rites" (cf. 891, 1205).[22] But Ismene protests Creon's denial of Antigone's individuality. The betrothal of Antigone and Haemon was unique in its fitness. Ismene points to their concordance in a legal relationship; she cannot bring herself to say that they love one another (cf. 73). Creon again generalizes: "I loathe bad wives for sons." Antigone is

---

[21] Almost as paradoxical as Antigone's assertion is Pl. *Lgs.* 927a1–3: αἱ τῶν τελευτησάντων ψυχαὶ δύναμιν ἔχουσίν τινα τελευτήσασαι, ᾗ τῶν κατ᾽ ἀνθρώπους πραγμάτων ἐπιμελοῦνται.

[22] See Porson on Eur. *Or.* 1051.

no more unique morally than she is sexually. Ismene then despairs of dissuading Creon, for he holds his son's wishes to be of no account. In calling Haemon "dearest," Ismene underlines, not only how far Creon has gone in the dismissal of his own (cf. 486-7), but how much her own hope rests on Haemon. But Creon brushes Ismene aside: she and her talk of marriage annoy him.

35.2. There are three objections to giving line 572 to Antigone. First, we must then suppose that Creon's dishonoring of Haemon consists in his calling Antigone a bad wife; but Creon does not criticize his son. Antigone is as bad for Haemon as she is bad in herself; Creon hates her on both counts (cf. 495-6). Creon, moreover, would then be saying to Antigone that he has no patience with her and her marriage; but Antigone neither speaks of marriage (even if line 572 be hers), nor has she been pleading for pardon on this or any other account. Creon could not answer Antigone in terms of what Ismene had said.[23] His reply to Antigone would have to have been: "I do not dishonor him in loathing you." And, finally, ἄγαν γε λυπεῖς suits Creon's annoyance with Ismene, but not his violent hatred of Antigone (cf. 760, 1084; Ai. 589, 592; fr. 314, 1.393P).[24]

36 (574-81). 36.1. Creon now faces his third opponent, the Chorus, whose remonstrance is so mild that they can hardly be said to oppose him. They do not take up Antigone's argument that she obeys a divine law, nor even Ismene's first plea that a deranged Antigone should not be punished, but merely repeat with a tone of wonder Ismene's second plea: "Is it really certain that you will deprive your own offspring of her?" They are surprised that Creon will not relent merely to indulge his son. The Chorus know nothing of the law, either in its sacredness or in its mercy. "It is the nature of Hades," Creon replies, "to put a stop to this marriage."[25] Creon means that he is not going to put to death Antigone the bride—his son's wife is of little importance one way or the other—but Antigone's death guarantees the end of Haemon's marriage. It seems proper that Creon should thus rebuke the Chorus for speaking so girlishly. Yet Creon's refusal to be a fond parent precipitates the destruction of his family. The worst reason in light of the law proves to be the strongest argument in light of individuals. If Creon had been "un-principled,"

---

[23]Cf. Schneidewin.

[24]For the pros and cons on the attribution of this line, see Müller, 109. His arguments for Antigone as the speaker do not come to grips with the difficulties. Creon's reply is correctly interpreted by A. Taccone, *Mouseion* 1923, 187.

[25]L's ἐμοί puts too great a stress on Creon's satisfaction in killing his son's fiancee; his satisfaction still largely consists in killing a lawbreaker.

he would have gone unpunished. That a concession, moreover, the very reverse of holy—a father gratifying a son's desires—would have made Creon do what is holy (ὅσια δρᾶν) brings out as nothing else could the uncanniness of Antigone's piety (cf. 9.3). It is one thing to act in accordance with the sacred, it is another to live it from within. The Chorus, at any rate, have just shown that it is one thing to act prudently, it is another to be wise (cf. 11.2, 4).

36.2. The Chorus inadvertently introduce for the first time since Ismene's entrance a quasi-political note: "It is resolved, it seems, that she be killed." Creon is quick to pick up the cue: "Yes, resolved by you as well as by me." Creon reminds the Chorus of his request, to which they never assented, that they stand fast against those who break the law (219-20). But his decree, even if accepted by the Chorus, would still not thereby become the city's resolution—he could not have said *καὶ σοί γε κἀμοὶ καὶ πόλει δεδογμέν' ἦν (cf. 749, *OT* 64), for Creon convened the Chorus because he mistook their adaptability to circumstance for their loyalty to the royal house (cf. 12.3). Creon senses that the Chorus are lukewarm, as incapable of opposing as supporting him. If he wants anything to be done, he must rely on his own servants. The Chorus could no more guard two women than they could keep watch over a corpse (cf. 215-7). The word δμῶες, moreover, which does not recur in Sophocles (cf. 1189, 1249), indicates how unpolitical Creon himself has become. His domain is now restricted to his own household, in which Antigone is a slave (cf. 30.2).

36.3. Creon thinks that Antigone and Ismene, who each in her own way has rashly chosen death, will try to escape, now that they see Hades drawing close to their life. It is plain, however, why Ismene would not desert Antigone; but why Antigone should not do everything she can to avoid an unjust punishment cannot be based on the reasons Socrates (either Plato's or Xenophon's) gave to justify his acceptance of the Athenians' condemnation. Plato's Socrates does not know whether there is a Hades; Antigone never doubts its existence—she only hopes that her family will love her (897-9). A young Socrates might have escaped; Antigone seems to have as much to live for as to die for. Socrates accepts his punishment as the price he pays for his choice of remaining in Athens; Antigone accepts her punishment as the reward for her piety. Socrates divines but does not wish that the Athenians will be punished (*Ap.S.* 39c3-d3; cf. *Rep.* 366c3-d3); Antigone wishes but does not divine that Creon will be punished (925-8). These differences recall Solon's double account of human happiness (Her. 1. 30-2). When Croesus asked Solon who he thought was the happiest of men, Solon had "truthfully" answered Tellus; and when he asked who was in second place, Solon answered Cleobis and Biton. Solon's descriptions indicate why he ranked them as first and second. While Athens was flourishing, Tellus had "beautiful and good" sons, all of whom in turn had children that were still alive; he himself had a modest fortune and met with a "most brilliant end of life"; for in a battle at Eleusis he routed the enemy and died "most beautifully"; and "the Athenians buried him where he fell at public expense and honored him greatly." Cleobis and Biton were Argives, whose livelihood was "adequate" and whose "bodily strength" had won them prizes in athletic contests. A story was told that when their mother had to appear at a festival to Hera, and the oxen to draw her cart were not at hand, they put themselves under the yoke and drew it forty-five stades to the sanctuary; for which they obtained the "best end of life," since "god showed in their case that it is better for a man to die than to live." The Argive men "blessed the strength of the youths," the Argive women their mother, who "joyful at their deed and report" prayed to the statue of Hera to grant her sons, who had honored her greatly, "what is best for a man to obtain." Cleobis and Biton were found dead in the sanctuary, and the Argives made images of them, which they dedicated at Delphi, "thinking that they had proved to be the best men." The first story turns on seeing, the second on hearing. Solon knows about Tellus—Croesus asked him whom he had seen most happy; he only knows a "story" about Cleobis and Biton, whose mother prayed because of the φήμη her sons received. Tellus had "beautiful and good" sons; Cleobis and Biton were strong. Tellus had a "most brilliant death"; Cleobis and Biton had the best. Tellus was honored by the city and buried at public expense, for he had fought for the sake of the city. Cleobis and Biton had helped their own mother; nothing is said about who buried them. Tellus lived at a time when Athens was flourishing; nothing is said about Argos' prosperity—its preeminence had been at the time of Io's rape (1.1.2). Tellus dies in a political setting, Cleobis and Biton in a sanctuary. Tellus' death at a ripe age was the most brilliant from a civil point of view, Cleobis' and Biton's from the divine. Tellus freely chose to die; a god gave to Cleobis and Biton their end. Tellus lived and died within the human horizon, the horizon of the city. He obtained everything that men regard as desirable. Cleobis and Biton obtained what gods thought best for men. The city looks to the beautiful and fine things, the gods to the best. The human good and the divine good are not the same. One restricts the end to visible and tangible goods—money, beautiful children, grandchildren, public honor. The other cares more for nonpolitical and even antipolitical ends; it says that life is not worth living. Socrates' life resembles the political Tellus, Antigone's the holy Cleobis and Biton. Socrates, however, transcends the political and its καλά while retaining its estimate of the sweetness of human life (cf. Ap.S. 33c4, 41b5 and context); Antigone remains within the political and its καλά while transcending the human (cf. 27.3).

37 (582–625). 37.1. The theme of the second stasimon is human happiness and misery, but it is not easy to formulate its unity more exactly. Only three nouns occur in both strophic pairs: θεός, ἄτα, φρένες. One might there-

fore say that the Chorus are mainly concerned with how the gods and the human soul work together for man's destruction. But even if this does run through and bind together both strophic pairs, their differences seem to separate them more. The first strophic pair sees the individual as part of his family; the second sees him as part of mankind. The first strophic pair speaks of generation, root, and house (γενεά, γένος, ῥίζα, δόμος, οἶκοι); the second speaks of mortals and men (θνατοί, ἄνδρες). The first strophic pair contains no non-metaphoric substantive for the individual; the second contains no proper names except Olympus and Zeus. The stasimon, then, as a whole turns on the ambiguity of "kind" (γένος): man in his parentage and man in his humanity. The first strophic pair speaks of man's past (ἀρχαῖα) and his becoming and perishing (φθιτοί); the second speaks of man's future (ἐλπίς, ἔρως) and his existence (βίοτος)—sleep, old age, and time. The stasimon, however, nowhere considers man as part of the city, perhaps because the city does not properly constitute a γένος in any natural way (cf. 342-5).

37.2. The first strophe begins with a general statement, which the elaborate simile that follows it is meant to illustrate. The second strophe begins with a general statement, which the facts that follow it are meant to prove; and the second strophe ends with the statement of a law binding for all time. The first antistrophe begins with an example, which the Chorus have themselves seen, that confirms the first strophe's statement, the operation of which is then illustrated more particularly in the case of Antigone. The second antistrophe begins with an explanation of the law's universal validity, which it then illustrates in a homely way, and whose meaning is in turn revealed by a renowned adage. The first strophic pair is vivid and imprecise—every one of its substantives occurs elsewhere in Sophocles; the second is plain, and distinct—ὑπερβασία and δυνάστας occur only here, δύνασις only again at 951.[26] The first strophic pair seems to be the poetic interpretation, the second seems to be the wise (620) interpretation of human life. The second strophic pair explains why a god leads a man astray (ὑπερβασία); the first accounts for the continuance of disaster within a family but not for its initial subversion by the gods. The gods of the first strophic pair are chthonic, the gods of the second Olympian. The chthonic has to do with the irrational, which it itself represents, the Olympian with the immoral, whose delusions it brings. The first strophic pair seems to pardon Antigone, the second to condemn her.

37.3. The simile of the first strophe likens the Thracian winds that set the surge in motion to the gods who once they have shaken a house never let its tremors cease. The ruffled surge in racing across the darkness of the sea's depths, and from which it stirs up dark sand, must be the present generation of

---

[26]Cf. A. A. Long, *Language and Thought in Sophocles*, 57-8.

a family (all of whom now lie below in darkness),[27] which likewise stirs up the original ἄτη, and which the individual of this last generation confronts as a shore confronts the storm. But the simile, however vividly it conveys that of which it is a simile, still more looks forward to the antistrophe's description of Antigone. The parallelism is remarkable for its inversion. The surge that races over the nether darkness under the sea is turned upside down in the light of hope that stretches over the last root of Oedipus' house; the dark sand rolled up from the depths is echoed inversely in the blood-red dust of the nether gods that buries Antigone;[28] and the headlands in their groaning and rumbling are taken up, again backwards, in the senselessness of speech and fury of wits that Antigone adds to the sacred law of burial. Antigone once more enters poetry under duress (cf. 32.1). She resists the poetry; she is antigeneration, who cannot embody, as Ismene and the Chorus believe she does, the hope in generation. The Chorus cast her in this role only to discover that the original crime of her family (the dark sand) proves to be the blood-red dust owed to the nether gods. The paradox of equating a sacred law with an original crime can be avoided only by concluding that it is better not to be born. Thus there culminates in Antigone—manifest to the Chorus in her inherited savagery and to Creon in her inborn senselessness—the very character of her family,[29] which wiped out through Oedipus that succession of generations on which the Chorus' argument rests. But if the Labdacids' original crime consists in generation itself, Antigone strangely is the hope of her race, not in perpetuating but in reconstituting it in Hades (cf. 27.5); and her senselessness of speech and fury of wits are the deepest wisdom (cf. 22.10, 11). That which buries

---

[27]It cannot be accidental that ἔρεβος everywhere else in classical poetry is connected with Tartarus and death; cf. *OC* 1389-90; Trag. adesp. 377 N.

[28]ἀμᾷ is difficult if κόνις is kept, but I venture to suggest that it has nothing to do with the verb to mow, but that it is found in διαμάω (cut through) with the basic meaning *to dig, the nominal forms of which are ἄμη (mattock) and ἀμάρα (channel). καταμάω would then have the same sense as κατορύσσω. Frisk also thinks that two distinct roots might be involved (*Griechisches Etymologisches Wörterbuch*); but Chantraine does not (*Dictionnaire étymologique de grec*). See further N. B. Booth's defense, *CQ* 1959, 76-7. Heimreich's σκιᾷ (for ἀμᾷ) is to be preferred to κοπίς; but if κοπίς must be accepted, the best parallel to the whole passage would be Aesch. *Ch.* 286-90. Even κοπίς, however, makes the passage no easier to understand; for if λόγων ἄνοια and φρενῶν Ἐρινύς are in apposition to it, the Chorus can only be saying that Antigone's destruction is due to some chthonic power, which power can only be the law of burial.

[29]Laius was held to be the first homosexual.

Antigone is that which finally purifies her kind.

37.4 The second stasimon sings of all that the first stasimon had omitted (cf. 22.7, 25.2). Nothing remains of man's δεινότης—the light-witted birds that man snares become the light-witted desires that delude man—unless it be hope, to which the second antistrophe here ascribes the same moral neutrality as the second antistrophe there had ascribed to art. But the goodness of art depended on its alliance with the laws of the land and the justice of the gods; the goodness of far-ranging hope seems to depend on nothing. The city no longer mediates between the confrontation of gods and men, for it does not administer the law that the Chorus now lay down. Yet the benefits of hope without the city seem to be limited to the life untouched by evils, the life, according to the Chorus, of the happy. Such happiness is consistent with the guard's understanding of the greatest pleasure, the unexpected escape from evils (cf. 24.2), but neither with the splendor of Solon's Tellus nor with the happiness of tyranny (506-7). Everything beautiful and brilliant belongs to Olympian Zeus. Man's delusion consists in his hope that he can acquire for himself these prerogatives of Zeus; but he is always held in check. This check is formulated as a law, in which unfortunately the key term is corrupt; but the sense seems to have been that everything wholly loved and desired comes disastrously to man.[30] If one strips Antigone's devotion to her family both of its divine origin through generation and of its divine sanction in the unwritten law and looks upon it as an entirely individual and human phenomenon, no different in kind from Haemon's love of Antigone, then the Chorus simply condemn Antigone for her lack of moderation. But it is then not easy to say how Antigone transgresses the power of Zeus. Or do the Chorus mean that Antigone's love of her own offends Zeus through its denial of everything

---

[30]H. Lloyd-Jones has shown that Heath's πάμπολύ γ' is impossible (*CQ* 1957, 10-20); but his own βίοτος πάμπολυς (also proposed by Kayser) does not satisfy, for βίοτος is not ὄλβος, or is πάμμεγας πάμπολυς, and the hope of prosperity cannot by itself be the ground for the disastrousness of prosperity. πάμπολυς, moreover, does not occur in extant tragedy; it seems to be avoided in formal prose; Isocrates does not have it; see further Müller, 145, note 1. When Jebb paraphrases the impossible πάμπολύ γ' in order to explain the antistrophe's γάρ, he says, "No inordinate desire comes to men...." I suggest that either the unattested παμφιλές or προσφιλές. The other possibility is the often conjectured παντελές: "Nothing comes complete to human life except disaster," i.e., only ἄτη stands at the peak of human hopes. Possibly πὰρ πόδας should be read: "Nothing follows as closely on the heels of human life as ἄτη." Sophocles would have deformed the proverb, νέμεσις δέ γε πὰρ πόδα βαίνει (παρὰ πόδας codd.).

noble and splendid as much as the emulation of his splendor would? The Olympian gods would thus represent a twofold prohibition, forbidding equally the exclusive love of one's own, which turns away from everything higher than itself, and the exclusive love of the beautiful, which challenges their supremacy. The human embodiment of this twofold prohibition is the city, which looks up to the gods as both its defender and its aspiration. But the Chorus do not mention the city. Their silence would seem to indicate that they are aware that the city does not embody but rather uneasily contains this twofold prohibition. If, however, one keeps Antigone's character as an individual human being together with her character as the expression of her origins and of the sacred, Antigone herself looks like the perfect resolution between the love of one's own and the love of the beautiful (cf. 9.3,4). But Antigone is a monster in the eyes of the Chorus (cf. 23.1). It seems, in any case, to be the counsel of despair if the perfect resolution necessarily entails the love of death.

37.5 One might suppose that the second stasimon does not exclusively refer to Antigone, but that only the first strophic pair does, while the second refers to Creon. Creon is willfully, Antigone helplessly guilty. Human misery has two different sources, one to be traced back through one's own ancestors to an original crime, the other directly attributable to an individual's *hubris*. On this view, Antigone represents the final working out of her inheritance, and Creon the beginning of a new chain of disasters. Ismene does not yet pose a problem, for the Chorus believe that she will share in the fate of Antigone; but Creon not only commits the first crime, he sees its destructive force at work in his own family. There will be no later generations to assume Creon's crime. Creon's punishment, which lies in the loss of his family, illustrates the operation of inheritance so perfectly that it fails to illustrate the operation of inheritance. Ismene's survival, on the other hand, could be taken as auguring a fresh onset of Laius' crime (cf. second hypothesis). The second strophic pair, then, cannot be thus reconciled with the first. If, however, one ignores the Chorus' restriction in the first antistrophe to the individual's family, and generalizes it to pertain to man as man, the first crime of a race would become man's original sin. This sin could have been Prometheus' theft of fire, or, to keep to the presentation of the first stasimon, man's own invention of the arts, the punishment for which was, according to Hesiod, first Pandora and then the race of women, or, to keep again to the play, generation itself, of which no more telling example on either account could be found than the race of Laius. The second strophic pair would then come into its own as the proper pendant of the first. Although man's hope—the second, according to Aeschylus, of Prometheus' crimes (cf. 23.1), and the gift to man, according to Hesiod, of Pandora—is inevitably frustrated by Zeus' power, hope is both a blessing as the indispensable companion to man's ineradicable misery and a curse as the irresistible lure to transgression. The second stasimon would thus have been the Chorus' meditation on the first stasimon, to which the intervention of Antigone would have provoked them. It is a mark of Sophocles' restraint that he did not let the Chorus express this meditation; and it is a mark of his wisdom that he encouraged us to make it (cf. 11.4).

38 (626–38). 38.1. The Chorus tell Creon of Haemon's coming. They remind him that the hope of his own race depends on his only surviving son. They thus obliquely refer to Megareus (1303), whose sacrificial death in appeasing the wrath of Ares has just now helped to save Thebes. It would seem, then, that Creon has already shown that he rules in accordance with his own laws: he gave up his son for the sake of his fatherland. Yet he did not decide to glorify Megareus' death but strangely chose Eteocles' as the highest form of patriotism. The need to prove his own legitimacy apparently outweighed what no one would have rated at less than a pardonable pride in his own consistency. His punishment would surely have gained in poignancy if the loss of his elder son underlay his hatred of Polynices and Antigone.[31] But could a man who has just sacrificed his son in obedience to a soothsayer's word have failed to consult him about the prohibition of Polynices' burial? And if he had, would he then abuse Tiresias as Creon does? Creon has given no indication up to now that he has ever experienced suffering (cf. 27.2). Are we then to suppose that Creon was indifferent to his son's sacrifice and his own? Or that he regarded them as so obligatory that he ceased to count them as obligations? Creon does not impress us as a humble man. If, moreover, one accepts Euripides' version, that Creon tried to abet Megareus' (Menoiceus') ostensible avoidance of self-sacrifice (*Phoen.* 962–85), Creon would be nothing but a hypocrite, more than willing to save his own at the expense of his fatherland. One of two conclusions would then follow: either Creon punishes Antigone out of shame at his own lapse from patriotism, or Creon thinks Megareus' sacrifice was unnecessary, a pious invention of Tiresias. In the former case, one would expect some hint of a remorse that takes so spiteful a form; and in the latter, his claim to have never departed from Tiresias' advice would be demonstrably false (993). When, however, the Chorus ask whether Haemon has come in grief and pain for his blighted hopes, Creon gratuitously replies: "We shall soon know better than soothsayers." In the mouth of Creon μάντις is no more to be strictly understood than Ζεὺς ἑρκεῖος, unless, perhaps, Creon now shows his resentment of Tiresias, whose unerring advice might rankle. His glorification of Eteocles would be his way of getting back at Tiresias. Yet perhaps Creon cannot be simply explained. The truth about him might lie in his very lack of any overwhelming passion or principle.

---

[31]Creon's relation to Megareus is often misunderstood; see, e.g., Schneidewin, *Einleitung,* 8.

Nothing dominates but petty suspicion, spite, and resentment. He is cold without being magnanimous. It would then call for much reflection on the ways of the gods if Creon's punishment consists in the loss of those who have never meant much to him (cf. 63.1,3). He does not, at any rate, address the dead Haemon or Eurydice with one term of affection; and he then addresses the messenger as he had just addressed his son: ὦ παῖ (1289).[32]

38.2. The Chorus ask Creon whether Haemon has come in pain and grief; Creon asks Haemon whether he has come in fury and anger; but Creon asks the alternative as well, whether he remains dear to Haemon regardless of what he does. Creon does not ask whether Haemon remains loyal to him despite his pain. If he is angry with his father, he is against his father; if he loves his father, he approves of him. Creon refuses to take love and pain into account. But he expects a loyalty on the part of Haemon that he otherwise condemns, for Creon despised anyone who put his φίλος before his country (cf. 12.4). Haemon does not answer Creon's question. He defers to his judgment but not necessarily to his actions. That he is Creon's does not mean that Creon can do with him as he likes (cf. 29.3). As Creon is his guide because his judgment is sound, Haemon implies that he does not simply defer to him as a father. Haemon knows what a sound judgment is. Does he need then anyone at all to guide him? Haemon also knows that love does not and cannot affect his judgment. He is a competent judge of wisdom and free of self-interest. In order to prove the first, he would have to defer to someone whom Creon acknowledged to be wise—could he have cited at this point Tiresias?—and to prove the second, he would have to do something against his self-interest—offer, for example, to marry anyone of his father's choosing. It is partly because he does not do this that neither Creon nor the Chorus accept his silence about his love for Antigone as a proof of his disinterestedness (cf. 43.1). Haemon does not know how to argue; he knows only how to be right.

39 (639–80). 39.1.88[33] The theme of Creon's speech is hierarchy, whose two central lines concern the consequence of his failing to keep in order those who are naturally of his own kind. The speech falls into three parts: fathers and sons (639–54), the private and the public (655–67), obedience and disobedience (668–80). In each part Antigone exemplifies something different: the bad wife (651), the improper claims of the private (658), and woman (678). Cnly in the first part does Creon speak directly to Haemon (639, 648), though not even there does he ever use the second person pronoun, which,

---

[32]Hermann remarks that this ordinary form of address is absent from tragedy except here and Aesch. *Ch.* 653-4: for Creon only the master-slave relation counts (cf. 479).

[33]I do not accept Seidler's displacement of 668–71; see below 39.3.

indeed, in the entire confrontation with Haemon he uses but twice, first to ask whether Haemon is unqualifiedly loyal to him (634), last to declare that Haemon's speech is wholly on Antigone's behalf (748).

39.2. Creon says that Haemon must hold to the sentiments he has expressed, which Creon interprets to mean that a son must set his father's judgment before everything else. Thebes no less than Antigone falls under this rule. Men pray that the offspring they beget—Creon does not restrict the prayer to sons—be obedient, in order that they requite their father's enemy with evil and honor their father's friend as their father does. Children are useless unless they conform to this purpose, for the father has then sown nothing but troubles for himself as well as his enemies' ridicule. Children are a calculated risk that can pay off in benefits; they have nothing to do with pleasure or love. One wonders what Creon would have said about the duty of sons to bury their fathers (cf. Lys. 13.45; Isae. 2.25.4). Creon himself, moreover, is aware of a difficulty. Sons get married and become fathers in their own homes (ἐν δόμοις); they do not as a rule stay at home (ἐν δόμοις ἔχειν), forever obedient to their fathers. The son acquires his own φίλοι, whom he could not expect his father in turn to honor. Creon therefore has to imply that no enemy of his is good and no friend bad; so Haemon, simply on the basis of calculation (εἰδώς), should not marry Antigone, unless he wants to inflict troubles on himself. Creon thus gives a tripartite argument, the inner coherence of which is not self-evident. It would follow at once from the subordination of everything to a father's judgment that Haemon must reject Antigone, for Creon says that she is bad. The opposition between judgment and pleasure could not be more clear-cut. And yet Creon inserts between the premise and the conclusion the prayer of fathers. But why should Haemon obey Creon because Creon has prayed for his obedience? Haemon must obey because that is what Creon wants. The duty of the son is grounded in the pleasure of the father. But Creon does not want anything else than what would be good for Haemon. Creon, however, can give no other reason why he wants Haemon's good except that it is his own good. He does not say that he cares for Haemon. His argument founders on the tension between a father's judgment and judgment simply, which he in vain tries to ease through prayer.

39.3. Creon knows that Haemon cannot loathe Antigone simply on Creon's command; he is content if Haemon will let her go as if (ὡσεί) she were ill-disposed to him. Creon does not ask that Haemon literally fulfill the prayer of fathers; he does not have to be his father's champion. Creon goes even further. It makes no difference whether Haemon obeys him or not; he will kill Antigone—he has always before spoken euphemistically of killing (308, 489, 581) or let someone else give it its name (220, 497, 576)—because as she alone out of the whole city was openly disobedient—he does not forget for a moment his secret enemies (291)—he will not prove himself false to the city. The "ethical dative" πόλει is ambiguous. It can mean either that Creon will not pardon Antigone because he could not then bear the city's mockery of his indulgence to Haemon or that Antigone's disobedience threatens the supremacy of the city. Antigone can harp all she wants on Ζεὺς ξύναιμος. Zeus is again in Creon's mouth an empty term (cf. 29.3). Creon takes only the Olympian and celestial Zeus seriously (184, 758, 1040–1; cf. 37.2). He pretends that Antigone's appeal to the Zeus of kinship is the same as her asking for pardon on the basis of her kinship with him. The natural relation between Creon and Antigone does not differ from the allegedly sacred relation between Antigone and Polynices. To cherish one's own natural kind to the point of disorder entails the encouragement of disorder in the city. Creon implies that he would not hesitate to kill Haemon if he found him disobedient. What can only be a father's prayer to hope for becomes a ruler's power to enforce. Lines 661–2 look as though they could mean only one of two things: either that whoever is just in his dealings with his own will be just in his dealings with the city (cf. Her. 5.29) or that whoever as ruler subordinates his own good to the city's good—ἐν τοῖς οἰκείοισιν ἀνὴρ χρηστός—is a just ruler. Creon, however, can mean neither of them. If the ὅστις of 663 is the same as the ὅστις of 661, and it means the ruler, the ruler's justice consists in his obedience to the city's laws; but since the law in question is Creon's own decree, Creon has to replace it with the ruler's will, from which it follows that the ruler obeys his own self-interest. If, on the other hand, the ὅστις of 663 is the same as the ὅστις of 661, but it means the subject, the subject is just if he obeys the ruler whom he, along with the other citizens, has established; but his justice then consists in an obedience that is independent of justice; he simply subordinates his own interests to the ruler's. If Creon thinks that the ruler's interests are identical with the subject's, it would be very easy to be good in dealing with one's own. Only out of mistaken self-interest could the private man disobey. But how does the private man know that his own interests coincide with the ruler's? It would seem that the subject banks on his becoming a ruler in turn. The city is nothing but a mutual exploitation society, in which every citizen has his chance as ruler to compensate for the injustices he has suffered as subject. Creon, however, cannot say that. The obedient subject is the noble ruler. He is noble because he subordinates his own interests to the city and its laws; but the laws of the city are Creon's decree. Creon could avoid this consequence, which no less faces him as ruler, if he supposes that the tacit obedience of the citizens to his decree is equivalent to their subordination of their own interests to the city. He would thus imply that everyone regards τὰ ἐγγενῆ φύσει of Creon as his own οἰκεῖα. As this cannot literally be true, Creon must mean that every citizen sees in Antigone a threat to his rule within his own family. Every citizen is a father or potential father, who must base his present or future rule on the superiority of men. Creon seems to oppose the city to the family; but he in fact models the city on the family (cf. 30.2). Obedience to the unjust ruler depends on obedience to the father, and not vice versa. Lines 661–2, then, mean: "Whoever keeps his own family in its proper order will also maintain the proper order of the city." Creon, however, has to admit that the family is not an actual model, for fathers have to pray for obedient children. The actual family therefore needs the city in order for it to become the model family. Without the other fathers no father could be certain of obedience. The city guarantees that the superior male be the actually superior father. But the city exacts a *quid pro quo*: the city will support the family in all its dignity if the family subordinates itself to the city; but the family cannot exist in all its dignity if it is subordinate to the city. Creon does not see this vicious circle because he is the ruler of the city. He can thus subordinate the family to the city at the same time that he can maintain the dignity of the father.

39.4. Whoever scrupulously obeys the city's ruler would be a noble ruler, a good subject, and in a storm of spears would stick to his assigned post, a just and good comrade-in-arms. That he would be a good subject follows only if obedience by itself turns him into the perfect instrument of the ruler's will; and that he be a just and good παραστάτης follows only if his martial competence can be presumed; but that he would be a noble ruler follows at once on his realization that the ruler must exact obedience. The threefold consequence of obedience seems to be matched by the threefold consequence of disobedience, which Creon treats as being equivalent to lack of order. When it does occur to him that πειθαρχία and ἀναρχία could fall together, he relies on the subordination of women to men, which is far more firmly established than either the subordination of children to fathers, which depends on prayer and the city, or the subordination of wives to husbands, which depends on judgment overriding pleasure. Disobedience destroys cities, ruins households, and routs an army in battle. The third consequence of disobedience is the counterpart of the third consequence of obedience, which, however, Creon now admits, does not invariably guarantee success. The first consequence of disobedience is the counterpart of the first and second consequence of obedience; but the second consequence of disobedience—the ruination of households— cannot have its proper correlate, for the father does not give up his own rule when he obeys the city's ruler, nor does a son prove his competence to rule in his obedience to his father, a wife in her obedience to her husband, or a woman in her obedience to a man. Creon's praise of unqualified obedience, so that whoever practices it automatically acquires the right to rule, undercuts the very basis of the hierarchy on which Creon models political rule. Creon avoids the self-contradiction by explicitly restricting the right to rule to men (τοῦτον τὸν ἄνδρα) and implicitly to fathers. The Chorus, at any rate, though they think that Creon speaks prudently, wonder whether they have not been

deceived by time (681–2). As loyal old men, all of whom could by now have
been fathers, they cannot but be pleased with Creon's granting them the right
to rule (cf. 988). Haemon, on the other hand, cannot be much moved by an
argument that promises him the right to rule as a man while it deprives him of
the way to become a father.

40 (683–723). 40.1. The theme of Haemon's speech is wisdom, whose
center consists of two parallel sentences, the first saying that Haemon has no
more prized possession than his father's success, the second asking what
greater delight could children have than their father's glory, or a father than
his children's. The speech turns on three *sententiae*, each of which contradicts
in turn the three parts of Creon's speech. To Creon's demand that a son must
set his father's judgment before everything else, Haemon answers that judgment does not reside with fathers *qua* fathers (683–4); to Creon's claim that
whoever is good in his own things will be just in the city, Haemon answers
that whoever thinks most highly of his own understanding is empty (708–9);
and to Creon's praise of unqualified obedience, Haemon answers that it can be
only the second-best (720–3). Haemon connects his threefold opposition to
Creon's opinions with a threefold attack on Creon himself: his ignorance (688–
91), his pride (705–6), his obduracy (711, 718). Throughout his speech
Haemon speaks directly to Creon. The second person pronoun and possessive
adjective here occur seven times, and in the exchange that follows seven times
more (cf. 39.1).

40.2. Creon began with the superiority of a father's judgment and ended
with the superiority of men; Haemon begins with the gods implanting
(φύουσιν) sense (φρένες) in human beings, the highest of human possessions
κτημάτων Lˢ; cf. 1050, fr. 210, 36P), and ends with his assigning the highest
rank to the man who is by nature (φῦναι) wholly full of knowledge
(ἐπιστήμη). Haemon is incapable, nor does he wish to be capable, of denying
the correctness of what Creon has said. But his own incapacity, which seems to
be due as much to the gods' unequal distribution of wisdom as to his own filial
piety, does not prevent him from reporting the criticism of others. Although
Creon inspires terror in the ordinary citizen (δημότης), Haemon relies not only
on his adopting the messenger's role (cf. 277) but on his father's affection to
offset his displeasure. But the impossible task Haemon has thus set himself
wipes out any gain his self-effacement might have won him. He must now
prove that the ordinary Theban is the wise man. And Haemon faces another
difficulty. Creon does not need Haemon to learn of the city's disapproval; he
counted his disregard of it as his greatest merit (178–81). He is not ignorant of
either the secret murmuring of his enemies (290–1) or the hidden defiance of
his rule (655). Haemon tries to sidestep the first difficulty by shifting from the
correctness (ὀρθῶς) of Creon's speech to the moral beauty (καλῶς) of a
counter view (cf. 706, 723). And he tries to sidestep the second difficulty by

appealing to Creon's own concern for reputation. Creon betrayed such a concern twice: he spoke of the mockery of a father's enemies (647), and he refused to be called a woman's inferior (680). Haemon exploits this concern in a peculiar way. He virtually identifies Creon's good fortune with Creon's glory; and he urges his own cherishing of the one and delight in the other. For Haemon to cite Antigone's glory while appealing to Creon's only looks absurd; he in fact obliquely threatens Creon with the power of the city. He could lose everything if the city acts on its now-secret opinion (ἐρεμνὴ φάτις), for Antigone can obtain the golden honor (χρυσῆς τιμῆς) she deserves only if the city publicly grants it. Haemon therefore puts Creon's good fortune and repute in terms of his own possession and delight in order to show that he would take no pleasure in Creon's downfall. Yet he adds that a father has no greater delight than in his children's glory. Is he thinking of his brother Megareus (cf. 38.1)? Or does he insinuate that Creon can bask through Haemon in Antigone's glory? However this may be, Haemon tries to link wisdom as the highest human possession with public opinion through his own most precious possession, the good fortune of Creon. In the absence of his own wisdom, Haemon must esteem most highly what can be his; and Creon's success can flourish and thus remain Haemon's only if Creon abides by public opinion, his knowledge of which depends on his devoted son. It is Haemon's care for Creon that eases the tension between public opinion and wisdom (cf. 39.2).

40.3. According to the city, Antigone's most glorious deed—the city does not say *ἀπ' ἔργων εὐσεβεστάτων—consists in the burial of her brother fallen in bloody slaughter (ἐν φοναῖς), whom she did not allow to be destroyed (ὀλέσθαι) by ravenous dogs or any bird (cf. 1314). The city does not say that Polynices died in battle (*ἐν μάχῃ); indeed, it speaks more euphemistically of his death than of his threatened consumption by beasts (cf. 1018, 1029). It prefers to forget, as the Chorus had advised themselves to do (150-1), both the war and the kind of war in which Polynices was engaged. The city, therefore, does not say, any more than Haemon does, that Antigone's glory lies in her resistance to Creon's decree. The city speaks cryptically even outside of Creon's hearing. It speaks as if the very handling of her brother's body, and not the fulfillment of a divine law, distinguished Antigone. The city speaks of neither the divine law nor Antigone's piety. It interprets Antigone's deed as intended to prevent dogs and birds from destroying Polynices.[34] Antigone

---

[34]On the inexactness of the city's speech, see A. B. Drachmann, *Hermes* 1908, 69. It is of a piece with the city's (or Antigone's) misunderstanding of the reason for Creon's calling the extraordinary assembly of the Chorus; cf. note 7.

saved her brother. That she saved a corpse no one mentions:neither νέκυς nor νεκρός occurs between 515 and 818.[35] Creon, however, just spoke of the many bodies (σώματα) that obedience saves (676). The city understands Antigone militarily. It tries to assimilate her deed as much as possible to a victory like Tellus' (cf. 36.3). Thebes does not see Antigone as Argos saw Cleobis and Biton. Creon had ordered Polynices' body (δέμας) to be left unburied in order that the city might see the birds and dogs eat and disgrace it (cf. 4.6). The city itself, however, speaks of the brother being eaten and perishing. Antigone is to die disgracefully κάκιστα φθίνει; Polynices would have suffered something more, the loss of self. Tiresias can speak of the unholy consequences of Polynices' punishment, and hence of the sacred reasons for the divine law (cf. 52); and he can speak as well of its meanness (1029–30); but the city knows nothing about any of this. Just to be eaten, and nothing else, constitutes in the city's opinion the whole meaning of lack of burial. To be incorporated into the nonhuman, the literal bestialization of man, one can say, is the primal terror (cf. 1081).[36] The question whether this terror is part of the core out of which man's need for gods arises or whether the gods, having given man his humanity, enjoin through the law that man live up to their gift underlies all of *Antigone*. Antigone herself seems to point to the truth of either answer (cf. 28.1).

40.4. Haemon follows up the veiled threat of the city with an argument that seems to have nothing to do with the city. He has wisdom yield to public opinion only to have public opinion yield in turn to moderation. Regardless of the city and regardless of what the issue is, Creon must in himself (ἐν σαυτῷ) be more adaptable. The Chorus, not Antigone, should be his model. Haemon now adopts for his own purposes two remarks of Creon. The triad of ψυχή, φρόνημα, and γνώμη, which Creon had said come to sight only in rule (cf. 12.4), becomes the triad of φρονεῖν, γλῶσσα, and ψυχή; and the two

---

[35]Their joint abstention from the word seems to be in accordance with Athenian speech: no Thucydidean speaker (unlike Herodotus) ever uses νεκρός. When Socrates refers to the shipwrecked corpses the generals failed to recover at Arginousae, he says τοὺς ἐκ τῆς ναυμαχίας (Pl. *Ap.S.* 32b3); likewise Lysias 5.36. When orators use νεκρός, it almost invariably refers to the dead buried at Marathon. On no Greek verse inscription is νεκρός/νέκυς used, as far as I know, before the third century; see W. Peek, *Griechische Grabgedichte,* numbers 129, 195, 220. Peek's remark about the increasingly euphemistic language about death (p. 37) would have to be modified.

[36]Cf. Moschion fr. 6, 30–3 N: κἀκ τοῦδε τοὺς θανόντας ὥρισεν νόμος/ τύμβοις καλύπτειν κἀπομοιρᾶσθαι κόνιν/ νεκροῖς ἀθάπτοις, μηδ᾽ ἐν ὀφθαλμοῖς ἐᾶν/ τῆς πρόσθε θοινῆς μνημόνευμα δυσσεβοῦς.

likenesses that Creon had used to illustrate Antigone's character and his way of dealing with it—overtempered iron and spirited horses (cf. 29.2)—are matched by the likenesses of trees facing a winter torrent and a seaman overstraining the sail's sheet. Haemon's triad, however, does not exactly correspond with Creon's; it resembles much more the first stasimon's triad of φθέγμα, φρόνημα, and ἀστυνόμοι ὀργαί (cf. 22.11). Since Haemon has to attack Creon in his pride—his fearless resolve (φρόνημα) to maintain what he is most devoted to (ψυχή)—and the question of argument (γνώμη)—is hence irrelevant, Haemon presents Creon's resolution as vanity, his arguments as specious, and his devotion as hollow. Creon's distinction between rulers and nonrulers is false. What comes to sight in the ruler must be the same as that which is latent in everyone else. The ruler's laws (cf. 191) must be the hidden opinion that the city has at any moment. Haemon speaks of the people and later of the gods but never of the city's laws (cf. 52.3). Between the divine law and the opinion of the people, which Haemon tacitly likens to the irresistible force of a stormy stream or sea (cf. Her. 3.81.2), there is nothing to guide the ruler. The ruler's moderation consists solely in doing anything to save his own skin. Haemon thus shows his care for Creon: he argues self-preservation at the expense of a futile but possibly noble resistance. Creon's high-mindedness, he believes, is mere bluster, concealing a fear for his own safety. He is the typical tyrant, according to Thucydides, who takes no risks (1.17). It is for this reason that Haemon keeps silent for so long about the divine law, for he does not know whether its violation involves punishment.

40.5. According to Creon, Antigone is unskillful art and/or artless nature; according to Haemon, though Creon runs the risk of becoming the same, he does not have to be like the uprooted trees or the unskillful seaman who drowns. He can restrain his nature (ἦθος) or improve his skill. He can yield to what cannot be resisted (τὸ μὴ τείνειν ἄγαν) or he can accept the opinion of others (τὸ μανθάνειν πολλά). They are equivalent, for the opinion of others is what cannot be resisted. Creon could object, however, that it is pointless to learn mere opinion (φάτις) and base to yield to it. Haemon therefore has to go further. The best thing is to be born wise; but as that rarely happens, it is noble too to learn from others who speak well. To speak well is the result of either being born wise or learning from still others who speak well. As Haemon can hardly claim that everyone in Thebes was born wise except Creon (cf. Pl. *Ap.S.* 24d3–35a11), he implies that the people learnt their wisdom from others, who must be either their more than human ancestors or the gods themselves. Haemon defers to his father's wisdom only to establish the wisdom of his father's fathers. He thus presents a sophisticated version of Antigone's appeal to the unwritten laws of the gods (cf. 27.2). These live in the φάτις of the city, which has inherited the wisdom the gods implanted in human beings long ago. Haemon can therefore replace the divine punishment for the law's violation, which Antigone saw in her pain, with the people's punishment, which now threatens to sweep Creon away.

41 (724-7). 41.1. The Chorus now speak the only ridiculous lines in the play. They advise Creon to learn from Haemon and Haemon to learn from Creon, "for it is well said on both sides." The Chorus show their wisdom to be only a mimicry of wisdom. They suggest that Creon, who argues for the paternal authority of the ruler, can compromise with Haemon, who argues for the divine authority of the city's voice. Fathers, however, are not ancestors. They begin to become ancestors as soon as they are dead (cf. *OT* 987).[37] Such a transformation can occur only through burial rites, which declare that the father is not carrion and does not perish (cf. 40.3). Now Creon talks of fathers as begetters (φύσαντες), who pray for obedient children (γονάς), Haemon of the gods begetting wisdom (φύουσιν φρένας). To endow parents with the authority of wisdom, it is first of all necessary to look upon them as nonsexual beings, i.e., as not possible objects of sexual desire. The prohibition against incest embodies this reverence.[38] It thus belongs together with the injunction to bury one's parents under the prohibition against seeing them naked (cf. 16.2). Antigone's burial of her brother only points to this issue; it is the confrontation between father and son that makes it plain.

41.2. Creon asks the Chorus whether "we old men" (οἱ τηλικοίδε)— perhaps he means the Chorus as well as himself (cf. 39.4)—are to be taught by a man as young as Haemon is by nature (τὴν φύσιν). Creon does not add that "we" too are old men by nature, for nature links age as closely with decay as with wisdom. Something more than natural aging is needed to turn men into respected fathers. But Creon does not see fathers except as begetters; and fathers cannot become more than begetters unless they pattern themselves after the ancestors, which Creon could do only if he abandoned his position (cf. 1113-4). He conceives of his own interests too narrowly to ally himself for long with the ancestral. Once he has finished with Antigone, he never again argues the case of the fatherland against Polynices.

42 (728-65). 42.1. The exchange between Haemon and Creon falls into three parts, in each of which Creon tries to force Haemon's capitulation, first through argument (728-39), next through abuse (740-9, 756), and last through threats, to which Haemon finally replies in kind (757, 754-5, 750-3, 758-65).[39] The theme of the exchange is reverence and devotion, or, better per-

---

[37] Cf. Pl. *Lgs.* 717d7-el.

[38] Cf. Thomas *Summa contra gentiles* III.124.

[39] Some rearrangement of the lines seems necessary; and I accept Enger's transposition of 756-7 and Pallis' of 750-3. I understand the sequence thus: Creon upbraids Haemon for trying to avoid affirming his total devotion to Antigone (756); Haemon asks whether Creon will just revile him or listen to

haps, honor and love: what one looks up to and what one cares for (cf. 12.7). The exchange begins with Haemon's interruption of the Chorus, before they can answer Creon's question. His disrespect toward the Chorus prepares for his refusal to defer to Creon and admit his own youthfulness to be a defect (cf. 719-20). He says that his teaching is not unjust and that Creon should examine, not what time has made him, but what he himself has done.[40] Creon asks whether Haemon's reverence of the unruly is something to be proud of. Haemon probably meant that to warn Creon of the city's mood, which could cost Creon his life, showed his devotion to his father's welfare. Creon prefers, however, to ignore his self-interest and argue his case on its merits. Haemon does not directly answer Creon; rather than deny Antigone's unruliness, he denies that he would even urge the show of reverence toward the bad.[41] The good citizen, he implies, is not necessarily the good man. Creon then asks an ambiguous question. He can mean either that Antigone is bad or that Antigone reverenced the bad Polynices. If he means the latter, Haemon's answer would be startling: all the people of Thebes now think that Eteocles was in the wrong. If he means the former, Creon drops the issue of Polynices' criminality in favor of convicting Antigone of disobedience, regardless of whether that disobedience violated the city or his pride. His long silence on Polynices suggests that he has abandoned for good any political justification. But it is Creon, one should not forget, who interprets his question and hence Haemon's answer as being solely concerned with Antigone. Haemon's answer could still imply that Creon's enemies have now won over the whole city. The threat that Haemon's similes disguised in his speech would be all the more menacing if it involved a repudiation of the war that Creon "the general" had won. When the Chorus celebrated the Theban victory, they did not praise Eteocles or blame Polynices (cf. 116-7). Precisely what Creon brought about but strove to

---

argument (757); Creon says that the witless Haemon will regret his attempt at instruction (754); Haemon says that Creon must be insane (755, cf. 765); Creon threatens and Haemon issues a counterthreat, which he says cannot be a threat to a man as devoid of understanding as Creon, i.e., one who does not know that Haemon's threat is a last effort to put some sense in Creon (750-3). If the lines are not rearranged, 757 must be read as a statement (cf. J. H. Kells, *CR* 1961, 191-2); but this still leaves Haemon's threat at the wrong point.

[40]So I understand the difficult τᾀργα. Jebb's interpretation of it as "merits" could be supported by Pl. *Chrm.* 163b1-c4, where Critias says that Hesiod restricted ἔργα to things nobly and beneficially done; cf. *Iliad* IX, 319-20; Xen. *Mem.* 1.2.56-7.

[41]Cf. J. D. Denniston, *CR* 1936, 115-6.

prevent might now have happened: the politicization of burial (cf. 13.2). Haemon's answers, in any case, up to his scornful, "You would be a fine ruler of an empty land," are as compatible with the city's approval of Polynices as with its approval of Antigone. Even his threat that Antigone's death will destroy someone could be a further warning of revolution (751). Creon now asks whether the city is to say what he should ordain. Haemon takes it as a foolish question, but Creon explains that to be a ruler means not to carry out the orders of another ruler: "Isn't the city customarily held (νομίζεται) to belong to the ruler?" Haemon answers that there is no city if it belongs to one man. Creon as ruler must simply execute what the city says. If Haemon does not only mean that Creon must take his bearings by public opinion in order to survive, he implies that Creon must look up to (εὐσεβεῖν) public opinion, for the people are never bad. Creon thought that the city was in itself good (cf. 19.4), but he had not drawn the conclusion that its citizens must be good. He supposes that the city is something other than its people (cf. 666).[42] He turns to the Chorus to remark that Haemon seems to be Antigone's ally, for the Chorus are the proof that Haemon's ὁμόπτολις λεώς exaggerates the city's unanimity. The Chorus are composed of the rich (843), whom both Antigone and Tiresias address as the rulers of Thebes (940, 988). They are not the δημόται who fear, according to Haemon, to tell Creon to his face what they think (690-1). The Chorus intervene on Ismene's behalf, and Creon gratefully accepts their correction (770-1); and when they later hear Tiresias, they do not hesitate to advise Creon, and Creon again obeys (1099). The factionalism of the city, on which Creon relies as he denies it (cf. 12.3), makes the citizens as such an impossible object of reverence. Haemon tries to dignify public opinion and ruins his case.

42.2. The weakest part of Haemon's defense of Antigone is Antigone; he has not dared up to now to defend her openly on the grounds she herself chose; and his respect for her seems to depend wholly on public opinion. Creon therefore tries to goad him into an admission of his subservience to her. All Haemon's talk of respect and reverence conceals the real object of his care. Haemon proclaimed on his entrance that he was wholly Creon's (635); and he now almost says that Creon is his only care. He does not say that he cares for the city. The reverence due its opinions does not entail any devotion to its interests. The way of Megareus is not Haemon's. When Creon says that his speech is wholly on Antigone's behalf, Haemon answers that it is also in the interest of Creon, himself, and the nether gods. He does not say *καὶ σοῦ γε κἀμοῦ καὶ πόλεως τῆς συμπάσης (cf. 36.2). The gods suddenly replace the city as the issue. Creon calls Haemon totally bad in separating, as he does, his

---

[42]Cf. L. Strauss, *Socrates and Aristophanes*, 94.

care for Creon from his respect for his father. Justice must be grounded in the gods, not in opinion. Haemon's answer is that Creon is unjust. He at last reveals that he never accepted the correctness of Creon's speech, one of whose points was that the ruler (father) must be obeyed regardless of his injustice. Creon now wants to know how he can be unjust if he merely cultivates the respect his office is due. Haemon replies that he cannot do so if he tramples on the honors of the gods. It is not true that the ruler democratically executes the people's wishes; the gods tell him what he shou' ! ordain. The ruler, then, does rule under the guidance of others; but they are the gods, not the city. Justice must be grounded in the gods, not in opinion, however unanimous (cf. 369). What Haemon has done his best to avoid has finally happened: he has been forced to adopt Antigone's position. Creon is triumphant: "Defiled nature ($\hat{\eta}\theta o\varsigma$) Lower than a woman!" Creon seems to identify piety with womanishness.[43] His greatest abuse of Haemon, at any rate, coincides with Haemon's appeal to the gods. One wonders whether his harping on Antigone the woman has not been his way of replying to Antigone's argument about the divine law. Male and female would reflect in his simple understanding the distinction between Olympian and chthonic gods (cf. 37.2, 39.2).

42.3. The coincidence of the city's opinion with what the nether gods demand as their due raises the question of whether the city and Hades have something in common. A passage in Aeschylus' *Agamemnon* points the way to an answer. The herald from the army opens his speech with an invocation of the "paternal ground of the Argive land"; and he goes on to say that out of all 'iis shattered hopes he has obtained but one, "to have a share on my death in the dearest grave" (503-7). The herald, whose special protector is Hermes (514-5), "greatest herald of those above and below" (*Ch.* 164), never says that he longed to return to his parents, wife, or children; the longing for what is his is not a private longing like Menelaus' (cf. 414-9), nor does he look forward to any comfort except the future glory of the army (567-81). When the Chorus greet him, he reiterates his joy on his return by saying that he does not now refuse to be dead (539).[44] The love for his fatherland manifests itself solely in the willingness to die there. That the Chorus interpret him to mean, through their personalizing of his love of country (540-5), that the present circumstances are so intolerable that they too welcome death (550), does not affect his original declaration. The way in which patriotism reaches the same level of intensity as private desires does not consist in the desire to die for one's country but in the desire to be buried there. Haemon, then, might not so much replace the city with the nether gods as unwittingly point to Hades as the core

---

[43]*Ibid.*, 233-4.
[44]The exact wording is not recoverable; cf. Fraenkel, *ad loc.*

of the city. Even if Thebes still regards Polynices as unjust and has not repudiated Eteocles, as the drift of Haemon's remarks has made us doubt, yet Antigone's love of death, from which all attachment to the family as generated has been drained, suggests that Antigone in herself represents the link between the city and Hades. Antigone had to reconstitute her family in Hades in order to cleanse it of its incestuous character (cf. 27.5). But the family without *erōs* is the city, for fraternity, which in itself has nothing to do with *erōs* is the highest degree of attachment that citizens can possibly have to one another.[45] The "fraternal" bond that Creon mistakenly saw between his soul's laws and his decree (192), between patriotism and the denial of burial to a brother, should in fact be the bond among citizens, of whom Creon never speaks (cf. 30.2). Antigone's silence about the war, Polynices' crime, and the mutual fratricide of her brothers thus take on a deeper significance. Her exclusion of every other concern than that her brother lies unburied—the city believes it merits golden honor—combined with the impartiality of her natural love for both her brothers despite their own enmity (523), makes her the representative of the city as the city itself would wish to be. But, as Antigone shows and Creon confirms (cf. 31.1), that for which the city longs is only possible in Hades, where the fraternal bond in its purity, apart from its source and the nature of the bonded, can be established. Creon's κάτω νυν ἐλθοῦσ', εἰ φιλητέον φίλει κείνους (524-5) buries the city's hopes along with Antigone (cf. 46.8).

42.4. Haemon does more than admit that he is also arguing on Antigone's behalf; his threat to Creon proves that his deepest care is for Antigone. If that is what Creon wanted him to say, he indirectly confesses to it; for his threat cannot be understood merely as a final effort to bring Creon to his senses. Although Creon is merely spiteful and cruel in wanting Haemon to see Antigone die, Haemon threatens suicide out of more than spite. He loves his father and thinks that Creon loves him; so for Creon no longer to see his head with his own eyes would pain him (cf. 1.1). One might therefore suppose that Haemon, in the absence of divine sanctions (cf. 40.4), and unsure of whether the city will act on its opinion, takes upon himself the duty to punish Creon. But would he have done so if Ismene had buried Polynices? His silence about the innocent Ismene, which the city's silence does not altogether justify, tells against him. And if the nether gods were so much his concern, he could have

---

[45]Cf. Pl. *Menex*. 237b6-3: αὐτόχθονας καὶ τῷ ὄντι ἐν πατρίδι οἰκοῦντας καὶ ζῶντας καὶ τρεφομένους οὐχ ὑπὸ μητρυίας ὡς οἱ ἄλλοι, ἀλλ᾿ ὑπὸ μητρὸς τῆς χώρας ἐν ᾗ ᾤκουν, καὶ νῦν κεῖσθαι τελευτήσαντας ἐν οἰκείοις τόποις τῆς τεκούσης καὶ θρεψάσης καὶ ὑποδεξαμένης; 239al: μιᾶς μητρὸς πάντες ἀδελφοὶ φύντες.

threatened to duplicate Antigone's holy crime. But the truth is that he can no more live without Antigone than Ismene says she can. Ismene's protestations when set next to Haemon's silence only underline the difference between φιλία and ἔρως. Haemon, then, begins as the city's spokesman, becomes the gods', and ends by cherishing Antigone unto death.

43 (766-80). 43.1. The Chorus warn Creon that a mind as young as Haemon's is, in pain, oppressive to its owner. Creon dismisses the warning; the contemplation of suicide, let alone suicide itself, is beyond the human. He forgets Jocasta (cf. 8.3). To risk death for the sake of monetary gain Creon can understand (221-2); but to die because of pain is unintelligible to him (cf. 27.2). As Haemon could never bring himself to carry out his threat, any more than Antigone and Ismene could face death unflinchingly (580-1), Creon's resolve to kill both girls is unchanged. The Chorus, however, easily save Ismene (cf. 34.1), and Creon decides to forgo Antigone's public execution (cf. 30.2). Haemon seems to have convinced him that the people would not stone Antigone to death; but he suspects that the people would not interfere if he kills her in a remote part of the country, and in such a way that no one's hand has to be raised against her. Just as he frees Ismene because she did not touch Polynices' corpse, so he frees the city from touching Antigone. The whole city will remain innocent if he meticulously prevents the city from being polluted (cf. 13.2). We do not know whether the formal purity of Antigone's execution would appease the city. Would the city forget its injustice, of which only Haemon on his own has spoken (728, 743), if Creon exactly complies with the demands of piety? The Chorus, at any rate, do not object. Perhaps they understand it as an example of ἀστυνόμοι ὀργαί, which though morally neutral are one of the glories of man's δεινότης (cf. 22.10).

43.2. Creon presents Antigone's suit of Hades for life as incapable of being fulfilled, for Hades is not a god like other gods who can grant or withhold a favor. If Hades is at work, he cannot produce his opposite. To worship him and what belongs to him is useless labor. It does not pay. The lesson Antigone's punishment will teach her is that her punishment is what she worships. The killing of Antigone is the education of Antigone (cf. 30.1). But precisely what offends Creon, who holds to the view of the marketplace that all χάρις is reciprocal (cf. 4.7), reveals Antigone as the perfect worshiper. Her reverence must be disinterested, for she worships the one god who cannot reward her. It is this very purity that, according to Creon, will prove to be too heavy a burden for her (cf. 29.2). And if she herself believes that her piety will be rewarded, that only confirms for Creon her madness and the ease with which she can be broken.

44 (781-801). 44.1. The Chorus of old men sing of Eros. For the first time in lyrics they use the second person pronoun.[46] In the parodos they

addressed the eye of the golden day (103) and in the second stasimon Zeus (609), but in neither case did they go beyond the vocative and a verb in the second person. In the parodos, however, they exhorted themselves and the rest of Thebes to visit all the temples of the gods with night-long dances (150-4); in the first stasimon they wished that the culprit not be of their own hearth (372); and in the second they spoke of the unceasing sorrows they had seen befall the Labdacids (594). But the song to Eros is, despite the repeated "you," almost entirely impersonal. Were it not for the deictic τόδε (793), it could be read as an independent poem. It is somehow akin to the first stasimon, which sang of man's δεινότης and in which man was a neuter "this" (cf. 22.6). The old men remind one of the elders of Troy who, on seeing Helen, "like unto the terrible beauty of the goddesses," do not begrudge the war, though they at once throw off her spell (Γ 156-60). The Chorus, however, do not sing of Eros while looking at Antigone; and when they do catch sight of her, they are silent about her beauty and speak of their own tears (cf. 32.1, 45.1). In the song itself Eros is the cause of madness, injustice, and strife, but not of tenderness, harmony, or self-sacrifice. The Chorus do not think of Antigone as acting through Eros.

44.2. The song is composed of eleven statements about love, the central one of which says that he whom Eros possesses is mad. Around this center the two sets of five statements each are balanced. The pendant to Ἔρως ἀνίκατε μάχαν is that not even the just can resist him; to Eros' swooping attack on what is one's own (κτήμασι), cf. 684, 702, 1050; fr. 210, 36P[47] is the pointing to the turbulent strife of kindred blood (ξύναιμον) that he has caused; to Eros' keeping watch on soft cheeks of a girl is the manifest evocation of triumphant desire in the eyes of a marriageable girl; to Eros' restless motion over sea and land is desire's office as the assessor of the great ordinances; and to the impossibility of either any immortal or human being escaping Eros is the goddess Aphrodite, who effortlessly wins every battle. It is not easy to say, as this summary reveals, how the Chorus understand Eros. The only other occurrence of erōs is in the second stasimon, where the Chorus speak of hope and the "deceit of light-witted desires" (cf. 27.4). The question to what degree the Chorus' animation of Eros reflects their belief in his divinity reminds one of the parodos, where the Chorus characterized eleven different beings in eleven different ways (cf. 11.4). There too the center was occupied by madness, the

---

[46]Cf. E. Norden, *Agnostos Theos*, 158.

[47]For this very broad sense of κτήματα see pseudo-Arist. *Oec.* 1345a26-30; Pl. *Grg.* 461c5-6. This economic understanding of what is one's own is indicative of how close the Chorus are to Creon; cf. 29.3, 53.2. Note also that Sophocles uses κτῆσιος as almost the equivalent of οἰκεῖος (*Tr.* 690).

Bacchic frenzy of Capaneus. But here, unlike the parodos, nothing as literally human as the miserable Polynices and Eteocles is found; nor do Eros and Aphrodite appear, like Dionysus and Zeus, as a god to whom one can pray or offer tribute. Eros far more resembles Hades, who when he is at work does what he is (cf. 43.2). The Chorus seem to treat as equivalent Eros, desire (ἵμερος), and Aphrodite; but one cannot take even ἵμερος literally, for apart from its "poeticization" it is set in apposition to τῶν μεγάλων πάρεδρος ἐν ἀρχαῖς θεσμῶν, which animates it at least as much as the "clatter of Ares" was galvanized into life in being juxtaposed to ἀντιπάλου δυσχείρωμα δράκοντος (126-7). Perhaps one could say that the night-watch of Eros on the cheeks of a girl does not divinize him more than "piney Hephaestus" (123) divinizes fire; and that the fusion of Polynices and eagle (112-21) is as little literal as the swooping attack of Eros on one's own. But Aphrodite is a goddess, and her playfulness no more detracts from her divinity than Dionysus' leading of the dance, for which the Chorus once wished (153-4), detracts from his. The ubiquity of Eros, moreover, to whom wilderness or dividing sea is no obstacle, and his power, which overcomes the gods as easily as men who live for a day, seem to make him the highest god. His ubiquity resembles man's own δεινότης, which set aside the apparent limits imposed on him by sea and Earth, the highest of the gods (cf. 22.7). Eros seems to supply the missing cause of man's δεινότης (cf. 22.1; Eur. *Med.* 844-5). The Chorus, then, seem to replace Earth with Eros or Aphrodite, and now assert that, while Eros is the cause of human transgression, Eros limits Zeus, whose splendor and immutability apparently checked human transgression (cf. 37.4). Does Eros lead astray the Zeus who justly punished Capaneus? The Chorus imply that there is no Eros for justice. They seem at first to understand the core of Eros as sexual, manifest in young girls, but they also say that desire holds sway over the great ordinances. If the text is sound,[48] they suggest that the great ordinances too are a part of Eros' domain. The love of country, the love of parents for children, and that of children for parents will belong to Eros. His power shows itself in his being both the love of one's own and the love that destroys one's own. It is desire's indifference to the goodness of either that makes the Chorus speak of Aphrodite's playfulness. Antigone, however, has shown that the love of one's own, when carried to its extreme, entails the love of death; and the extreme of the love that destroys one's own is equally the love of death, for one's own in the strict sense is oneself, which even Antigone (however unwittingly) admitted (cf. 2.2). The latter consequence would not follow were Creon wrong and Hades could grant Antigone life: but Antigone

---

[48]If my interpretation of πάρεδρος is correct, the issue would turn on the possibility of a proceleusmatic here; see Müller, 174-6.

is silent about the afterlife. Her soul has long been dead. Antigone would thus seem to embody Eros, the love of one's own that destroys one's own, and the Chorus' song to Eros an ode to death. But the Chorus understand Eros as primarily sexual, and Antigone's denial of sexual generation, which the Olympian gods share with men, sets her above Eros. Antigone seems to over-step the one limit that limits the gods. The question, then, which Eros' pos-sible divinity poses, is this: does Antigone offend against someone or some-thing divine that lends to the gods some of their splendor? Is her justice stricter than the gods', and her suicide a divine punishment?

45 (801–5). 45.1. When the Chorus beheld Antigone after they had sung of man's daring artfulness, they looked upon her as a monster, so different was she from the culprit they had envisioned (cf. 23.1); and now, after they have impersonally sung of Eros, they confess on seeing Antigone again that they too are carried outside the limits (θεσμοί) and cannot restrain their tears. The limits that the Chorus transgress would seem at first to be the great ordinances over which Eros presides; but the Chorus do not acknowledge compassion to be an effect of love; and in so far as it is implicit in the great ordinances that com-mand the love of one's own, they cannot be carried outside of them and yet be under their sway. They do not weep because they love Antigone and suddenly recognize her as one of their own (cf. 11.1). They weep against their will, for her cause is unjust (853–5). Their tears are solely caused by her approaching death. They are unloving and impersonal tears (cf. 527) that well up from a source almost beyond the consciousness of the Chorus. Theirs are not the tears of pity. The Chorus never speak of pity; indeed, *Antigone* is the only extant play of Sophocles' in which no word for pity occurs, though no other play has less than six instances (*Ajax*) of οἶκτος, οἰκτρός, ἐλεεινός and their several cognates.[49] There is, however, one exception: a messenger later says that Polynices' dog-mangled body still lay unpitied (1197). The Chorus' tears, then, arise from the same source as that which prompted Antigone to imply that her hopeless misery consists in man's mortality (cf. 27.3). It is this θεσμός that the Chorus of old men on seeing Antigone find themselves carried beyond;

---

[49]LA's reading οἶκτον at 858 is indefensible. *Antigone* differs in two other related ways from the rest of Sophocles' extant plays: πρὸς θεῶν as a form of supplication or invocation occurs only once (838), whereas other plays (except *Trachiniae* with two) have no less than five (*OC*); and all the rest have persons other than the Chorus call on Zeus in the vocative; here only the Chorus do so once (604). Antigone's πρὸς θεῶν, moreover, is the only case in Sophocles where the phrase occurs in a request that the speaker does not wish to be true.

and whatever pity they feel is mostly for themselves.[50] Antigone therefore rightly calls their heartless consolation a mockery of herself (839).

45.2. The Chorus say that Antigone approaches the bridal chamber (θάλαμον) where all sleep. The forcible joining of Eros and Hades is strange, for the Chorus, though pitiless, do not so much scorn Antigone as to take the view of Creon that she should marry in Hades (654). Everyone dies in that bridal chamber. If love is primarily sexual and its end generation, the Chorus point to the acknowledgment in love itself of death. One unwittingly accepts one's own death in the generation of another self. The survival of one's own is the death of oneself. In granting a kind of immortality, Eros compels each man to see himself as living for a day (cf. 789-90). It is the sight of Antigone that brings out a truth about Eros that the Chorus had ignored in singing of Eros. But Antigone herself is antigeneration; she has so far acknowledged the death but not the life in Eros. Her painful recognition of it is the burden of the kommos.

46 (806-82). 46.1. The kommos consist of nine parts, of which five are sung by Antigone and four by the Chorus. The Chorus' parts are paired: the first pair concerns Antigone's glory, which is offered as a consolation for her mortality (817-22, 834-8); the second pair concerns her crime, which is linked with her inheritance (cf. 37.1). Antigone's parts, on the other hand, fall metrically into three, two stanzas and an epode; but thematically they can be sorted differently. In the two strophes Antigone appeals to the Chorus, first, as fellow-citizens of a common fatherland, to see her imminent death and then, as the rich men of the city, to wait until her death before they mock her. In the two antistrophes she voices her reflections, first on what she has heard of Niobe, then on the incest of her parents. Each stanza, however, also hangs together: the first is Antigone's desperate attempt to normalize what she is and assimilate herself to things known, while in the second she accepts what she is and delineates her uniqueness. She thus begins with an address to her fellow citizens but ends with an address to her brother, who can as easily be Oedipus as Polynices. Only in the second antistrophe does she use ἐγώ (866, 868).

46.2. Antigone now speaks of marriage for the first time. She wants the Chorus to see her as one of their own, whose death will come before her wedding song. She therefore presents Hades, not Creon or the city, as her executioner (cf. 575, 847), and throughout the kommos remains silent on her deed. Antigone is no longer certain, and her uncertainty is soon confirmed, that the Chorus, were they not afraid of Creon, would approve of her deed (504-9). But she cannot throw off her strangeness or do more than mouth the

---

[50]Cf. *IG* I²972 (=48 Peek):Ἀντιλόχου ποτὶ σῆμ᾽ ἀγαθοῦ καὶ σώφρονος ἀνδρὸς/ [δάκρ]υ [κ]άταρξον, ἐπεὶ καὶ σὲ μένει θάνατος.

role of a girl deprived of her marriage. Not only does she fail to mention Haemon but she never speaks of the husband and (in the kommos) of the children she will never have (cf. *El.* 165, 187–8). The most she can bring herself to do in eliciting pity is to speak of marriage by itself and particularly of its ceremonies. She knows its rites but not its substance. She cannot bring to her loss of marriage the vividness she brought to Polynices' lack of burial (cf. 4.6). She understands marriage in the way that others understand burial, something one goes through for form's sake (cf. 22.10).

46.3. The Chorus disregard Antigone's self-normalization and insist on her uniqueness. They seem to speak as if her fame is due, not to what she did, but solely to the manner of her death, as if, that is, no mortal but Antigone had ever killed himself. They too, like Creon, forget Jocasta (cf. 43.1). The Chorus, moreover, do not speak exactly. Antigone will not descend to Hades alive; she is no Orpheus or Heracles. Creon intends to hide her in a man-made underground chamber where she will starve to death (774–5). The Chorus thus seem to confuse a hidden chamber with τόδ'...κεῦθος νεκύων, for the task of consoling Antigone so poorly suits them that they can only exaggerate her uniqueness to the point of nonsense. No "demythologization" of their language can rid it of its nonsense. They do not mean that Antigone will die alive: such a paradox does not fit the Chorus' understanding of Antigone. It would not be surprising, however, if Antigone did hear their words as genuine praise. When they say that she is independent of any law but her own (αὐτόνομος), Antigone doubtless takes them to mean that she uniquely holds to or even embodies the divine law itself; and when they add that she alone of mortals will descend to Hades alive, she must think that she has at last found someone who understands her. The uniqueness of her living descent into Hades lies in nothing else but in her living of the law of burial (cf. 34.3). It is this misunderstanding of the Chorus' words that impels Antigone to explain herself through her likeness to Niobe.

46.4. Antigone seems to forget that she does not resemble Niobe in three ways: the reason for Niobe's punishment (her boasting), the occasion of her boasting (her children), and the agents of her punishment (the gods). Antigone tries to make up for the last dissimilarity by saying that a *daimōn* lays her to rest; but how can she ignore the vanity of Niobe the mother? In order to normalize herself, she is driven to liken herself to a mother, just as the guard could account for her actions only in terms of a mother bird (cf. 25.3). But Antigone picks a comparison that is itself strange and needs a likeness—the only one Antigone ever uses[51]—to make it familiar. The gods rewarded Niobe

---

[51] Antigone seems to speak in trimeters much less poetically than the others. She says nothing as contrived as Ismene's καλχαίνουσ' (20) or as metaphoric as Ismene's ξύμπλουν (541); Creon's language is also not as plain (cf.

in death; they recognized in her boasting that challenged the gods the extreme case of the love of one's own; and to compensate for the loss of her own, they transformed her into a living growth of rock eternally weeping for the loss of her own. Nothing remains of Niobe but the signs of sorrow, the rain and snow that never leave her as she melts away. She is one with her grief. Antigone too is one with her grief, but her grief does not show itself in her own tears (cf. 32.1) but in the eternally living law of burial (456-7). Nothing remains of Antigone but the law ($a\dot{v}\tau o\nu \acute{o}\mu o\varsigma$). Her life is the law. She thus surpasses Niobe, for Niobe's love of her own led to the death of her own, while Antigone's love of her own is based on the death of her own. She is piously in accord with the divine. She is not a boaster. The love of her own never made her vain. In recalling Niobe's fate, she does not think of her own future recompense, whether it be from the gods or from men. She does not even want very much the Chorus' pity. There is, in a sense, nothing pitiable in the "most mournful perishing" of Niobe. Antigone, rather, wants the Chorus to see in her life the same kind of all-consuming devotion that the report of men attributes to Niobe. The truth about Eros is shown as much in her law-abiding self-sacrifice as in madness, injustice, and strife (cf. 44.1). The Chorus, however, mistake her meaning and thus, instead of consoling, mock Antigone.[52]

46.5. The Chorus remind Antigone that Niobe was a god and born of gods, while she, like themselves, is mortal and born of mortals. They suppose that Antigone was boasting that she would divinely obtain in her death the fate of Niobe. Contrary to the literal meaning of their words, which they think Antigone has misinterpreted, Antigone will not descend to Hades alive. They do not understand that it is her life in death that most resembles Niobe's tears. They therefore can only console her for her death but not praise her for her life: "It is a great thing when you have perished to have it said [$\tau \dot{\alpha}\kappa o\hat{v}\sigma\alpha\iota$ Wecklein] of you that in your life and then in your death you did share in the lot of the godlike."[53] If the Chorus had said that it is a great thing to be like Niobe, there would have been no ridicule in their words, for they then would have agreed with Antigone that in the love of her own she rivals Niobe. But

---

163, 190, 291-2, 474-8, 531-2, 1033, 1037-9), nor is Haemon's (690, 700, 712-7). Antigone never indulges in so artificial an opposition as Ismene's $\mu\iota\hat{\alpha}$ $\dot{\eta}\mu\acute{e}\rho\alpha$ $\delta\iota\pi\lambda\hat{\eta}$ $\chi\epsilon\iota\rho\acute{\iota}$ (14, cf. 13, 55) or Creon's $\pi\rho\grave{o}\varsigma$ $\delta\iota\pi\lambda\hat{\eta}\varsigma$ $\mu o\acute{\iota}\rho\alpha\varsigma$ $\mu\acute{\iota}\alpha\nu$ $\kappa\alpha\theta$' $\dot{\eta}\mu\acute{e}\rho\alpha\nu$ (170-1).

[52]Cf. Müller, 186-7.

[53]I understand ($\zeta\hat{\omega}\sigma\alpha\nu$ $\kappa\alpha\grave{\iota}$ $\check{e}\pi\epsilon\iota\tau\alpha$ $\theta\alpha\nuo\hat{v}\sigma\alpha\nu$ as a corrective of $\zeta\hat{\omega}\sigma$'...$\H{A}\iota\delta\eta\nu$ $\kappa\alpha\tau\alpha\beta\acute{\eta}\sigma\eta$ but as still referring only to the manner of Antigone's death.

the two additions of φθιμένα and τἀκοῦσαι humiliate Antigone. After the Chorus' insistence on the gulf that separates her from Niobe, ἀκοῦσαι implies that she will resemble Niobe in fame (ὡς φάτις ἀνδρῶν) but not in principle— the superficial similarity of her death to Niobe's will alone be remembered, and φθιμένα denies at a stroke all her greatness—what she did can be of importance only to herself.

46.6. Antigone now turns away from the Chorus. Their incomprehension makes her swear—the first and only time—by her father's(s') gods. Those whom she took to belong to her fatherland have proved to be merely the representatives of the present regime (cf. 12.5). She therefore must go beyond them and call on the unchanging elements of her country to bear her witness: the springs of Dirce and the sacred ground (ἄλσος) of Thebes. The sacred and the ancestral, which first come to sight as places and things, replace the old men of the Chorus, whose wealth Antigone mentions in order perhaps to remind them of the reason why the city, as it now stands, satisfies them. They would never do anything that could possibly lead to the confiscation of their estates. Their replacement reminds one of the shift Creon was forced to make in defining Polynices' crime (cf. 19.2). Creon had first presented Polynices' crime as his desire to destroy his fatherland and native gods, commit fratricide, and enslave the Thebans (199-202); but later the Chorus' dread that the gods might have buried Polynices compelled Creon to restate his crime: Polynices had come to destroy the temples, dedications, land, and laws of the gods (285-7). Creon thus transformed Polynices' crime into sacrilege at the price of suppressing his crime against living beings. The sacredness of divine things replaced the life of Polynices' own gods, brother, and people. So Antigone, in despairing of the Chorus, tries to find support for herself in the hoped-for indignation of sacred places. But Antigone invests Dirce and Thebes with a kind of life. They can make up for the absence of friends to weep for her and thus imitate the living growth of rock that is Niobe. And yet (ἔμπας) Antigone knows that the eternally weeping Niobe is just a story she has heard; the primary truth is what the Chorus see: Antigone is now seeing the sun for the last time. To live is to see the sun (cf. 3.4); it is not to be a rain-drenched brow and neck of rock, let alone a spring and piece of land, however sacred. Antigone begins to admit that the loss of life weighs heavily upon her, for she will not say that there is life in Hades (cf. 9.6). She thus prepares the way for her qualified defense of her deed (cf. 48).

46.7. The Chorus reject Antigone's denial of the justice of the laws under which she will suffer; but they try to soften their assertion of her injustice. They address her affectionately for the first time (ὦ τέκνον, cf. 987), and they adopt the same (and similar) measures as those that Antigone had just employed. They are the first to accuse Antigone to her face of injustice, for she has just spurned them and invoked sacred places to witness her so-called lawful (οἵοις νόμοις) punishment. The Chorus resent the double implication: they are Theban patriots, not Creon's partisans; and her punishment, being strictly according to the law, is just (cf. 43.1). And not to be outdone by Antigone's appeal to the sacred, the Chorus endow Creon's decree with all the majesty of a god. Antigone has struck against the lofty foundation of Justice.[54] They too must animate the inanimate; but whether they are as aware as is the desperate Antigone that indignation alone does not fully make for life remains doubtful. The juxtaposition, in any case, of ὑψηλόν with βάθρον reminds one of the first stasimon, where Earth was described as the highest of the gods (cf. 22.7). The Chorus there were compelled, in the absence of any other god than Hades acting as a limit to human daring, to assign to Earth the prerogatives of the Olympian gods. Here Justice is that limit; and she seems to reach as high as the Olympian gods and as low as the nether gods, among whom, according to Antigone, Justice dwells (451). The Chorus themselves indicate how this could be, for they suggest that Antigone is paying for the ordeal of her father. She is paying for the dead as well as for herself. But her own rashness is not unconnected with her paternal inheritance. The Chorus had discerned in her savagery the savagery of Oedipus (cf. 28.1). Her father's nature has thus made her pay for her father's crime.

46.8. That the same words or sounds in the second antistrophe occupy the metrical position they had in the strophe (ἐπίφαντον-πρόπαντος, ἰὼ Διρκαῖαι—ἰὼ ματρῷαι, οἵα-οἵων, πρός-πρός, ἰὼ δύστανος-ἰὼ δυσπότμων) serves only to bring out the differences between them. The strophe began with Antigone's outcry at the Chorus' mockery and humiliation of herself; the antistrophe begins with her confession that the Chorus have now touched on her most painful care (cf. 34.3). The strophe turned away from Antigone's fellow-citizens (the Chorus) to the sacred places of her country; the antistrophe dwells on the unholy marriage of her mother and father. The strophe appealed to the sacred places to witness the suffering the laws have dealt her; the antistrophe presents her misery as the very nature she received from her incestuous parents (cf. 6.1). The strophe spoke of her going, unwept by friends, to a strange kind of tomb; the antistrophe speaks of her going, unmarried, to dwell with her parents. The strophe ended with her dwelling with neither the living nor the dead; the antistrophe ends with an address to her brother, through whose ill-fated marriage she is slain. Antigone thus accepts the Chorus' second charge that she is paying for her father's ordeal, while denying their first charge, which they had somehow connected with the second, that she suffers justly. One is due to her nature by birth, the other is due

---

[54]Müller rightly reads προσέπαισας and rejects Lesky's defense of προσέπεσες.

to unjust jaws. The unholiness of her origins does not stand in the way of her invoking the sacred; rather, it promotes such an invocation, for the sacredness of Thebes partly rests on the incestuous relation among her earth-born people. The bond forbidden within the family is the indispensable bond for the city—it is what guarantees that its citizens be brothers (cf. 42.3), But Antigone cannot imagine herself as anything but accursed when she thinks of her parents (cf. 27.5). Her unmarried state means that she does not belong to any other family than her own; and that which she has longed for, to lie with her own (cf. 9.6), entails that she confront in her parents that which accounts for her love of her own. As their incest is the love of one's own writ large, Antigone cannot maintain her piety unless she condones their impiety (cf. *OC* 1698). This tension within Antigone parallels the tension within the city between the neutrality and the impiety of art (cf. 22.12–3). Out of art's impiety its moral neutrality arises; out of her parents' impiety arises Antigone's neuterization of her family. Both impieties and neutralizations converge in the fourfold makeup of the city. The city rests on art's violation of Earth as it aspires to the incest of Oedipus; and the city rests on the neutrality of art as it aspires to the antigeneration of Antigone (cf. 34.2). But what constitutes the holiness of the city in one respect (Oedipus) condemns it to unholiness in the other (art); and what constitutes the fraternity of the city in one respect (Antigone) condemns it to disunity in the other (art). It is not accidental therefore that Oedipus should "solve" the riddle of man and violate the sacred, any more than that the artful man should be a neuter "this" and turn out to be Antigone (cf. 22.6).

46.9. Antigone herself perhaps could not tell us whether her exclamation at her brother's ill-fated marriage refers to Oedipus' or Polynices'. No matter for whose we opt, Antigone despairs of finding any rest in Hades. If she means Polynices' marriage, Antigone somehow connects it with the marriage of her parents and her own unmarried state. Polynices settled in another city in order to destroy his own city. He overcame his incestuous origin only to commit fratricide. He thus compelled Antigone to give up any hope she might have had of renormalizing her family through marriage. Polynices has made her die accursed in her own eyes. If, on the other hand, Antigone means Oedipus' marriage, she recognizes in her father another brother, whose incest, while being the source of her suicidal devotion to Polynices, makes it impossible for her to embrace her death without shame. In these circumstances life becomes very precious to her.

46.10. The Chorus in answering Antigone seem to rephrase, rearrange, and reinterpret the elements of their original accusation. Antigone's extreme rashness becomes her self-willed temper; the high foundation of Justice becomes Creon's authority; and Antigone's paying for her father's ordeal (τιν' ἆθλον) becomes a certain kind of piety. The Chorus had causally connected Antigone's rashness with her offense against justice, but they had not explained how that involved her paternal inheritance; and now they causally link her qualified piety with her offense against authority, but they do not explain how that involves her temper; indeed, just as σὲ δ᾽ αὐτόγνωτος ὤλεσ᾽ ὀργά suggests that her willfulness alone, regardless of any lack in her piety, sufficed to destroy her, so πατρῷον δ᾽ ἐκτίνεις τιν᾽ ἆθλον suggested that her own injustice had little or nothing to do with her punishment. Oedipus is the source of both Antigone's temper and Antigone's piety. Her inborn temper made her offend against divine justice; her reverence for the divine made her offend against authority. The second offense, however, looks less serious than the first. Authority is not divine; whoever has it in his care cannot allow it to be transgressed. Antigone would thus seem to have offended merely against Creon's own self-willed temper. But the Chorus do not admit that Antigone's piety is pious; she has not fully practiced reverence for the divine. Some divinity therefore must cling to authority as such: κράτος must be an indispensable ingredient of Δίκη. A goddess cleanses Creon's authority of its willfulness. He is the selfless caretaker of a divine principle. Intransigent piety, on the other hand, is self-contradictory. Since piety does not demand self-sacrifice in the defense of piety, piety by itself could not so incandesce Antigone as to consume her self. Piety cannot be a goddess, for the gods stand apart from whatever beings or relations they establish as holy. The gods themselves are not holy.[55] They cannot be loved.[56] Antigone's devotion to her brother, therefore, cannot be grounded solely in her devotion to the gods. The incivility of her temper has no warrant from the gods. The love of her own contaminates her piety (cf. 52.3).

46.11. Antigone repeats in the epode several elements of her former songs: ἄκλαυτος ἄφιλος picks up φίλων ἄκλαυτος of the second strophe; ἀνυμέναιος compresses into one the conjunction οὔθ᾽ ὑμεναίων...οὔτ᾽...ὕμνησεν of the first strophe; ταλαίφρων already occurred in the second antistrophe; ἄγομαι τὰν ἑτοίμαν ὁδόν rephrases two expressions of the first strophe, even as οὐκέτι μοι... ὁρᾶν seems to do;[57] τὸν ἐμὸν πότμον

---

[55]Neither ἱερός nor ὅσιος is applied to the gods, and ἁγνός only in the restricted sense of "pure."

[56]In Plato's *Euthyphro*, neither Euthyphro nor Socrates ever suggests that the holy, which the gods love, is the gods themselves. This is partly due to polytheism.

[57]Antigone calls herself τάλαινα only here: Ajax (838), Oedipus (*OT* 1363), and Deianeira (705) also use τάλας of themselves only once. *Antigone* has seven instances of τάλας, of which three are in the mouth of Creon (1211, 1295, 1298); *OT* has four; no other play has less than eleven (*Aias*); see note 75.

recalls ἁμετέρου πότμου of the second antistrophe, and ἀδάκρυτον... στενάζει the first two words of the epode. But Antigone does not exactly repeat herself. She has said that she now sees the light of the sun for the last time; but she here presents that fact in a peculiar way: "I am no longer sanctioned to see the sacred eye of the torch" (λαμπάς). Antigone seems to speak of sacred law (θέμις) "for form's sake" (cf. 22.10), for she surely does not mean that Creon's decree, which condemns her to death, is a sacred law that prohibits her from seeing the sun. The decay of οὐκέτι μοι θέμις into an empty phrase, no stronger than οὐκέτι μοι ἔξεστι, not only in itself seems strange on the lips of Antigone, who has resisted this kind of decay in the case of burial, but its conjunction with the sacred forces one to restore to it (or at least think of) its original meaning. Or is "this sacred eye of the torch" also an empty phrase? That Antigone should animate the sun to indicate her recognition of what the loss of life primarily means is not surprising; but that she should sanctify the sun while calling it an artifact is surprising.[58] Antigone seems to deanimate the sun while animating it, and to sanctify the sun while robbing θέμις of its holiness. If, however, her own accursedness in light of her most painful care still grips Antigone, she might mean that the holy eye of the sun abhors her presence. She might regard herself as defiled as her father, whom Creon once begged to hide his taint in shame from the earth, the sacred rain, and the all-feeding light of Lord Helios (OT 1425-8). Antigone, then, might not call her fate tearless to express her isolation—could she forget Haemon as well as Ismene?—but to deny the possibility that any friend could weep in the face of the horror she and her family must inspire. But why does she call the sun a torch? According to Prometheus, the blind hopes he gave to man deprived man of his ever seeing death except within the horizon of fire and the arts (cf. 23.1). But Antigone is pre-Promethean, without hope and without art. As the death she always longed for presses upon her, Antigone speaks of the sun as an artificial fire, from whose holiness she is excommunicated (cf. 52.4). The artless and hopeless Antigone has no right to look upon the divine source of art and hope. Her piety is the obstacle to perfect piety (cf. 25.4).[59]

---

[58]I know of no similar expression in classical poetry, for elsewhere there always seems to be a defining genitive, such as ἡλίου or the like (cf. 104, Eur. IT 194, IA 1506, Ar. Ach. 1184-5 (=Trag. adesp. 45 N). For the night lamp endowed with sight see fr. 789P; L. Strauss, Aristophanes and Socrates, 263.

[59]This interpretation restores to θέμις its full meaning and sacred family right; cf. E. Benveniste, Le vocabulaire des institutions i-e, vol. 2, 99–105.

A READING OF SOPHOCLES' *ANTIGONE:* III

47 (883-90). 47.1 Creon's speech consists of three parts: a rhetorical question to Antigone and the Chorus (883-4), a command to his servants (885-7a), and, closely linked with his command, a justification of his way of dealing with Antigone (887b-90). Only when he comes to his own justification does Creon explicitly speak of, and point to, Antigone. "This girl" is opposed to "we." Apart from that opposition Antigone does not exist (cf. 567).

47.2. Creon speaks as if he had interrupted Antigone and the Chorus before they could begin another kommos. He seems not to recognize Antigone's words as putting an end to any further sharing with the Chorus. He is unaware of the extent to which the Chorus have been his spokesman. He further takes it for granted that no song of grief could possibly dissuade him or anyone else. By universalizing the subject (οὐδ' ἂν εἷς) and omitting every circumstance but one (πρὸ τοῦ θανεῖν), Creon turns Antigone's death before her time (896) into the common lot of men. Her fate becomes the paradigm of mortality. Creon unconsciously makes himself out to be as inexorable as Hades, for Hades must do the work that Creon's scrupulous piety forbids him from doing. Creon must speak of Antigone's death as fated if he is to remain innocent of her execution. He therefore cannot help beginning as if he were offering a conventional piece of consolation. Were it not for πρὸ τοῦ θανεῖν ("instead of getting killed"), it would have been perfect as such: "Don't you know that dirges would never cease if one was not fated to stop saying them?" But Antigone was not singing a γόος, which strictly applies to ritual lamentation for someone already dead (cf. 427, 1247). But as Creon cannot acknowledge the right of ritual lamentation without undermining his case (cf. 13.2), he must adopt the standpoint of the god whose will the γόοι of men do not alter. He can punish Antigone only by submitting to her terms as he himself understands them (cf. 777-80).

47.3. Creon combines a brutality of intent with a certain delicacy of expression (cf. 665). He tells his servants to imprison Antigone in her grave as if they were to wrap her in a garment (περιπτύξαντες); and she is to be left alone and isolated in such a dwelling (στέγη) as if she were some sacred beast left to roam a distant pasture (ἄφετε μόνην ἐρῆμον). Forced to speak piously "for form's sake," he must reject the fate that he had just invoked when cutting short the threnodies of Antigone. Antigone now has a choice. If she chooses suicide, Creon will be plainly ἁγνός. If she chooses to live, so as to keep up her burial practices underground (τυμβεύειν),[1] Creon has only offered Antigone the means of literally fulfilling her own wishes. Creon's way of punishing Antigone, which suspends the issue of her death, duplicates the way in which Antigone herself understood the rites of burial. Creon has inadvertently discovered the most telling mockery of Antigone's life in death. It forces her at last to reassess the ground of her devotion.

47.4. Creon sees Antigone as deprived of any share in what is here above (μετοικίας τῆς ἄνω). He implies that she has been an alien in and to this world (cf. 35.1). Antigone herself had twice sung of her status as a μέτοικος, first as an alien among the living and the dead (852), and then as an alien to her incestuous parents (868, cf. 46.8). She saw herself as forced to be with either those with whom she cannot fully share because she is unlike them or those who, because she shares everything with them, find her abhorrent. Antigone is everywhere a metic (see 3.4).

48 (891–928). 48.1. Antigone, in her third and last defense, gives an account of herself in a threefold way: Antigone and her family apart from Polynices (891–902a), Antigone and Polynices (902b–14a), Antigone and Creon (914b–28). Family links the first and second parts: the family she has and the family she hypothetically spurns in favor of her brother. And family again links the second and third parts: the family she has just spurned and the family she can never have because of her devotion to her brother. In design, her speech resembles her second defense, where death was the link between the gods of the first part and the pain of the third (cf. 17.1). Oedipus, Jocasta, and Eteocles now gloss the connection between gods and law that she had there tried to establish (Phersephassa displaces Zeus and Dike); the irreplaceability of Polynices now glosses the inevitability of her death; and the punishment she hopes Creon will undergo now glosses the pain she would have had if she had not buried Polynices. That law, however, now appears only in the second part, where any trace of its connection with the gods seems to have vanished, shows how much Antigone's imminent punishment has affected her understanding of what she has done. Creon has, in a sense, managed to shatter Antigone, but only to ₌eveal the core within the core of her resolve. Antigone had ended her second defense by charging Creon with folly; she now hopes that Creon will suffer no less than she has suffered.

---

[1]Morstadt's νυμφεύειν should be rejected; but τυμβεύειν should not be taken intransitively; it is too common a word to bear it; cf. T. M. Barker, *CR* 1907, 48.

48.2. The triple invocation with which Antigone begins characterizes the three parts of her speech. She calls the place where she is going to meet her own a grave, a bridal chamber, and a deep-dug dwelling that keeps eternal watch. What begins as a literal designation (τύμβος) of her place of punishment becomes through the metaphorical νυμφεῖον the region where she will dwell (οἴκησις) forever with the rest of her family. The grave that deprives her of being with a husband allows her to be with her family, for τύμβος, in replacing νυμφεῖον, replaces as well the οἴκησις that could not be on the earth (cf. 9.6). To stay at home with Oedipus and Jocasta is no less impossible for Antigone than marriage. κατασκαφὴ οἴκησις ἀείφρουρος describes not only Creon's underground chamber but Hades, which Antigone later calls θανόντων κατασκαφαί, and to which she will descend while still alive (920). This fusion of grave and Hades, which Creon has forced Antigone to reenact in her own death, and which the apparent redundancy in the coupling of ἐν νεκροῖς and ὀλολώτων here exemplifies, is for Antigone indispensable, for on it rests the sanctity of burial. Antigone can no more give up her own body in death than abandon Polynices' corpse to birds. If she cannot go as herself to Hades, she cannot defend the obligation under which she has acted. The strange argument to which she now resorts arises from the need to keep Polynices' burial and her own death strictly together.

48.3. Antigone contrasts the hospitable reception (δέδεκται) that Phersephassa has extended to her own with her own most miserable descent before her time (cf. 59). Antigone no doubt continues to ignore the mutual killing of Eteocles and Polynices; and she still must regard her own evils as outside the evils that Zeus has inflicted on her family (cf. 2.2); but the misery that overwhelms her now was the secret burden of the kommos: no one will do for her what she did for her father, mother, and brothers. No one remains to wash, adorn, or pour her libations. Ismene will not risk doing for her what she would not risk doing for Polynices, for the same prudential considerations now apply even more. Antigone's greatest sacrifice consists in depriving herself of burial rites (cf. 848-9 with 80-1). She must now confront her family without the rites that were indispensable for them. She therefore can do no more than nourish the hope that they will hold her ritual devotion to them as greater than her own lack of sanctity (cf. 867). She must appeal to them over the head of Persephassa, on whom she cannot rely to be gracious. Perhaps this consideration more than any other prevented Antigone from ever asserting that burial rites alone can assure one's passage to Hades. It now prevents her in any case from plainly distinguishing between Hades and the grave.

48.4. Antigone seems to think of her family together, but she speaks of or to them separately. She will come φίλη to her father, whom she does not address, προσφιλής to her mother, whom she does, and φίλη again to Eteocles, whom she calls κασίγνητον κάρα (cf. 1.3). She cannot bring herself to say that she will come beloved to them all (cf. 75, 89); indeed, she no longer speaks of Polynices' love (cf. 73), for whom she has not done all that she did for the others (cf. 33.4). Only in so far as her family were corpses and the objects of her ritual devotions do they belong to one another. Antigone's performance of burial rites is the only nonsacrilegious bond her family has. Her family is not a γένος (cf. 8.6).

48.5. Antigone now knowingly lies for the first time. She had come close to it in saying that she would heap up a tomb for Polynices (cf. 10.1); but now she says that she laid out Polynices' body for burial. The technical verb περιστέλλω embraces even more than the three rites she has just mentioned; but whatever else she did, we know that she could not have either washed or dressed Polynices (cf. 7.1). That she now invokes Polynices by name—the only time she does so—indicates the extent to which she depends on his good will to make up for her failings in ritual piety. The wise (and Antigone told Ismene who they were [557]) know that she honored Polynices; but to honor is not the same as to bury (cf. 13.2): the very argument Antigone uses to confirm the honor confirms the difference. The sacral terms περιστέλλω and δέμας[2]— only here does Antigone refer to a corpse as a body—signify Antigone's attempt to adhere to piety as piety "for form's sake" despite her own living of its truth. To keep together the surface and the heart of the law is as difficult as to separate Hades from the grave.

48.6. To favor a brother over against a hypothetical husband or son seems to be absurd when it means to favor a brother already dead; but the absurdity is due to the need to compare incomparable things. It is precisely because death makes all the difference that any argument about burial must appeal to what does not suit the argument. The Chorus of Sophocles' *Electra* see in the stork the most fitting way to praise Electra for her devotion to the dead Agamemnon: "We see the wisest birds above carefully tending those from whom they grow and receive support—why is it that we do not perform

---

[2]The sacred character of δέμας, which it shares with all neuters with the same suffix (cf. note 55), is plain in Δανάας δέμας (944-5); and that Creon is indifferent to this nuance (205) is a sign of his consistency and on a par with his use of σῶμα (cf. 20.2). For the difference between δέμας and σῶμα, see Xenophanes, fr. 15, 4–5, where Xenophanes has the animals make the σώματα of the gods such as to be like their own δέμας. Greek, like English, often opposed head to body (cf. Her. 2.66.4; 3.110; 4.75.3, 103.3; 7.75.1); it is therefore significant that Antigone calls Polynices by name when she refers to his body but calls Eteocles κασίγνητον κάρα when she speaks of his loving her, and again Polynices is κασίγντον κάρα when she speaks to him of Creon's injustice.

these duties equally?" (1058–62; cf. 25.3). The Chorus must ignore the absence of stork burial rites; and Antigone likewise seems to ignore the same difference, which is what makes her adaptation of Herodotus' story so damaging to her piety (Her. 3.118–9). Yet to defend Antigone in this way and hence the authenticity of the passage misses the import of her words. Intaphernes' wife was given the choice of saving her husband, her children, or her brother; Antigone has to invent choices in order to give the semblance of choice to the inevitable. The way in which she presents these choices reconfirms the lack of choice. She says that if one husband died she could have another; and if one child died she could have another from another husband. Antigone, however, seems to run the two cases together, for in ordering them chiastically she speaks at first of her children's life (τέκνων μήτηρ ἔφυν) but of her husband's death (πόσις κατθανὼν ἐτήκετο). She thus assumes that if her son died she would need another husband to have another son; and only one condition would make that inevitable: if her son were her husband (cf. 486–7). Antigone imagines herself to be another Jocasta. Even *ex hypothesi* she takes her family to be the model family. Even *ex hypothesi* she does not depart from the antigeneration of her name: the husband of her supposition is merely a lawful husband, a πόσις and not an ἀνήρ (cf. *Tr.* 550–1), and the brother that could be born were her mother and father still alive would grow (βλάστοι). Antigone, however, does not mean what she seems at first to imply, that if her mother and father were alive she would not have done what she did, for she could not then make her action depend on a contingency over which she would have no control—the birth of another brother.[3] Lines 911–2 mean something very different: there is no growth from those who can legitimately be a family only in Hades (cf. 27.5). Her mother and father are now concealed in Hades; they should always have been concealed there and never have seen the light. Antigone cannot wish that Oedipus and Jocasta could still supply her with a living brother. The duties to her husband would cease because she could acquire another; but the duties to her brother cannot cease because she would even wish that no one in her family had ever been born. Antigone imagines herself to be a mother for no other reason than to repudiate in advance the very possibilities she envisions. It is her way of making a retroactive wish against all generation; and such a wish allows her in turn to call an apparently special case a law.

48.7. Antigone would not bury a husband despite the citizens because she could have another husband; she must bury her brother because she cannot wish to have a brother. In order to prove the need to bury Polynices, Antigone

---

[3]No more than she thinks it possible at 450 that Zeus could have told her not to bury Polynices.

must assume that "to have" or "to be with" primarily means "to live with" (cf. 9.6): she could have a second husband because she would then be without (ἤπλακον) the first, and she would be without a husband because he had withered away (ἐτήκετο). To bury a husband is second-best; to be with a husband is best simply (Euripides *Supplices* 1054–1071). Antigone, then, must bury Polynices because she cannot be with him; but in burying him she dies and hence is with him. Her obedience to the law thus looks like a rationalization of her desire to die; but the spirit of the law informs that desire, for it says that to bury means to be with the buried. The rites for the dead are the means for being with the dead. They therefore compel Antigone's return to the corpse, but they cannot satisfy her (cf. 25.4). Antigone's pain at ever being apart from her family—her desire to overcome the endless repetition of ritual— forces her beyond burial to suicide; and indeed the law of burial contains within itself the inducement to commit suicide; but that inducement can come to light only within an incestuous family, where the impossibility of ever living with one another necessarily entails being with one another in death. The truth of the law, however, destroys the heart of the law for any lawfully constituted family; and so the law becomes in practice something done "for form's sake." Only the incestuous family can fulfill the spirit of the law, for it alone must regard "the being with" that burial affords as the primary sense of "to be with." The law that enjoins burial thus seems to enjoin incest; but the law can avoid that consequence through the demand for consanguinity without generation. The law demands the reconstitution of the family in Hades; it is in perfect agreement with Antigone.

48.8. Antigone speaks three times of her nature. It is her nature not to share with her brothers in their mutual hatred but to join them through the love of her own (523; cf. 31.1); it is her nature to have been born from incestuous parents (866; cf. 46.8); and if her nature were to be the mother of children, she would not have defied the citizens of Thebes (905). Merely to put these three ἔφυν together reveals that the link between the first and second is the *per impossibile* hypothesis of the third. Antigone's origin precludes her possible motherhood as it makes inevitable that the love of her own manifest itself in burial rites. And yet she cannot help but wish away the condition of her piety (cf. 46.8). She must long to be a mother as totally as she is now the embodied denial of generation: she must regret not having been a wife (N.B. τον, 917) and mother four lines after she has shown that she would not have done what she did for a husband's or child's sake. A mother might die to save her child's life; she would not die to give him burial. The divine law does not hold in such a case because a child is always replaceable. A mother's nature is to be the perpetual giver of life; but the τροφή of children does not include burial. Antigone does more than imagine herself to be like the earth itself, παμμήτωρ (cf. 22.9, 61.1): with her parents dead no brother could grow. Antigone has to die in order to escape from the repetition of burial ritual and guarantee her being or lying forever with her own; when she considers the alternative, she no less holds fast to eternity, the eternal succession of generations, on account of which no individual can be preferred over against the perpetuation of the race. Not only inexperience blinds Antigone to the possibility that a mother's love for a son might not stop with his death. Her family has so colored her imagination that only incest can properly express the love of one's own. She cannot think of being a mother without holding up Jocasta as a model at the same time that she longs to be a mother just to be free from the love of her own. She forgets Niobe (cf. 46.4).

48.9. The last part of Antigone's speech turns on three triads: wrongdoing (921, 926, 927), gods (921, 922, 925), and justice (921, 925, 928). One might suppose that Antigone would see their relation as simple: Creon has done wrong in the eyes of the gods and she has done right; the gods will punish him and reward her. Antigone, however, thinks that she can only wish that such a relation hold. The execution of her punishment—to go alive to the deep-dug chambers of the dead, friendless, unmarried, and childless—follows at once on Creon's judgment of her wrongdoing: but the gods have delayed the confirmation of her justice. Antigone suggests that she has been expecting the gods to interfere all along. Her piety should have been recognized as piety and not been qualified by the Chorus and ignored by the city (cf. 40.3, 46.10). The gods should have brought about a change of heart in everyone but Creon; but since they have failed to do so, Antigone might suffer still more and be forced to acknowledge her error. What error does she have in mind? Does she suspect that the law she has just promulgated does not have the gods' sanction? Or that her belief in her reward as she has imagined it is not the way of the gods? To discover that her reward will consist solely in Creon's punishment and not in any reunion with her family would be enough to break her. Antigone might be innocent of transgression against the gods' justice, yet not be deserving of recompense for her death. Antigone, however, assumes that the just and the noble ($\kappa\alpha\lambda\delta\nu$) coincide (cf. Pl. *Leg.* 859d2–860c3). But her action in itself might be just without being noble; she might have done what simply had to be done, and the risk she willingly ran to do it might not affect the gods' estimate of its worth, particularly if the risk entails a reward (death) that is nothing but the truth of the law itself. But in this speech Antigone never speaks of her own death; and just in this lies the difference between her second and third defense; she has replaced through her new law the gain of death with the gain of being with her family. Antigone cannot see that her justice might no more be noble than Creon's suffering for his injustice would be. In hoping that Creon suffer as many evils as she unjustly has, Antigone counts his suffering as her own reward. She thus makes herself out to be the instrument of the gods' punishment of Creon but as such an instrument she supposes she will obtain the other hope on which she has been nourished, to come beloved to Oedipus, Jocasta, and Eteocles. It is the tension within this double hope that makes her, if anything does, "tragic."

49 (929-43). 49.1. The Chorus do not discern any difference between the Antigone who convicted Creon of folly and the Antigone who would condemn him to suffering. The same onrush of her soul's selfsame winds still possesses her. The Chorus had spoken of ῥιπαὶ ἀνέμων before: Capaneus in a Bacchic frenzy breathed against Thebes the onrushing winds of hatred (137). Antigone is another Capaneus, possessed as he was with hatred and impious defiance; but Capaneus was divinely inspired (βακχεύων), Antigone owes her possession to her own soul. The Chorus now ascribe to her soul what they had formerly ascribed to her father (cf. 28) But the Chorus virtually identify soul and winds; and they had likened to Thracian blasts the gods, who once they have shaken a family let disasters pursue it from generation to generation (cf. 37.3). The metaphorical use of wind would seem to be the Chorus' sole consistency (cf. 353, 1146). Gods and soul equally account for Antigone; but they are linked through Oedipus, who inherited the Labdacids' fate and passed it on. The Chorus, then, have left it dark whether τῶν αὐτῶν ἀνέμων αὐταὶ ῥιπαί refers to Antigone or her family. They might understand Antigone just now to have been the spokesman for her whole family. The savagery she inherited from Oedipus might have its roots in the gods.

49.2. Creon then takes up obliquely what the Chorus have said: "It is a consequence of this that those who lead her will regret their slowness." Since Antigone has not confessed her error—she did not even try to escape (557-80)—the only thing to do is to hasten her death, the slow execution of which Creon supposes has let her keep up the show of her intransigence. Creon takes out his failure to break Antigone on his servants: someone must learn through suffering, someone must cry. Creon, however, does succeed in forcing Antigone to acknowledge her own death, on which she was silent throughout her third defense (cf. 48.9). The οἴμοι testifies to the collapse of that defense. It is the signal for her suicide, which is equally compounded of hope and despair—hope that she will be reunited with her family, despair that such a reunion can ever be more than parasitic on life. Out of that despair she now asks the gods, whom she thought she should no longer look to for help (922-3), to look upon her. The gods she calls on are gods of generation (cf. 8.6), without whom she can face Hades but not death.

49.3. Antigone addresses her last words to her father's city of Thebes, her ancestral gods, and the Chorus, whom she calls the rulers of Thebes (cf. 988). She implicitly rebukes the Chorus for letting perish the last link Thebes has to its past. She thus ends where Creon had begun. He had put forward a twofold title to rule: he was nearest in kinship to the royal house and wholly devoted to the city (cf. 12). Antigone now adopts this argument for herself:

she is last in the royal line and wholly pious. Creon failed to keep his two titles together, for he both confounded and divorced the city and its regime. Antigone, however, succeeds, for she connects the ancestral city with her piety through the gods who founded Thebes. Creon spoke of Cadmeans but never of Thebes (cf. 30.2); and he spoke of θεοὶ ἐγγενεῖς but never of θεοὶ προγενεῖς or θεοὶ πατρῷοι (199, 838). He is unaware of the city's divine origin; his link with the Spartoi means nothing to him. His laws were as silent as Antigone's about the gods; but whereas Antigone's silence merely hid her law's ultimate reliance on the gods, Creon's reflects his partial failure to politicize the gods (cf. 19.2). Antigone, on the other hand, remains oblivious of the political to the end: she invokes the ἄστυ, not the πόλις, of her father (cf. 46.6).

49.4. The suicides of Haemon and Eurydice are verbally prepared. Haemon angrily makes a scarcely veiled threat to that effect, as the Chorus recognize (cf. 43.1), and Eurydice's silent departure provokes the Chorus and the messenger to a similar foreboding. Antigone, however, ends with "by my reverent exercise of piety," and the Chorus then console her in a way that wholly fails to notice that she has resolved to kill herself. Her suicide occurs sometime during the interval that Tiresias' confrontation with Creon and the Chorus' hymn to Dionysus occupy. It is thus introduced by Antigone's avowal of her piety, and it occurs in that part of the play where the issue of the gods is most prominent. One is forced to wonder then whether piety and suicide necessarily go together.[4] Perhaps the peculiar uniqueness of her circumstances allows Antigone to see more deeply than Tiresias into the gods (cf. 52.4).

50 (944–87). 50.1. The fourth stasimon falls into three parts, of which the first describes the punishment of Danae, the second Lycurgus', and the third Cleopatra's and her sons'. It seems to have little to do with Antigone, whom the Chorus address twice at the beginning and once at the end (949, 987); Lycurgus as the only man seems the least relevant.[5] The stasimon's irrelevance could be partly due to the Chorus' lack of agreement with, and compassion for, Antigone; it would show the strain they are under to prove their perfect adaptability to any situation; and the best they can do for the τέρας Antigone is to cite three examples of fate. To urge Antigone's compliance with fate would seem to be the precept best suited for showing off their own moderation. Yet this explanation fails to account for Lycurgus, in whose connection the Chorus do not mention fate and abstain from drawing a moral: neither Danae nor Cleopatra, unlike Lycurgus, was guilty of any crime. Lycurgus, then, forces one to look more closely at the Chorus' intention. Even

[4]Cf. L. Strauss, *Aristophanes and Socrates,* 82–3; S. Benardete, *Herodotean Inquiries,* 49.

[5]Cf. Wolff-Bellermann's analysis.

if one comprehends the three examples under the rubric "imprisonment," despite the Chorus' silence about it in Cleopatra's case,[6] one cannot extract a meaningful parallel for Antigone, for none of them died in prison. Danae's prison ($\tau \upsilon \mu \beta \acute{\eta} \rho \eta \varsigma$ $\theta \acute{\alpha} \lambda \alpha \mu o \varsigma$) was figuratively a grave and literally a marriage chamber; Antigone's will be just the reverse (cf. 48.2). But this difference might indicate that the Chorus lag behind Antigone's final understanding of death (cf. 49.2) and that deliberately or not they are more compassionate than they seem.

50.2. "Fate" and "high birth" put together Danae and Cleopatra, "imprisonment" Danae and Lycurgus, and "Thrace" Lycurgus and Cleopatra, but nothing seems to put all three together. The stasimon's coherence therefore might be thought to lie in its very incoherence. Since the Chorus point the moral in the first strophe (the second antistrophe merely repeats it), and all things considered Danae does seem to fit Antigone better than the other two, the Chorus during the rest of the stasimon, one could argue, are induced despite themselves to sing of the irrelevant Lycurgus and the distracting addition of Cleopatra's sons. They then are caught in the grip of something like inspiration, which carries them outside the limits they had set for themselves (cf. 801–2). The second strophe, at any rate, is more ornately "poetic" than anything the Chorus have sung before. The Chorus would thus experience for an instance an equivalent to the "gusts of her soul's self-same winds" that always possess Antigone and we should get to know Antigone's peculiar inspiration through our hearing a more conventional Muse. Through the Chorus' adoption of a voice not their own we should begin to sense what it must entail for Antigone to live a divine law. It would be as well a fitting punishment for the Chorus: they would never recognize that they had been possessed.

50.3. Such an explanation, however, ignores the stasimon's apparent continuity. It begins at least as a reply to Antigone's last words; but it does not reply to everything she said. The ancestral city, their own ruling, and Antigone's piety find no echo in the Chorus. They are rather struck by Antigone's royal descent and her kinship with the gods (cf. 46.5). They directly link Antigone to Danae, not through imprisonment or fate's dread power, but because Danae was of high birth too and the treasurer of Zeus' son. Lycurgus, on the other hand, denied the divine birth of Dionysus, while Cleopatra was the offspring of the gods. That the gods generate with mortals is the theme of the stasimon, in which Danae represents its promise for the future, Lycurgus its denial in the present (the only verb in the present tense occurs in the first antistrophe), and Cleopatra its claim from the past. The

---

[6]See Pearson on Sophocles' *Phineus*, 311, n. 1.

Chorus' inspiration is not in the poetry or the moral but in this theme, of which, I think, they are wholly unaware, for otherwise they would have reserved the phrase ματρὸς ἔχοντες ἀνύμφευτον γονάν (980) for Oedipus and his children (cf. *OT* 1214-5, 1403-8) and much of ἀρατὸν ἕλκος...κερκίδων ἀκμαῖσιν (972-6) for his own self-blinding (cf. 51-2, *OT* 1276). The Chorus stick as always to the immediate likeness, which they then poetically elaborate before drawing the moral. All the choral odes suffer to some degree from the tension between the moral, which lends itself to poetry, and the theme, which does not (they thereby imitate the tension between the law as it is practiced "for form's sake" and the law as it is lived); and the fourth stasimon, as the Chorus' confession of bafflement before Antigone, necessarily suffers from it the most. For its theme, but not for its moral, Lycurgus is central. Antigone angers the Muses as much as Lycurgus did (cf. 32.1, 37.3). Her crime is his. As Lycurgus tried in speech to disrupt the continuity of divine generation, so Antigone disrupts in fact the continuity of human generation. As antigeneration she embodies the denial of Eros' divinity (cf. 44.2). Aphrodite and Dionysus are in her lineage but not in her future. She has no right to appeal to θεοὶ προγενεῖς if she forgets Ismene (cf. 8.1).

51 (988-97). 51.1. Tiresias is the only character with a proper name whose arrival the Chorus do not announce (cf. 155, 376, 386, 526, 626, 801, 1180, 1257). He shares with the watchman and the two later messengers the role of reporter; and like the watchman he neither did nor saw what he speaks of (238-9, 1012), though Creon believes in the complicity of them both and for the same reason; and again like the watchman on his first entrance, he takes the Chorus and Creon by surprise. The Chorus had concluded just before the watchman's entrance that no one would disobey Creon's decree because plainly no one is in love with death; and they now advise Antigone to resign herself to fate just before the knower of fate, Tiresias, enters. He, however, begins by offering hope, but he ends by confirming the fatefulness that the Chorus had divined. The two scenes are the joints on which the play's action hinges. The first dealt with the soul, the second deals with the gods; and gods and soul are united in the question of burial (cf. 19.4). The watchman needed three speeches and eighteen lines to protest his innocence and quiet his own fears (cf. 237) before he described the signs, or rather the lack of them, attendant on Polynices' burial; Tiresias needs three speeches of a line each to remind Creon of his own infallibility and arouse Creon's fears (cf. 997) before he describes the signs he heard and heard about at his place of augury (cf. 257, 990, 252, 1004, 1013). When the watchman left, he gave thanks to the gods for his unhoped-for salvation (σωθείς); when Creon now leaves, he fears that it be best throughout one's life to keep safe (σῴζοντα) the established laws (1113-4). Creon gave the watchman a second chance; the gods give Creon none at all. Creon learns too late the difference between a decree and a law.

51.2 The lords of Thebes, whom Tiresias addresses, seem to be the Chorus; but since Tiresias does not object to Creon's answering for them, he apparently regards Creon as the Chorus' spokesman. They would in that case be as guilty as Creon (cf. 577). That they are in no way punished would underline how indispensable Antigone is in order that Creon be punished (cf. 17.5). Tiresias, at any rate, says nothing to terrify the Chorus (cf. *OT* 316–8). He talks to them as if they knew as little about his blindness in particular as about blindness in general; and this despite their having just sung of the blinding of Cleopatra's sons and their long acquaintance with Tiresias (1092–3). Tiresias, however, might not know any of this; he might know nothing of the Chorus and their political position. His boy-servant, then, would have said to him as they approached something like, "Tiresias, the lords of Thebes are gathered here," and Tiresias simply repeated what he was told. The error in the address, if it is an error, suggests that a part of the city agrees with Antigone and holds the Chorus to be the active partisans of Creon (cf. 46.6). But this may not be the full or the only possible explanation of Tiresias' words. He might address the Chorus proleptically (cf. 1155; *OT* 631, 911, 1223). Creon would already be finished, and Tiresias would then proceed to give him advice he could not act upon. If Tiresias thus toys with Creon, he warns the Chorus, as the future rulers of Thebes, that they can never even once afford to act without him (cf. 1058). He must therefore speak to them as if they were ignorant of him in order to charge them with forgetfulness (cf. *OT* 297–9). They had in the first stasimon been silent about divination (cf. 22.5). Without any risk to themselves, they could have suggested to Creon, as soon as they heard the decree, that Tiresias be consulted. That they suspected Creon's prudence but not his competence to act as he did shows the degree to which the sacred not only has decayed but, in light of Antigone, must always be in decay. Her appeal to the divine law did not impress the Chorus.

51.3. On 993–5 see 38.1. Tiresias tells Creon that he stands on the razor's edge; and he surely speaks as if Creon had a choice. Unless Creon was fated to reply as he does, his immediate acquiescence at line 1033 would apparently have canceled his fate. The opportunity has passed seventy-two lines later (1105). Whether that interval would have been enough to stay Antigone's suicide is not an altogether idle question; perhaps her reprieve, we should suppose, would have so altered her that she would then have been content to bury Polynices and no longer be with him and her family. But Creon, even if he had at once acquiesced, might still not have gone unpunished; and perhaps all he would have gained might have been his ignorance of his fate (cf. 54.1). Tiresias, at any rate, does not connect the signs of his art from which he infers that the city is polluted with his foreknowledge of Creon's fate (cf. 55). He might have come to save the city and not Creon. We, however, could not perhaps have borne the city's redemption if Creon had not railed against

Tiresias; for it is Creon's distrust of Tiresias' public-spiritedness that seems to justify his punishment (cf. 61.2). Creon in this scene never mentions the city (cf. 30.2, 56.1).

52 (998–1032). 52.1. The first seventeen lines of Tiresias' speech deal with the signs of his art (998–1014), the last seventeen with the conclusions Tiresias draws from those signs (1016–32). What links them is καὶ ταῦτα τῆς σῆς ἐκ φρενὸς νοσεῖ πόλις (1015). The first and second parts are each in two sections: (1) the sounds Tiresias heard himself (99–1004), (2) the sights he heard about from his servant (1005–14), (3) his interpretation of the signs (1016–22), (4) his counsel (1023–32). So the whole speech consists of three parts: signs, their interpretation, and advice. That the speech allows a twofold analysis of its plan points directly to the apparent misalignment between Tiresias' art and Tiresias' advice, of which one is couched in the most exact and particular language and the other mostly consists of nonspecific generalities. Tiresias disregards the unholiness of Creon's deed—he returns to it when he foretells Creon's punishment (1068–73, 1080–3)—and stresses instead its meanness: "Why kill once more the dead?" Tiresias argues that Creon has made a mistake—every human being makes mistakes—and not that he has committed sacrilege. He needs his art to convict Creon of error; but he does not use it to condemn him. The signs are inauspicious but corrigible; Tiresias is silent as to whether the single crime for which they stand—Creon's failure to bury Polynices, not his burial of Antigone—admits of correction. He thus veils Creon's future punishment behind the possibility of Creon's future happiness; but the happiness lies in Creon's service to his country—the restoration of favorable communication between the city and the gods. Tiresias demands of Creon a sacrifice as unrewarding for himself as Megareus' was in light of Creon's own failure to memorialize his son (cf. 38.1). Creon is to benefit the city without recompense. If he abandons at once the position in which he has so much invested, he will be acting justly but not nobly.

52.2. At his place of augury Tiresias heard the unintelligible and barbaric cries of birds, and he knew at once that they were murderously clawing at one another. Tiresias' art primarily consists in his knowledge of a language not known to other Greeks (cf. 1094); when bird cries are as dark to him as they always are to everyone else, he knows that something is amiss. But he does not know what those cries signify before he "tastes" burnt offerings at the altar. The "dying oracles from non-prophetic rites" tell him that the fault lies in birds and dogs infecting public and private altars with Polynices' flesh. But for all his exactness of description Tiresias does not explain how birds and dogs infect the city. He talks as if Polynices were a sacrificial victim whose flesh refused to burn properly; yet that could literally hold true only if birds and dogs, having eaten Polynices, were themselves sacrificed. Tiresias could have avoided this difficulty if he had argued as follows. He cannot understand the birds because the corruption of a dead man's fat has rebarbarized their voices. In order to keep them "hellenized," the gods must on each occasion accept the sacrifices that are offered; and that these now fail to burn proves that the gods have withdrawn this favor. But Tiresias does not go directly from line 1015 to line 1019. He inserts between them a conclusion that universalizes his own experience (N.B. (N.B. ἡμῖν, ἡμῶν, 1016, 1020), as if each citizen at his own altar could understand the cries of birds. The infection of the city and its altars therefore seems to be symbolic. Not until Tiresias predicts Creon's downfall does he suggest that an unholy smell in the mouths of birds interferes with the smell of sacrifice (1080-3). He now omits that key to his account because he wants to join as closely as possible two different aspects of himself, soothsayer and citizen. He thus minimizes his own importance while implying that the city depends entirely on him. His speech, accordingly, suffers from the strain of arguing for Polynices' burial on both a universal and a particular ground. The particular ground is Tiresias' own art, which cannot work unless birds of omen do not contaminate the messages they convey. The universal ground, on the other hand, holds good regardless of whether anyone understands the cries of birds. The universal ground says that every city must prevent carrion from polluting its sacrifices, for otherwise the gods do not welcome the sacrificial prayers of its citizens; the particular ground says that Thebes must prevent its birds from lapsing into savagery, for otherwise the gods do not inform Tiresias of their plans and wishes. Yet Tiresias cannot help but imply that even in the general case birds take precedence over dogs and wild beasts. They "hallow" the corpse they mangle, but only birds pollute the city with all its hearths (cf. 53.1).[7]

52.3. Antigone's bestiality was evident to the Chorus (cf. 28), but they did not connect it with her devotion to a law of the gods, gods who, as Tiresias now explains, are the mainstay of civility. The gods forbid human sacrifice in any form, for they reject carrion for themselves and for their messengers (cf. 1081). Antigone, however, could not have resorted to an argument that so entirely disregards the law's injunction to bury one's own. On the basis of what Tiresias says, Antigone should have defied Creon even if Polynices had not been her brother and had been besides most hateful to her (cf. 10). She would then have been acting on behalf of Tiresias and Thebes; but Antigone would never have done what she did unless the law had not only supported but been grounded in the love of her own, which made what offended the gods and

---

[7]Perhaps ἑστιοῦχος πόλις should be taken as a case of transferred epithet, i.e., as ἑστίαι ἑστιοῦχοι; cf. the easier Aesch. fr. 343 Mette (= Pap. Oxy. 2245, col. ii, line 5): παρ᾽ ἑστιοῦχον σέλας = παρ᾽ ἑστίαν σέλας ἔχουσαν.

barbarized the birds, the consumption and the stench of Polynices' corpse, something innocuous, and more than innocuous, to herself. Tiresias, however, mentions neither the law nor Antigone's devotion to it. He is silent about the blood relation between the "soul" Creon buries and the "corpse" he does not (1069-71). He shares with Antigone nothing but her conviction that Creon is in error. Yet his intervention has the effect of restoring to "the established laws"—"law" does not recur after Creon uses that phrase (1113)—the obligation to obey them. He succeeds, against Creon, in making that obligation political; and he succeeds, against Antigone, in keeping it unqualified. He makes the obligation political through the city's need of his art; and he keeps it unqualified through the suppression of the soul (cf. 9.8). Burial no longer engages the soul of the living—Antigone's ἡ δ᾽ ἐμὴ ψυχὴ πάλαι τέθνηκεν is now impossible—or involves the issue of body and soul of the dead, for the benefits of burial are wholly in this world (cf. 55).

52.4. The only god Tiresias names is Hephaestus. The god of fire, who is fire, guarantees that the smoldering sacrifices are significant. If fire were under man's control, Tiresias could not have inferred from the sacrifices' failure to burn the displeasure of the gods.[8] In this light, Polynices' attempt to have "piney Hephaestus" fire Thebes was in itself impious (123); and it in turn must have determined the Chorus' choice of depicting the fire-bearing Capaneus, whom Zeus destroyed with a cast of fire (cf. 11.4). In the first stasimon, however, the Chorus were silent about fire (none of the nine examples of man's δεινότης entailed man's possession of it; cf. 373); in the second stasimon they made use of a proverb like "once burnt twice shy" to illustrate hope as "the deceitfulness of light-witted desires" (cf. 265; *El.* 619); in the fourth stasimon they counted Lycurgus' prohibition of "Dionysian fire" as one of his three crimes (964); and finally in the hyporchema they call on Dionysus as the choral leader of the fire-breathing stars (1146-7; cf. 1126). Fire runs an underground course through the play only to emerge in Tiresias' tasting of the ἔμπυρα; but the reason for its unnoticed presence has to wait for the play's greatest shock: Creon's servants burn Polynices' remains (1202). Nowhere else is cremation even hinted at. To bury has always meant heretofore to bury a body in the earth (cf. 4.1, 16.2). Antigone talked of how she prepared the bodies of her family for burial, and she once boasted that she would heap up a tomb for Polynices (cf. 10.1); but she seems to have been indifferent to, or

---

[8]Cf. Eur. *IA* 1602. Aeschylus' Clytemestra, in order to answer the Chorus' question as to who of messengers could come so quickly from Troy, was forced to say Hephaestus (*Ag.* 281): φρυκτός (282) or the like would not have sufficed; indeed, not until 293 sq. does she mention human beings and have them kindle the light.

rather wholly unaware of, the alternative to interment. Cremation is equally compatible with the law but not with Antigone's devotion to it. Interment allowed, if it did not promote, Antigone's blurring of the distinction between body and soul, Hades and the grave; but it no less diminished, if it did not prevent, the possibility of Antigone's arguing that only the burial of Polynices' body could grant his soul access to Hades.[9] The structure of the play is doubly gracious to Antigone. She does not hear Tiresias propose an interpretation of the gods that undercuts her understanding of the law; and she does not live to learn that Polynices is burnt before he is buried. The two favors are related, for the smell of carrion but not of burning flesh offends the gods and barbarizes their messengers. The burnt and the raw are polarized in the way that the holy and the unholy are. The first pair is the marker for the second; and the Chorus called Antigone and her father raw right after she had cited the divine law as her defense. Antigone is in the strictest sense pre-Promethean (cf. 23.1). She antedates the prohibition against cannibalism, which ancient authors often associate with the eating of raw flesh (cf. Her. 3.99; Arist. *EN* 1148b19–24); indeed, it can only be the discovery of fire that makes Plato's Athenian Stranger head a list of the arts with the prohibition against cannibalism: the second art he mentions is the making of bread (*Epin.* 975a5–b2).[10] By standing outside the arts Antigone had threatened the link between the holy and civility (cf. 28.1); through burnt sacrifices Tiresias restores it. But all that Antigone stood for cannot survive its restoration.

52.5. Creon must be astonished that Tiresias does not differ from Haemon in the moral he draws from completely different premises (cf. 40). The sameness of the moral, however, does not extend to the language in which it is expressed. Haemon's was so vivid that it concealed the political threat it contained; Tiresias' is flat because he conceals the threat from the gods behind a proverbial wisdom. Creon, Tiresias says, is willfully in error; but he can change, and the change will profit him. Even the change itself will be pleasant, for he will not have to learn through suffering. Haemon had told Creon that it

---

[9]Cremation is rarely mentioned in early grave epigrams. How inconceivable it would be for Antigone is shown by this late fifth-century distich: σάρκας μὲν πῦρ ὄμματ᾽ ἀφείλετο τῆδε ᾽Ονησοῦς,/ ὀστέα δ᾽ ἀνθεμόεις χῶρος ὅδ᾽ ἀμφὶς ἔχει (*IG* II/III: 1237=58 Peek).

[10]Cf. Juvenal 15. 78–87: *ast illum in plurima sectum/ frusta et particulas, ut multis mortuus unus/ sufficeret, totum corrosis ossibus edit/ victrix turba, nec ardenti decoxit aeno/ aut veribus; longum usque adeo tardumque putavit/ expectare focos, contenta cadavere crudo. / hic gaudere libet, quod non violaverit ignem,/ quem summa caeli raptum de parte Prometheus/ donavit terris. elemento gratulor et te/ exultare reor.*

was as noble to learn from good speakers as to be naturally wise oneself. He did not put it in terms of pleasure, for the prosperity or glory he promised Creon if he relented would be no more Creon's than his own. He urged Creon to give in to the people's judgment; Tiresias urges him to give in to the dead Polynices. The people had judged Antigone's deed most glorious because she tried to stop Polynices from utterly perishing. They could not have argued as Tiresias does now that Creon's efforts to rekill the dead are unworthy of him.[11] The flesh-eating dogs horrify them more than the birds. They do not imagine that Creon's crime is sacrilege and has infected themselves (1015); that it has deprived them of the fruits of the victory he had brought about; and that as long as Polynices remains unburied the celebration at the temples of the gods, which the Chorus had proposed in the parodos, cannot take place. Not until Hephaestus lights the sacrifices once more can Dionysus answer the Chorus' request that he lead Thebes in night-long dances.

53 (1033-47). 53.1. Creon addresses Tiresias as respectfully now as he had on his entrance (991, 1033, 1045). Tiresias is corrupt, but Creon cannot help deferring to him (cf. 1053). Tiresias could not except willfully make an error; and his error is so gross that it betrays the profiteering behind it. Tiresias is in the pay of Creon's political enemies; but no matter how far his avarice will induce him to lie, Creon will not cravenly submit, even if, he implies, Tiresias succeeds in hoodwinking the rest of the city (cf. 178-81). The most extravagant lie Creon can imagine Tiresias asserting would be that the eagles of Zeus have brought Polynices' flesh to the seat of Zeus; but since no human being in any form can pollute the gods, Creon sees no reason for taking seriously Tiresias' much weaker interpretation. Creon's silence about Tiresias' own art points to the difference between the soothsayer's interest in keeping the birds uncontaminated and the citizen's interest in having the gods accept his sacrifices. His silence further suggests that he does not think that Tiresias' wisdom, which he never doubts, depends on the cries of birds. Tiresias, in any case, does not refer to that point again. Creon limits the issue to the mechanics of pollution, which Tiresias had left obscure. If birds, Creon argues, have brought Polynices' flesh to the altars and thus polluted them, then, according to Tiresias, eagles should be able to pollute Zeus himself. The sacred cannot be susceptible to what the gods are not (cf. 46.10). Creon points somewhat obliquely to the weakness in Tiresias' account. Why should any

---

[11]Tiresias' ἀλκή, the refusal to yield in combat before one's enemy, is the opposite of his εἶκε (cf. E. Benveniste, *Le vocabulaire des institutions i-e,* vol. 2, 72-4). For the difference between τῷ θανόντι and ὀλωλότα (1029) see Th. 7.75.3: οἱ ζῶντες καταλειπόμενοι...πολὺ τῶν τεθνεώτων τοῖς ζῶσιν λυπηρότεροι ἦσαν καὶ τῶν ἀπολωλότων ἀθλιώτεροι.

beast have to link the stench of carrion with its interference with the city's sacrifices? It is not the beasts themselves that make such a stench unholy. Even if Polynices' corpse had remained as undefiled as Hector's was, Creon would still have committed sacrilege (cf. 1070-73). Tiresias ignores both the horror the city felt at Polynices' annihilation by dogs and the tenderness with which Antigone regarded Polynices' corpse, so that even its consumption by birds was something precious to her. If the birds whose cries Tiresias can no longer interpret had not touched Polynices, Tiresias could still have argued that the gods are depriving the city of his art because a divine law has been violated, which would equally follow from the failure of the sacrifices to burn without dogs and birds having polluted the altars. But Tiresias does not appeal to the divine law; he replaces its violation with the pollution of altars, to which, however, he needlessly adds the notion of their pollution through beasts. The birds and dogs he invokes vivify his account, but they essentially belong to Antigone's devotion to Polynices and the city's recognition of it; they are not indispensable for Tiresias' understanding of the gods. To make them indispensable would have required Tiresias to integrate the divine law as Antigone lives it into his own account. Such an integration seems to be impossible. That birds have consumed Polynices' fat, as the blind Tiresias declares, is plausible but false; dogs alone mangled it (1198).

53.2. Creon denounces Tiresias' avarice as hyperbolically as he disproves Tiresias' divination; but nothing else seems to connect the two main parts of his speech. He does not, however, harp on avarice now just because, though he loathes it, it is the only thing he understands and therefore sees everywhere. The drift of his speech suggests not only that Tiresias trades on the gods but that he trades with the gods. Sacrifice and omens are established currency (cf. 19.4), and piety is a kind of commerce between gods and men (cf. Pl. *Euthyphro* 14e6-8). Creon surely misunderstands Tiresias, but Tiresias is partly to blame. Instead of simply citing the divine law, the obedience to which would be automatic, he chose to replace its authority with his own knowledge; and his knowledge could only replace the holy with the ledger. He spoke of Creon's profit but not of his repentance. Tiresias tried at first to rationalize the holy; later he tries to do it justice; but he then cannot offer Creon any choice. The divine seems to admit of choice when it is speciously rational; when it is holy, it is inexorable.

54 (1048-63). 54.1. Creon's speech prompts Tiresias to a general reflection, which Creon interrupts before he can complete it, as if he knew that it would be as trivial as the last part of Tiresias' previous speech. And it is trivial in content, but paradoxical in phrasing: who does not know that prudence is the best of possessions (cf. 40.2)? Tiresias, however, means by prudence a certain kind of prudence, the submission to his own authority. Creon cannot accuse Tiresias of false divination without convicting himself of an inborn

imprudence. Tiresias, it seems, had intended more to remind Creon of his wisdom than once again to prove it. If Creon cannot take a friendly reminder for what it is, he should not be spared foreknowledge of his fate. The profitable and most pleasant learning Tiresias held out to Creon was ignorance. He would not terrify Creon and thus delude him with hope if Creon were only willing to reacknowledge his subservience. Tiresias anticipates the gods' punishment with his own. It is as though he suspected that the gods' punishment would not be sufficient punishment for Creon (cf. 38.1).

54.2. Creon, in order to justify his abuse of Tiresias, explains that the abuse was directed against all soothsayers indiscriminately (cf. 1035). Love of money is their class characteristic; and as nothing Creon heard from Tiresias differed at all from what any soothsayer would have said, he concluded that Tiresias had betrayed himself in adopting the usual patter of his class. Tiresias' attempt at reasonableness backfires. Creon needs to hear something that reveals Tiresias' special position before he will consider his advice. If, then, Tiresias' first speech really offered Creon the chance to alter his fate, not just to save the city (cf. 51.3, 52.1), the reason would be that Creon's immediate submission to Tiresias would have shown his regard for the sacred in its everydayness. The reasonable—why rekill the dead ?—and the sacred in its everydayness are hardly distinguishable. The civil and the decent cover them both. To Creon's charge that he is the typical soothsayer, Tiresias replies that he is the typical tyrant: he loves base gain. Tiresias here tries to convince Creon of his unreasonableness and warn him of his impiety. To prohibit Polynices' burial is a form of base gain, for it is an attempt to profit from either what is profitless or what should not be turned to profit. If Creon refuses to understand the first point and has to be instructed in the second—why burial in itself is mandatory, apart from the consequences for the citizens' sacrifices and Tiresias' art if it is not done—Creon is past saving. Creon cannot learn the divine ground of the holy without learning at the same time of his divine punishment. He would be punished not so much for his being unmovable (ἀκίνητος, 1027) as for his prying into the unmovable (τἀκίνητα, 1060).

55 (1064-90). 55.1. Tiresias' second speech is harder to understand than his first (the dispute about lines 1080-3, both as to their meaning and authenticity, proves it), but they do resemble one another. A central line here too divides the speech into two equal parts, each of thirteen lines. The first part deals with three things—Creon's punishment (1064-7), Creon's crime (1068-73), and the divine aspects of his punishment (1074-6); the second part also deals with three things—the domestic consequences of Creon's crime (1078b-9), its political consequences (1080-3), and Tiresias as the human agent of his punishment (1084-90). The first part is inspired; the second seems to be its prosaic translation: οὐ μακροῦ χρόνου τριβή replaces μὴ πολλοὺς ἔτι...τελῶν (cf. fr. 664P). The first part explains the penalty Creon must pay

and the reasons for it; the second explains the suffering he causes—κωκύματα (1079), ἔχθρα (1080), λυπεῖς (1084)—and now undergoes himself. The first part concerns the relation of gods to men and one another, the second with the relation of men to themselves. The bond between them is the unholy; but in the first part it is the unholy corpse (1071), in the second its unholy smell (1083).

55.2. The symmetry between the two parts of Tiresias' speech is plain; but how deep it goes or what it means is not as evident. The one who came from Creon's flesh and blood[12] to be his payment for corpses will provoke the ritual lamentation of men and women in his house; but do these ritual lamentations include those on behalf of Eurydice? Does Tiresias know of her suicide? The balance of payments would be more nearly equal if Haemon pays for Polynices and Eurydice for Antigone; but Tiresias presents Haemon alone (ἕνα) as paying for both of Creon's crimes. To conclude from this, however, that Tiresias knows nothing of Eurydice is not warranted. He might suppress his knowledge, not to spare Creon, but to gloss over his own contribution to her death. Eurydice curses Creon for the death of both her sons, Megareus and Haemon (1302–5, 1312–3); but Tiresias could not have accused Creon of Megareus' death without condemning himself (cf. 38.1). Tiresias recognized in Megareus' suicide a sacred necessity; he does not recognize it in Antigone's. Haemon's death looks very different if only in the eyes of men but not in the eyes of the gods it is in payment for Antigone's. Tiresias, then, might have been closer to the truth when he held Creon's only crime, or rather error, to be his failure to bury Polynices (cf. 52.1). His art might inform him better than his inspiration about the sacred.

55.3. Tiresias predicts that within not many circuits of the sun Creon will be punished; and he calls the Furies ὑστεροφθόροι and says that no long time will pass before lamentations fill Creon's house. Tiresias thrice deludes Creon (and the Chorus) into believing that his fate is not yet foreclosed; he still has time to make amends (cf. 1103–4). Since the events prove otherwise, we are again forced to think about Tiresias' knowledge. If he did not know that Creon would be punished before the day was out, his ignorance would explain the hopefulness of his first speech. If the city's loss cannot frighten Creon into

---

[12]In light of the hieratic tone of Tiresias' prophecy, nothing perhaps should be made of σπλάγχνα; but since σπλάγχνα are technically the parts of a sacrificial victim eaten by men as opposed to the thigh bones reserved for the gods, Tiresias could mean that Creon will pay for the gods' rejection of thigh bones with what otherwise would be his. The ἀντίδοσις would be superficially an exchange of human corpse for human corpses, but essentially an exchange of human corpse for bestial sacrifice.

correcting his error, the threatened loss of his son might; and the second speech too would be meant to be hopeful. Tiresias, on the other hand, could have concealed his more exact knowledge: Creon was not to know that the gods are unforgiving and repentance unrewarded. The delusion of hope would be a divine favor. Creon could come to believe that had he just reversed himself sooner, he would have saved his son. But that would only be Creon's consolation; the truth would be that Creon through his crime alone and not through his obduracy merited punishment. If, however, all men err, as Tiresias says, the punishment would have then seemed to men excessive. Perhaps Tiresias out of compassion spared us all the truth about sacrilege: the reasonable and the sacred in its everydayness are not as alike as Tiresias had pretended. Creon rejected their equation only to learn his fate; but his fate was phrased in such a way as to keep him in ignorance about the gods. To sustain Creon's hope, moreover, in order that he never learn that an act of sacrilege is not the same as an act of imprudence, would not be incompatible with sustaining it for a different reason. To cast Creon into total despair would delay what Tiresias and the city most need—the immediate burial of Polynices.

55.4. Creon's crimes are (1) to have cast below someone who belongs with those above, for he has ruthlessly settled a life ($\psi\nu\chi\dot{\eta}$) in a grave, and (2) to have kept here (above) a corpse that belongs to the gods below, for he has prevented it from receiving due burial rites. Tiresias then explains still further the second crime: neither Creon nor the gods above have any share in corpses. Tiresias thinks it unnecessary to give a fuller explanation of Creon's other crime. Could he have said that neither he nor the gods below have any share in souls? Or that Creon has forcibly deprived the gods above of Antigone? To have asserted the former would have entailed the denial that there are souls in Hades; to have asserted the latter would have implied some confusion between the region of οἱ ἄνω and the region of οἱ ἄνω θεοί. We are above in relation to the gods below, but where are we in relation to the gods above? The living cannot belong to the gods above because they alone are alive, any more than the dead can belong to the gods below because they too are dead. This difficulty cannot be separated from another: does the κάτω of 1068 mean the same as ἐν τάφῳ κατῴκισας (1069) and the κάτωθεν of 1070? If they mean the same, Tiresias shares with Antigone a confusion of Hades with the grave. If, on the other hand, Tiresias means that Creon has put Antigone in a kind of limbo Creon's crime consists, not in his killing of Antigone, but in the way he killed her, the very way Creon had chosen in order to avoid pollution for the entire city (cf. 43.1). Creon would have committed the same crime twice— ἄμοιρος, ἀκτέριστος, ἀνόσιος apply equally to Polynices and Antigone (cf. 1207)—and therefore would have to pay only once. The parallelism Tiresias draws between Polynices and Antigone—he calls them both corpses (1067)— conceals his denigration of Antigone. He cannot recall Creon to his original crime, which Creon had almost forgotten in the face of Antigone's defiance (cf. 41.2), without making what Antigone stands for of little or no importance. And if Tiresias cannot do Antigone justice, the reason must lie in a link between the gods and men above that excludes her: they alone share in generation (cf. 50.3). Creon's own flesh and blood must pay for his crime of exposing the dead in the region of the life-renewing sun.

55.5. Tiresias' prophecy strictly ends at 1076; what follows from 1078b up to 1083 translates the prophecy into human suffering and at the same time replies to Creon's argument at 1040–4. The translation and the reply are in a sense the same: the signs of Tiresias' art forebode human suffering, not divine pollution. Tiresias begins with the ritual lamentations in Creon's own house. The asyndeton of ἀνδρῶν γυναικῶν shows that, though κωκύματα are strictly a woman's way of grieving, the rites of burial are not, as Creon had supposed, female (cf. 1206, 1227; 42.4). σοῖς δόμοις, in turn, points back to σῶν σπλάγχνων and the difference between Creon the father and Creon the master. Creon's payment for his crime is his son, but the experience and expression of his crime are sexually undifferentiable. These ritual lamentations, moreover, recall the barbaric cries of birds: Plato calls a kind of dirge the "Carian Muse" (Lgs. 800c2–3; 25.3).[13] Tiresias would thus be deepening his original interpretation in light of his prophecy: his own failure to understand the cries of birds merely anticipates the unintelligible cries of mourning in Creon's house. His apparently self-interested argument turns out to be in the interest of Creon. Tiresias then goes further in playing down his own importance when he reargues the second sign. What is now at issue is not the fact of pollution but the belief in pollution. The mangled bits of corpses that dogs, beasts, or birds hallow stir up hatred in every city.[14] The human effect of a crime like Creon's against all the gods is manifest in the universal loathing of all cities. Regardless of what Creon himself thinks of pollution, it would be to his self-interest to avoid such hatred in Thebes. The city, no less than the gods, can punish when every citizen thinks himself threatened at his own hearth (cf. 22.14). The city is its hearths: the ἐσχαραί count more than the βωμοί (1016). Nothing, according to Tiresias' prophecy, mediates between οἱ ἄνω and οἱ ἄνω θεοί; but, according to his translation, sacrifices mediate between the city and the gods. The unholy corpse does not belong to those above, its unholy smell does not belong at the city's hearths. The city seems not altogether to belong to those above. It has a share in the nether gods as well (22.9).[15]

---

[13]Cf. Wilamowitz, *Griechische Verskunst*, 28–9.

[14]Böckh (275–6) rightly denies that Tiresias could be referring to the second expedition against Thebes, but he wrongly keeps ἐχθραί (sc. τοῖς θεοῖς; only Reiske's ἔχθρᾳ gives coherence to Tiresias' speech.

[15]Note the syntax of σπαράγματα, whose antecedent is strictly πόλεις.

55.6. Tiresias ends his speech with somewhat the same triad as Haemon had used (cf. 40.4). Creon should express his anger (θυμός) at those younger than Tiresias (i.e., those ignorant of his fate), learn to cherish a quieter tongue (γλῶσσα) and have a mind (νοῦς) better than his present wits (φρένες). Haemon said that whoever thinks he alone is sensible (φρονεῖν) and has a tongue (γλῶσσα) and soul (ψυχή) superior to any other is empty within. Haemon's triad recalled the triad of speech (φθέγμα), thought (φρόνημα), and civility (ἀστυνόμοι ὀργαί) that the Chorus had ascribed to man's δεινότης, (cf. 22.11); and that triad, in turn, pointed back to Creon's own triad, soul (ψυχή), resolve (φρόνημα), and judgment (γνώμη), which Creon held to be evident only in a ruler (cf. 12.4). Tiresias now tells Creon that he proposed the wrong test. It is not what one loves that is decisive, let alone the degree to which one is devoted to it, but civility. Civility would at least have spared him the anguish of foreknowledge (καρδίας τοξεύματα βέβαια), and perhaps have even checked him from issuing his decree (cf. 1113-4). Tiresias' message has nothing to do with Antigone.

56 (1091-1114). 56.1. The Chorus and Creon equally realize that Tiresias has never yet prophesied falsely to the city. Neither can see a reason as to why he should do so now (cf. 61.4), yet neither thinks Creon's fate to be unavoidable: prudence (εὐβουλία) can put everything right. Do they think, then, that prudence could have saved Oedipus or Megareus, and therefore condemn retroactively the one for his persistence in uncovering the truth or the other for patriotism? As the Chorus' patriotism cannot be in doubt, whatever one may think of Creon's, the parallel must be with Oedipus. But when should Oedipus have stopped his search? If he had not been public-spirited, he could have failed to consult the oracle or at least kept silent about it (cf. *OT* 93-4); and if he had not thought that Jocasta despised him for his origins, he could have stopped when she begged him to. In the first case, the plague would have continued until the city banished him for his lack of concern (cf. *OT* 47-50); and in the second, he would have gained no more than a respite, until he learned of Jocasta's suicide. Oedipus, then, could have shown his patriotism without discovering his origins only if he had never summoned Tiresias but relied solely on the testimony of the one survivor from Laius' retinue. He would then have been a regicide and nothing else. Does Tiresias have a similar role in mind for Creon? If Tiresias had stayed away and sent his servant, or even if a nameless citizen had come to report the failure of the sacrifices to burn, Creon could perhaps have avoided his fate. Such a report by itself, without any of Tiresias' authority behind it, should have been enough to tell Creon that he had gone against the practices of custom. Creon comes to fear that this indeed was the case (1113-4). The Chorus, however, seem to delude him into believing that he can outrun the swift-footed mischief of the gods (cf. 951-4). They advise him to release Antigone and bury Polynices; but Creon

first buries Polynices and then goes to Antigone's prison. Is this, then, Creon's mistake and what the Chorus mean by prudence? If Creon's fate depends on the timeliness of his actions, Creon's very patriotism, which makes him release the city from pollution before he attends to his own, destroys him (cf. 51.3). But the Chorus seem to have misunderstood Tiresias, for Tiresias spoke of Antigone as already a corpse (1067) and only put Haemon's death in the future; but since he also referred to Antigone as a soul, the Chorus took him to mean that she was still alive, whereas he really meant that Creon had killed her in an impious way (cf. 55.4). As Antigone's death seems to make Haemon's inevitable, there would seem to be no room for prudence. Not until one learns more about Haemon's suicide can one say whether or not the Chorus were simply wrong (cf. 61.5, 7).

56.2. Creon has some difficulty in adjusting to Tiresias' prophecy, the Chorus have none at all. Creon's mind and heart are in turmoil,[16] the Chorus have never invested much in any position. The hopeful construction they put on Tiresias' prophecy agrees with their politic lack of policy; and Creon readily believes that he too can drift with the necessity of circumstance. As soon as the Chorus repeat Tiresias' word "prudence," he hands himself over to them. He ceases to be his own master even before they remind him of the swiftness of divine punishment. His conversion seems precipitate only if one accepts his words (καρδίας ἐξίσταμαι τὸ δρᾶν) as implying that his principles were deeply rooted in his heart. His principles have long since eroded (cf. 42.1). He obeys the Chorus rather than Tiresias because Tiresias' loyalty has always been to the city (994, 1058) and the Chorus' loyalty (he does not doubt) to him. The confusion inherent in Creon's principles comes home to him (cf. 12.4).

56.3. The Chorus tell Creon not to entrust the freeing of Antigone and the burying of Polynices to anyone else; but Creon does not take them literally. He assumes that they mean he should supervise the work of his servants, to whom he assigns the whole task of burying Polynices while apparently reserving for himself that of freeing Antigone. He cannot, however, be taken literally either: he is present on both occasions and does no work himself. Creon could not have perhaps removed by himself the stones that block Antigone's prison; that Haemon does it proves nothing for Creon or, one might add, for Antigone (1216). But why should he think that his servants must bury Polynices? αὐτός τ' ἔδησα καὶ παρὼν ἐκλύσομαι, after all, applies as much to Polynices, if less literally, as to Antigone (cf. 40). Why, more

---

[16]Brunck's δειλόν is, I think, right, and Jackson's ἄτῃ 'μπαλάξαι τοὐμὸν ἐν δεινῷ κάρα (1097) near the mark, but I should prefer κέαρ (cf. Ai. 686, Tr. 629, 1246, OC but fr. 210, 45 P).

precisely, does Creon think at once of cremation and a barrow? Neither Tiresias nor the Chorus even hint that a simple interment would not suffice; and it would have sufficed if the city's pollution by dogs and birds were the issue (cf. 53.1). Creon seems to believe that Polynices is due rites almost as elaborate as those he gave Eteocles—the high mound he has raised would be conspicuous in the plain (1203)—but not that he should do them himself. The Chorus, however, might have meant that it was here and nowhere else that Creon's salvation lay: only if he were to handle the stinking, rotting, and mangled Polynices with his own hands could he find forgiveness from the gods (cf. 900). Only such an act would imply remorse (cf. Diodor. 1.77.7). But not only do the Chorus say nothing about remorse, Tiresias said nothing about it either (cf. 53.2). What genuine piety involves, rather than just piety "for form's sake," disappears from the play as soon as Antigone leaves. Creon never thinks of his crimes as impious; he continues to the end to talk of his unfortunate imprudence (1261, 1265, 1269).

57 (1115–54). 57.1. The Chorus now accept Creon's understanding of the priorities, but they go even further: since Tiresias never spoke of Antigone's death as politically relevant, the burial of Polynices, as far as the city is concerned, alone counts. The Chorus abandon Creon to his fate as soon as he is out of earshot; he can take care of his own without the help of Dionysus; but if the Thebans are to have Dionysus lead their dances, he must cleanse the city of the pollution that now violently grips it (cf. 52.5). The Chorus thus hark back to the end of the parodos (cf. 152–3, 1153–4), as if all that had happened between then and now were of no importance. What we have witnessed are the last traces of the war that the Chorus wanted Dionysus to help them forget. Dionysus now takes hold of them completely. The shaft of sunlight that the Chorus had greeted as their savior in the parodos yields to Iakchos the choral-master of the fire-breathing stars; μεγαλώνυμος Nike becomes πολυώνυμος Bakchos; and the frenzied Capaneus is forgotten in the hoped-for presence of the frenzied Thyiads (cf. 11.3). Dionysus is to wipe clean the Chorus' memory; and he succeeds. The moral they draw at the end almost repeats the moral they had put in the center of the parodos (127–8, 1348, 1353).

57.2. The hyporchema is the antithesis of the first stasimon.[17] That was almost wholly general, this is almost wholly particular; that had no proper

---

[17]Rhetorically, it is built up to a great extent out of triads. The first strophe consists of an opening invocation of three elements (πολυώνυμε, ἄγαλμα, γένος), followed by three verbal phrases (ἀμφέπεις, μέδεις, ναιετῶν), the last of which is expanded into a threefold description of Thebes. The first antistrophe, on the other hand, is held together by three nouns, the first two of which (λιγνύς, νᾶμα) share the same verb, while to the last is

names except Earth and Hades, this has seventeen, eight of which are place names; that called Earth, whom man wears away, the highest of the gods, this says Dionysus honors autochthonous Thebes most highly of all cities and presides with Demeter over Eleusis; that held man to be the conqueror of earth and sea, this begs Dionysus to come now over Parnassus or the Euripus; that presented man as the hunter of wild beasts, this traces the origin of Thebes back to a wild dragon; that spoke of man's taming of the mountain bull, this has the ivy-clad Nysaean mountains escort Dionysus to Thebes; that spoke of man's self-taught speech and thought, this hails Dionysus as master of nighttime voices and madness; and that said man contrives a cure for impossible diseases, this relies on Dionysus to cleanse the city of a violent disease. But despite these antitheses, the stasimon and hyporchema do share one thing in common: what is under the earth is as close to Dionysus as to man. Hades is not alone in closing it to man; man has no fire to mine the earth (cf. 52.4). He has no fire because it is divine and Dionysus is its master. Dionysus is the offspring of Zeus βαρυβρεμέτης, who cares for Thebes with his mother κεραυνία, is seen by the smoky flame of torches above Delphi, and leads the fire-breathing stars in dance. Fire comes down to earth only for sacred purposes: sacrifices, ordeals (264–5), festivals, or cremation. Sacrifices and festivals unite the city with the gods, and with none more closely than Dionysus; and cremation dissolves the Antigonean conflict between civility and holiness. Dionysus rightly represents this Tiresian solution, for he sponsors a frenzy in speech and mind different from Antigone's (603), and he has nothing to do with Hades (cf. 50.3).

58 (1155–71). 58.1. Antigone's entrance upset the moral of the first stasimon; the messenger reports nothing that does not harmonize with the hyporchema: the Chorus did not ask for Creon's safety. Once they have confirmation of Tiresias' prophecy they are not interested in Creon; and only the appearance of Eurydice distracts them from planning for the future, as the messenger advised (cf. *Ai.* 904, 981–2). The messenger resembles the watchman on his first entrance: both are reluctant to act as messengers. The watchman delayed his report until he had proved his innocence; the messenger delays just as long in order to show first how Creon exemplifies his own understanding of human life. From his understanding one could draw the moral that resignation is best; but whereas the watchman, though equally holding to resignation as his final hope, was resigned to his fate (cf. 15.2), the messenger has no hope, for

---

added another noun and two participial phrases. The sequence of places in the first strophic pair is: Thebes, Italy (Κασταλίας confirms Ἰταλίαν), Eleusis, Thebes, Delphi, Euboea, Thebes. The second antistrophe begins with a threefold invocation: χοραγέ, ἐπίσκοπε, γένεθλον.

there is nothing but chance. Chance replaces the gods (cf. 162-3, 1158-60). This is, in fact, the only scene in the play (1155-79) in which the gods are not mentioned either individually by name or collectively.[18] The messenger's standard for happiness is pleasure (cf. 24.2), his standard for misery is to be a corpse.

58.2. The messenger does not address the Chorus, as Tiresias had, as the rulers of Thebes (cf. 51.2); he calls them the neighbors of Cadmus' and Amphion's house. Cadmus founded Thebes, Amphion built its walls; but after the hyporchema the name of Thebes does not recur. The invocation of Dionysus succeeds in making the city as an issue disappear (cf. 1094, 1247). The city and the regime are replaced by the land and the earth (1162-64, 1203). The enjoyment of what is one's own, whether it be victory over the land's enemies, kingship (cf. 178), or children, alone counts: Amphion was the husband of Niobe. The messenger, of course, does not know what else Creon will lose, but his wife's death would be a redundant proof of chance's power: Eurydice learns of her son's death by chance (cf. 1182). The messenger seems to know nothing of Tiresias' prophecy (cf. 1212); and it seems to be Creon's inopportune presence, in his account, that occasions Haemon's suicide. The messenger's speech has three parts: chance (1156-60), Creon (1161-5a), pleasure (1161-5a). Creon supplies the link, one would suppose, because the messenger assumes that the loss of Haemon wipes out Creon's pleasure: but he needlessly refers to Creon's noble sons, and Creon never takes any notice of Megareus. The messenger, moreover, conceals Creon's loss of Haemon, which he does not mention, by holding Creon's victory over Argos and his kingship to be elements of his enviable life, one of which Creon cannot and the other Creon does not lose in any literal sense. The messenger therefore must shift from Creon's downfall, for which his thoughts on chance have presumably prepared us, to Creon's pleasures now that his son is dead. In order, however, to extract a moral from the death of Haemon, the messenger must put himself in Creon's place, for he is not certain that Creon experiences the moral he wishes to illustrate. He lets his imagination stretch beyond Creon's good fortune, where he sees great wealth and the pomp of tyranny— the tyrant's private wealth replacing Creon's victory over his country's enemies (cf. Th. 1.17)—and then declares such magnificence to be deficient if the man who has them takes no pleasure in them. Pleasure, then, comes entirely from one's children; everything else is hollow without them. The messenger does not think, as Creon had, that children are good only if they sup-

---

[18]There are nineteen scenes in the play, the central one of which is the Chorus' song to Eros. The guard initiates the fourth scene from the beginning, the messenger the fourth scene from the end.

port their father in his friendships and enmities (cf. 39.2). He does not praise the fortunate just because their fortune might change, but because there is no good fortune without children (cf. Th. 2.44.2); nor does he find the unfortunate not to be unfortunate just because their fortune too might change, but because even in the absence of good fortune one can delight in one's children. The instability of one's own life is not in itself a matter of regret; it is the impossibility of fixing the life of others on whom one depends.[19] The messenger rejects both the life lived for the city and the life lived against the city, for, if Creon is any model, either involves the loss of a son, Megareus or Haemon. This twofold rejection forces him into a paradox: one cannot divine what is established for mortals. Creon feared that the preservation of the established laws is the best policy throughout one's life; the messenger makes us fear that the truth lies in the literal meaning of Creon's words: it is best in preserving the established laws to end one's life. The messenger inadvertently vindicates Antigone. He vindicates, over against the ensouled corpse Creon, the dead soul Antigone (cf. 35.1).

59 (1172-9). 59.1. The Chorus have to ask the messenger three questions before they learn what he should have told them at once. Consistent with his first speech he is more interested in Creon than in Haemon; but he does not explain how he reconciles Creon's guilt with the moral of his first speech, which Creon exemplified precisely because chance showed its power in his case. Guilt seems to be as incompatible with chance as with necessity; and the messenger has to admit that Creon's hand was not raised against his son. Is Creon guilty, then, in the way that Oedipus was the cause of Jocasta's suicide? Or did chance just give Creon the opportunity to be guilty? There was no necessity that Haemon love Antigone. Antigone, however, seems to be furthest from anyone's thoughts. The Chorus ask about the grief of kings; and we might suppose that they include Antigone in the royal circle, even as the messenger's answer (τεθνᾶσιν) suggests that more than one has died; but since he also makes Creon into a plural, and the Chorus' next two questions are in the singular, it would seem that Antigone's suicide, which the messenger now calls murder, does not count among the royal griefs. Creon, at any rate, never holds himself responsible for her suicide. That he failed to save her must look like chance to him (cf. 61.3).[20]

59.2 The pun on Haemon's name (αἱμάσσεται) would seem to preclude any misunderstanding of the messenger's reply ("he made himself bloody with

---

[19]For this meaning of chance see Arist. *EN* 1135b18-9; Eur. *Hipp.* 258-60; and for Creon to be an ἔμψυχος νεκρός as the result of Haemon's death see Antiphon Tetr. 11.β.10: ἐπὶ τῇ ἐμαυτοῦ ἀπαιδίᾳ ζῶν ἔτι κατορυχθήσομαι.

[20]Cf. Müller, 253.

his own hand") but the Chorus suggest that the verb might be passive and αὐτόχειρ not have its literal meaning. To ask whether the messenger could possibly mean that Creon killed Haemon is a grammarian's question;[21] but the Chorus are impelled to ask it for several reasons. First, the messenger did imply that Creon was guilty, and the Chorus perhaps only recognize the guilt of deeds. They had urged Creon to release Ismene on the grounds that she had not handled Polynices' corpse (cf. 34.1); and just as Creon thought his way of killing Antigone absolved the whole city, so they surely do not see themselves as involved in Creon's guilt. Second, Creon had implied that he had the right to kill his own sons if they disobeyed him (cf. 39.3), and they cannot be certain that Creon on second thoughts had not gone back on his word. Third, they did not dispute Creon's assertion that it would be more than human for Haemon to carry out his threat of suicide (cf. 43.1). And finally, Tiresias predicted Haemon's death in such a way (αὐτὸς...ἀντιδοὺς ἔσῃ) as to be at least as compatible with murder as with suicide. They took, at any rate, Tiresias' prophecy—ἀνήρ, ἄναξ, βέβηκε δεινὰ θεσπίσας (1091)—more seriously than their own understanding of Haemon's anger— ἀνὴρ, ἄναξ, βέβηκεν ἐξ ὀργῆς ταχύς (766)—for they now exclaim at the rightness of Tiresias' prediction despite Tiresias' silence about Haemon's suicide and its cause and the messenger's confirmation of their own understanding on both counts. Not even the Chorus trust their own wisdom. For the messenger now to invite them to deliberate is unwittingly ironic.

60 (1180-91). 60.1. The entrance of Eurydice lets the Chorus avoid deliberation. They call her τάλαινα as they had called Antigone δύστηνος on her entrance (379). Once Antigone, however, had spoken in her defense, she never elicited from them again another expression of condolence. Eurydice, on the other hand, now says nothing to deprive her of their sympathy; but when they later learn that she cursed Creon for the death of Megareus and hence implicitly condemned Thebes for its self-defense, they do not hold Creon responsible, despite his self-accusation, for her suicide (cf. 64.1). Eurydice's death was not included in Tiresias' prophecy (cf. 55.2); and the Chorus cannot discern in it, as they do in Haemon's, its justice (cf. 1270). For the Chorus she is an unaccountable intrusion. There is no one to tell them what to think. Creon could convince them of Antigone's injustice, and Tiresias of Creon's; but neither prepared them for Eurydice, whose silent suffering lies outside their experience and immune to their advice. Without the mean vanity of Creon or the holy madness of Antigone she reminds us of a suffering that the city as such inflicts and no theodicy comprehends. Tiresias preferred to remain

---

[21]Cf. schol. 1176: τὸ χ ὅτι ἐρωτᾷ ποτέρα κτλ. ἀκούσας ἤδη ὅτι αὐτόχειρ ἀπέθανεν.

silent rather than try to explain why Eurydice justly had to suffer Creon's punishment.

60.2. The messenger had addressed the Chorus as house-dwellers; Eurydice addresses the Chorus and the messenger together as townspeople. The difference between citizen and servant means nothing to her. Even the messenger is more aware of the city than she is. He later hopes that her silence is due to her shame of expressing her private grief (πένθος οἰκεῖον) openly, ἐς πόλιν (1246-1249). She says that she overheard the messenger's report while leaving the palace in order to pray to Pallas Athena, from whom she intended, we can suppose, to ask what the Chorus had failed to ask for from Dionysus, the life of her son. She wanted the virgin goddess to save Haemon from the effects of Eros. She began, however, much too late. Athena's ability to defeat Eros the undefeatable is not put to the test. Chance, or perhaps more than chance, intervenes before one learns whether Eros is a god subject to other gods. Sophocles allows there to be no refutation in deed of the Chorus' unprincipled wisdom.

61 (1192-1243). 61.1. Eurydice could not have fainted before 1173 or much after 1177. She might know that either one of her own is dead or Haemon killed himself. She might therefore want the messenger either to repeat no more than what he has already told the Chorus or to explain the exact degree to which Creon is the cause of Haemon's suicide. The messenger assumes that she wants a full report, as if she doubted his charge against Creon. Eurydice is entitled to the truth, no matter how painful, neither because her recovery from a swoon has shown that she can take it nor because her experience of evils has steeled her to listen, but because any softened version that the messenger now might tell would be later proved false. The messenger believes that the truth can never be unjustified; but Eurydice's departure in silence forces him to hope that to be versed in evils (κακῶν γὰρ οὐκ ἄπειρος, 1191) is the same as to be versed in judgment (γνώμης γὰρ οὐκ ἄπειρος, 1250). He believes so firmly in the decency of his mistress that he forgets his own speech, in which he counted Creon a living corpse for losing the enjoyment of what Eurydice also loses; and Eurydice has no political pleasures to fall back upon (cf. 58.2). The messenger spoke for himself when he made pleasure the standard; he makes decency the standard when he speaks for his masters. He thus draws back from the conclusion that the lack of certain pleasures entails suicide. Chance, after all, could restore one to good fortune. One wonders whether he would have counseled Eurydice, in an argument like Antigone's, to have more children (cf. Th. 2.44.3). The second messenger calls her παμμήτωρ (cf. 48.8).

61.2. For νηλεές (1197), see 45.1; for κυνοσπάρακτον (1198), 53.1; for σῶμα (1198), 48.5; for συγκατήθομεν (1202), 52.4; for χθονός (1203), 22.9. The messenger frames his true account in such a way that the burial of

Polynices—three aorist participles articulate its description (αἰτήσαντες, λούσαντες, χώσαντες)[22]—seems to be nothing but a slight incident on the way to the rescue of Antigone. However important his burial is for the city, it is of no interest to Eurydice. Creon's servants prayed that Hecate, the goddess of roads,[23] and Plouton check their wrath and turn gracious. They seemed to have been afraid that the chthonic gods were not pleased with their uncovering of Polynices' body, which they had done on their own without the excuse of such a command from Creon (cf. 25.4). They did not pray to the gods above, who according to Tiresias were equally angry. But Tiresias had not suggested how Creon should propitiate the gods; indeed, he had not even indicated what rites should be accorded Polynices. Creon on his own decided that only the most elaborate rites were now appropriate: Polynices is buried in a conspicuous tomb of native earth. Piety would have been satisfied and patriotism maintained if he had been buried outside of Theban territory (cf. 12.7). Creon gave up his patriotism to save his son. He believed that Polynices had to be buried on the spot if he were to outrun the Furies. He thereby gave up his pleasure in his victory over Argos (cf. 58.2) and admitted that the conquest of Thebes was unjustly thwarted (cf. 42.1). Creon compensated for his crime against the gods by committing another crime against the city. He was tested in office and found wanting. His punishment could thus be due as much to his betrayal of his own principles as to his rejection of Antigone's (cf. 51.3).

61.3. The messenger, like Antigone herself, speaks of Antigone's prison as a bridal chamber (cf. 46.2); but he amplifies this aspect still more (λιθόστρωτον, παστάδα). It is, however, the presence of Haemon, who by embracing Antigone obtains his marriage rites in Hades (1224, 1240-1), rather than Antigone's marriage to Acheron (816), that dictates his choice of words. That Antigone has now rejoined her family, with all the horror that implies (cf. 46.8), means nothing to him. He calls Haemon but not Antigone miserable (1234, 1241 cf. 1272, 1310-1). Her suicide, like Polynices' burial, is just an incident in his account. No one ever regrets that they came too late to save her. Neither the Chorus nor Creon, on the other hand, had thought of stopping Haemon from entering her tomb. Creon had so confidently spoken against the possibility of Haemon's suicide that this precaution, which even on the ground that Haemon might try to free Antigone would have been sensible, eluded them. Creon must have expected her suicide as soon as he had listened to her (cf. 567); and he must have changed the way of punishing her, not out of a scrupulous piety, nor even out of fear that the city would not stone her to

---

[22]The change in construction (τὸν μέν...αὖθις) calls our attention to the shift from σῶμα Πολυνείκους (1198) to τόν (1199) and ὃ δή (1202).

[23]Fire is the constant attribute of Hecate; cf. fr. 535 P.

death, but in the knowledge that Antigone would do his work for him (cf. 43.1). The Chorus understood Antigone less well than Creon did; but it was because of their advice that he had to pretend that he still had a chance to save her. He must have known what Tiresias meant when he called her a corpse (cf. 56.1) and for that reason put the burial of Polynices before the rescue of Antigone.

61.4. A servant told Creon that he had just heard from afar the shrill cries of ritual lamentation near the tomb; but Creon did not act on this report before he had heard them for himself and seen the stones of the tomb's entrance wrenched apart. He then divined ($\mathring{\alpha}\rho$' $\varepsilon\mathring{\iota}\mu\mathring{\iota}$ $\mu\acute{\alpha}\nu\tau\iota\varsigma$) their source while they were still indistinct ($\mathring{\alpha}\sigma\eta\mu\alpha$); but, unlike Tiresias, to whom a servant reported $\mathring{\alpha}\sigma\eta\mu\alpha$ $\mathring{o}\rho\gamma\iota\alpha$, Creon was not sure of their interpretation (cf. 52). He wondered whether the gods were deluding him; but for what purpose he did not say. Could Creon have come to believe that Tiresias had deluded him with prophecy and that all Tiresias had wanted to do was put a scare into him? Tiresias could surely have relied on his former infallibility to put across so salutary a lie (cf. 55.3); and, despite the Chorus' exclamation at the rightness of his prophecy, nothing Tiresias said argues for a more than human source for its truth (cf. 59.2); indeed, he never mentioned Apollo.[24] Had Tiresias foretold the death of Eurydice, or given the circumstances of Haemon's suicide, he would have confirmed his inspiration as divine; but he would then have deprived Creon of hope, hope that concealed the severity of divine punishment and the difference between sacrilege and error (cf. 55.3).

61.5. Creon seemed to have been bent on self-punishment. He overheard Haemon's bewailing Antigone's death, his father's deeds, and his own marriage; and thinking perhaps that all was forgiven if Haemon could regret the cause no less than its effects, he tried to plead with Haemon without repenting any of his crimes. His speech would have been the same even if he had not revoked his decree. Creon did not ask Haemon for forgiveness but rather asked three questions calculated to enrage him—what deed had he done, what did he intend to do, and what circumstance distracted his wits. Since Creon saw what his servants did, Haemon embracing Antigone around her waist as she hung from a noose, and then asked him what he had done, what could Haemon have thought except that Creon now dared to charge him with Antigone's murder?[25] It would hardly have occurred to him that Creon might have meant his forcible entry into the tomb; and if he had had the sense to understand him so,

---

[24]It is perhaps because Tiresias fails to remind them of Apollo that the Chorus do not ask Apollo, the god of purification *par excellence*, to purify the city.

[25]Cf. S. M. Adams, *Sophocles the Playwright*, 57–8.

what could he have made of Creon's third question? ἐν τῷ συμφορᾶς διεφθάρης is not a question that a guilty man asks. Creon simply bungled his self-appointed task of dissuading Haemon. Anyone—why not Eurydice?—could have pleaded his case better than he did. Instead of giving Haemon time for his sorrow to abate, he opposed it at its flood. To face Haemon, after Haemon had promised that Creon would never see him again (763-4), could only have intensified Haemon's anger and frustration. Creon's imprudence, then, in word and deed was the proximate cause of Haemon's suicide. He is too heartless to be wise.

61.6. When Creon had finished speaking, Haemon wildly glared at him, spat in his face, and in silence drew his sword; but when Creon had succeeded in evading his attack, he grew angry at himself and slew himself. Haemon's suicide seemed to have arisen from a compound of regret, remorse, vengeance, and love—regret for having missed Creon, remorse for having contemplated patricide, vengeance for Creon's crime, and love for Antigone (cf. 1177). The remorse that Creon never shows for his transgression of one sacred law was shown by Haemon for his intention to transgress another; but this intention would never have brought Haemon to punish himself if he had not also wanted to punish Creon and join Antigone in death. Nothing could illustrate better the peculiar character pious remorse and divine punishment have in common than Creon's evasion of death and Haemon's suicide. Creon's death—did Tiresias know that Haemon would fail?—would have deprived him of the chance to atone through suffering, and the compound cause of Haemon's suicide suggests the difficulty of atoning for sacrilege. Oedipus rejected suicide on the ground that he could not bear looking upon his mother and father in Hades; and he chose self-blinding on the ground that he could not bear looking upon either his children or Thebes (cf. *OT* 1369-86). Oedipus' vain attempt to isolate himself from everyone and everything haunted Antigone (cf. *OT* 1349-56, 1386-90, 1409-15, 1466-70), whose own piety entailed a remorse for which she could never atone. Haemon, on the other hand, could satisfy his original desire to punish Creon while making amends for his unholy impulse. Punishment and self-punishment make him doubly just, but they could not make him noble (cf. 48.9).

61.7. No one would have faulted the messenger's truthfulness if he had spared Eurydice the details of Haemon's suicide and said no more about it than the second messenger will say about Eurydice's (1315); instead, he dwells on Haemon's still-living embrace of the virgin Antigone and the gush of blood on her cheek. The passage reads like a grim mockery of a sexual embrace; and the words τὰ νυμφικὰ τέλη λαχών make it almost certain that the messenger wanted to insinuate it. Forced to choose between two equally distasteful endings, a thwarted marriage or a thwarted patricide (their juxtaposition recalls Oedipus), the messenger preferred the ending to which he could more readily attach a moral: no greater evil than imprudence belongs to man. The moral, however, bears a peculiar message when applied. Since the context forbids its application to Creon's impiety, with which, in any case, the messenger never charges him, Creon can be reproached only for not having yielded at once to Haemon's love of Antigone (cf. 36.1). Creon should have let the love of his own override his sense of righteousness. If he had wanted to prevent their cold embrace, Haemon's pleasure should have guided him (cf. 648–50). It would have been prudent to be fond.

62 (1244–56). 62.1. The Chorus are bewildered by Eurydice's silent departure, and they are forced to ask the messenger about it; but they are not satisfied with his explanation (cf. 61.1). They either doubt that any grief (or at least Eurydice's) is publicly inexpressible (cf. Her. 3.14–5) or think Eurydice incapable of such restraint. They rightly suspect that her silence is ominous, but not that she might want to say something not fit for them to hear. They forget Megareus, upon whose death Eurydice might look differently from the city. Eurydice's silence, moreover, is no more distressing to the Chorus than if she had indulged in an excess of lamentation. A few words of sorrow would have allayed their suspicion. A moderate utterance, they imply, is incompatible with an extreme resolution, for the mean in speech is consonant only with the mean in deed. They thought Antigone's defense of the law a proof of her savagery, but her last words (τὴν εὐσέβειαν σεβίσασα) were so devoid of paradox and excess—unlike, for example, ὅσια πανουργήσασα (cf. 924)—that they never suspected that she had resolved to kill herself (cf. 49.4). The Chorus always measure the deed by the speech and therefore fail to see the extreme that sometimes lurks within the mean. This failure sets the limit to their wisdom (cf. 65.1).

63 (1257–1300). 63.1. The Chorus still regard Creon as their lord despite Tiresias' address to them (cf. 51.2); and so they hesitate to lay Haemon's death to his error. Their εἰ θέμις εἰπεῖν allows Creon the chance of pleading not guilty; but he obliges them with a confession.[26] They behold the killer and the killed (Haemon is in his arms), the consequence of his imprudence, but not, we must supply, of his impiety (*φρενῶν δυσσεβῶν). His ill-conceived plans have led to his own unhappiness and the early death of his son. That he blasted his son's happiness as well does not occur to him, for Antigone's death is not one of his errors. The justice he sees too late are the miserable toils of mortals, which, as his own overturned and trampled joy illustrates, the gods savagely inflict. Creon admits his guilt without accepting his punishment, for he had unwillingly killed Haemon and Eurydice (1340), and even Tiresias argued that

---

[26]Cf. Andocides II. 5–7 for the way in which Creon expresses his regret for his crimes.

error was common to all men. He does not suggest what punishment would have been fitting; and once he learns of Eurydice's death, he thinks fate, not a god—he never names any god but the unappeasable Hades—caused his suffering (1345-6). Creon bewails the unwilled effects of his impiety but not their willed cause. He must be silent about Antigone and piety if he is to take part in a kommos, for he cannot lament what he does not understand.

63.2. Creon mentions something that is almost as surprising as was the cremation of Polynices. He says to Haemon that in his death he was released (ἀπελύθης), and as if to confirm that his choice of words is not casual, he later asks the second messenger how Eurydice was slain and released (1314).[27] Perhaps Creon means no more than that they have "passed away"; but since the verb is unknown this early as a euphemism, and a euphemism joined with ἔθανες in Haemon's case and with ἐν φοναῖς in Eurydice's hardly qualifies as such, one wonders whether Creon, holding the corpse of his son and confronted with that of his wife, does not mean that their souls are now separated from their bodies. Creon would thus be opposed to Antigone to the end, for whom the separation of body and soul in death would have made her devotion to the law impossible. Creon, on the other hand, has to be reminded of his duty to bury the dead (1334-5; cf. 1101). The restoration of the established laws, to which Antigone contributed nothing (cf. 17.5), can only lead once more to their being forgotten (cf. 26.1).

63.3. Sophocles allows Creon just one strophe to grieve over Haemon alone: but this is not because Creon feels more deeply about Eurydice than about Haemon; indeed, he never calls her his wife or himself her husband (cf. 1196, 1282). She is in his eyes a wretched mother and nothing else. Yet the unexpected shock of her suicide does force Creon to drop all thought of his deficient counsel and the miserable toil of mortals (cf. 1317).[28] Tiresias had asked Creon what proof it was of his courage to rekill the dead (τίς ἀλκὴ τὸν θανόντ᾽ ἐπικτανεῖν, 1030); and Creon now tells the messenger that with this

---

[27]Read κἀπελύσατ᾽; see Müller.

[28]The frequency with which the same sounds occupy the same place in strophe and antistrophe, accompanied as it is by slight dislocations of the same word and by contrasting words or phrases in the same place, alerts us to the shift Creon undergoes (cf. 46.8): δυσφρόνων (1261)—δυσκάθαρτος (1284): (1262)—(1285); ἰὼ παῖ (1266)—τί φῄς, ὦ παῖ (1289; see 38.1); νέος νέῳ (1266)—νέον (1289); ἀπελύθης (1268)—ἐπ᾽ ὀλέθρῳ (1291); (1273)—(1296); ἔπαισεν ἐν (1274)—μὲν ἐν (1297); ἀντρέπων χάραν (1275)—ἔναντα προσβλέπω νεκρόν (1299); (1276)—(1300). See also Müller. For an example of a shift in thought accompanying close symmetry between strophe and antistrophe, see Aesch. *Eum.* 155-68.

news he has reexecuted a dead man (ὀλωλότ᾽ ἄνδρ᾽ ἐπεξειργάσω). Creon speaks of himself as a second Polynices (cf. 1077): the crime that he mistakenly thought in Polynices' case could never be atoned for would be his own. Creon thought, however, that his crime was the death of Haemon, not the prohibition of Polynices' burial; and he does not now admit his guilt on either count when he envisions his unending suffering. He does not put together φρενῶν δυσφρονῶν ἁμαρτήματα with ἰὼ δυσκάθαρτος Ἅιδου λιμήν, let alone his rekilling of Polynices with Hades' rekilling of himself. Mistaken as to his crime, Creon cannot see his suffering as his punishment, for even on his mistaken view, in terms of which his crime should double as his punishment, Creon still attributes his suffering to either a god or fate, but never to himself. As agent he is guilty, as patient he is innocent (cf. *OC* 266-7).

64 (1301-46). 64.1. The messenger answers Creon's question of 1296, though Creon perhaps did not expect that anyone could answer it. Eurydice prayed at the altar of the house just before her suicide for the ill-success of Creon.[29] She did not think that Haemon's death, let alone Megareus', would adequately punish Creon. Not the ὀξυκώκυτον πάθος (1316) of her son, which brought on her own death, but only κακαὶ πράξεις in the future can affect him. Eurydice seemed to have understood Creon's incapacity for the punishment of suffering. He now, at any rate, becomes terrified and for the only time speaks of his pain (cf. 27.2). The fear of punishment takes the place of remorse and prompts Creon to ask for his death (cf. 15.2, 29.1). Fear, which should be part of his punishment, makes him want to escape from it, for he seems to have no fear, as Antigone had, that he will be judged in Hades (459-60, 925-6), and he hardly thinks he will meet his wife and sons there. His immediate death would be the most beautiful of fates, for he then would not have to undergo another day of fear. Creon's fear, however, alternates with his guilt, and his guilt suggests to him another way. To the messenger's report that Eurydice held him guilty for both Megareus' and Haemon's deaths he responds with a question about the manner of her suicide. Creon thus avoids extending his guilt to include the death of Megareus, for he senses that it would ill become him to protest in the name of the city Eurydice's blanket condemnation. He prefers instead to admit his guilt for Eurydice's death, even though no one charges him with it and he himself is aware of the extravagance of his admission (φάμ᾽ ἔτυμον). He wants his servants to take him out of the way now that he is not even as much as a no-one. He is too empty to suffer any more. He is unable to atone. Creon is in his life less than the dead Polynices, for he has no one to pity him; but he does not complain, as

---

[29]Nothing seems certain in 1301 except βωμία; but I should be inclined to accept Seyffert's reading at 1303 because of 424-5.

Antigone did, of his lack of friends. He has too much self-pity to miss them;[30] and he seems to believe that if he is out of sight his guilt is out of mind. So little does his crime against the city mean to him that he does not think of exile or any other public punishment. The Chorus, therefore, are not ready to comfort Creon: the sooner his misfortunes are out of the way the greater is their own gain. They want to forget Creon in his troubles as they must have once forgotten Oedipus in his; and they renounce their loyalty to Creon in words that could equally have served against Oedipus. Indeed, their advice to Creon, not to pray for anything since the future does not properly concern mortals who must stick to what is before them, suits Oedipus far more exactly than Creon, whose fate scarcely deserves the name of destiny (cf. *OT* 1518-20).

65 (1347-53). 65.1. The Chorus draw a conclusion that they apparently did not need the play to learn (cf. 57.1). Man, according to the first stasimon, taught himself speech, thought, and civility, all three of which are morally neutral; but if, they now say, thought is good it is wisdom, if speech is bad it is boasting, and if civility is good it is piety (cf. 52.3-4). Yet there seem to be two kinds of wisdom. Wisdom consists solely in not acting impiously against the gods, and this non-Antigonean piety is the chief ingredient in happiness; and wisdom comes in old age solely through suffering, and happiness is thus impossible, for Creon can now be called wise but not happy (cf. 52.5). The Chorus, however, see no difficulty, for the precept that the wisdom of innocence trusts in from the start is the same as that which the wisdom of suffering learns late, and to the Chorus nothing matters but the precept, however learnt: Creon must do τὰ προκείμενα and disregard τὰν ποσὶν κακά. They never understand that civility is not self-taught but piety already in decay, the piety of precept. That one could live the precept, so that χρὴ τά γ᾽ ἐς θεοὺς μηδὲν ἀσεπτεῖν be transformed into Antigone's ὅσια πανουργήσασα, is wholly beyond them. They therefore can only regret that Creon, who had he followed the precept would have kept clear of trouble, forced them to confront the τέρας Antigone.

---

[30]Cf. 34.2.1. Antigone never calls herself μελέα or δειλαία, each of which Creon uses thrice (977, 1319, 1341; 1272, 1310-1). The one trait they have in common is tearlessness; but in Antigone's case it comes from her greatness of soul, in Creon's from his emptiness. Antigone is ταλαίφρων, not Creon.

Two Notes on Aeschylus' Septem

(1st Part)

I. The Parodos and First Stasimon

The Chorus sing twice about the Argive attack, first before and then after Eteocles has rebuked them. One question can be raised at once: How does Eteocles' rebuke change the content and tone of what they say? He offers his own prayer as a model for theirs (265-278). How closely, then, do they follow him, and how far do they depart from what they said as they entered? Eteocles bids them to leave the precinct of statues and sing, in the "Greek fashion of a sacrificial cry," a gracious or placatory ὀλολυγμός; and he then lists two kinds of gods to whom he and the citizens will sacrifice if the city is saved. It is clear from his conclusion (τοιαῦτ' ἐπεύχου...θεοῖς) that he expects the Chorus to echo his vows; but the Chorus do not mention sacrifices either past or future (cf. 230-1, 699-702). That the Chorus depart so much from Eteocles' instructions forces us to attend all the more closely to how they interpret his demand that they cease to be φιλόστονοι, "without vain and wild snortings," in their prayers (279-80).

Both structurally and metrically the parodos and stasimon differ as much as the intervention of Eteocles would lead one to expect. The parodos begins with almost 80 lines of non-strophic dochmiacs and iambs, and then continues with dochmiacs in strophic correspondence; while the stasimon is strophic throughout, and there are no dochmiacs except toward the end, where, however, less disturbing measures relieve them (cf. Wilamowitz' analysis). The first line of each chorus agrees with this difference. The parodos has θρέομαι φοβερὰ μεγάλ' ἄχη, the stasimon μέλει, φόβῳ δ' οὐχ ὑπνώσσει κέαρ. φοβερά can either mean "fear-provoking" or "fear-filled," but Eteocles considers their song and behavior dangerous because it might terrify the rest of the city (237, 262, cf. 270); and the Chorus' shouting of their fear most contrasts it with the fear they feel after Eteocles has addressed them. The movement seems to be from fear outside to fear inside the heart, and this turning inward characterizes the entire stasimon: γείτονες δὲ καρδίας μέριμναι ζωπυροῦσι τάρβος. No word for heart occurs in the parodos, and fear either is presented as "out there"—φόβος δ' ἀρείων ὅπλων (120)—or Poseidon is asked to relieve them from it (134). Fear is not a foreboding that ranges beyond the immediate cause for alarm. A settled fear in the stasimon replaces a momentary terror in the parodos. ὑπερδέδοικεν, πάντρομος, and προταρβῶ occur in the stasimon (292, 294 332), but nothing similar is found in the parodos, where the gods are asked to care for (μέλεσθε...μελόμενοι) the city's sacrifices (177-8), about which the Chorus are silent in the stasimon, whose first word is an uncoordinated μέλει (cf. Ag. 370). The main reason for this difference lies in the shift in the object of the Chorus' imaginings.[1] They shift from imagining the enemy to imagining the imminent condition of themselves and other citizens. The parodos is pictorial, the stasimon reflective. The Argive army βρέμει in the parodos (84), while in the stasimon βλαχαὶ...τῶν ἐπιμαστιδίων βρέμονται (348-350). In the parodos the city makes no noise, all the sound arises from the enemy; but in the stasimon the city is filled with sound. The noise of the enemy in the parodos accompanies their description as water and waves, whereas the enemy is later described as wild and the Chorus as tame animals (290-294, 328). The animation of the inanimate yields to the animate. δοριτίνακτος αἰθὴρ ἐπιμαίνεται (155) stands opposed to μαινόμενος δ' ἐπιπνεῖ...Ἄρης (343-4). Ares, who is invoked at first as the founder of Thebes, shows himself second as the frenzy of war (105, 135-139, cf. 244). Even when Ares appears as war's personification in the parodos, the context is the animated inanimate or rather the fusion of the animate and inanimate— κῦμα...ἀνδρῶν καχλάζει πνοαῖς Ἄρεος ὀρόμενον (114-5, cf. 630-634). He is not the madness-breathing Ares who pollutes piety (344). When Aristophanes has Aeschylus claim that he made the Septem full of Ares, the claim raises a question that lies at the heart of the drama. Which Ares? The Ares to whom Eteocles refers when he says that Melanippus descended from the sown men whom Ares spared, or the Ares of two lines later, who seems to be simply the fortunes of war: ἔργον δ' ἐν κύβοις Ἄρης κρινεῖ (412-414, cf. Schütz)? This ambiguity, I believe, points to *the* question of the Septem: τί ἐστὶν Ἄρης; Ares is, indeed, in a deeper sense than Zeus perhaps would allow, ἀλλοπρόσαλλος (E 889, cf. Bechtel, Lexilogus, s. v.).

The parodos and stasimon equally contain prayers to the gods, but they are entirely different in kind. In the stasimon no god is invoked by name, in the parodos eight gods are thus invoked. This anonymity of the gods seems to be occasioned by the Chorus' leaving their statues at Eteocles' behest, for the gods they first invoked by name were clearly present as statues before them.

---

[1]Cf. schol. on 79: ταῦτα δὲ φαντοζόμενα λέγουσιν ὡς ἀληθῆ, and on 100, 181.

The Chorus approach (πελαζόμεσθα) Aphrodite as they pray to her (144). Eteocles' ridicule of their reverence for images apparently compels them to avoid mentioning specific deities (185, 208-210). Only the Dircaean waters allow them to name but not to invoke Poseidon and the children of Tethys (307-311, cf. 273); and they name besides only Zeus, Hades, and Ares (301, 322, 344). Perhaps the most striking indication of the change is the different sense εὔεδρος obtains in each Chorus. First it refers to the statues of the gods to which, in their fixity, as all else is in upheaval, it is opportune to cling—ἰὼ μάκαρες εὔεδροι, ἀκμάζει βρετέων ἔχεσθαι (96-99)—but it later refers to the gods themselves as firm defenders of the city—πόλεως ῥύτορες εὔεδροι στάθητ' (318-9). The gods have become citizens (253). Whatever loss of vividness the absence of statues and divine names entails would seem to be compensated for in the gods' more intimate enrollment in the city's defense (cf. 304-307). But the Chorus' prayer is short-lived, and they dwell more on the disasters that await women and children if the city is captured than on the gods' confounding their enemies. The gods are not now assumed to see and hear as they were in the parodos (106, 110, 171). λιταὶ θεόκλυτοι become ὀξύγοοι λιταί (144, 320, cf. 172). The gods are no longer loving gods. Nothing in the stasimon corresponds to (πόλιν) εὐφιλήταν in reference to Ares (109), to φιλόμαχον κράτος in reference to Athena (128), to κήδεσαι ἐναργῶς again in reference to Ares (139), or to ἰὼ φίλοι δαίμονες and φιλοπόλιες (174, 176), to say nothing of Ἄρτεμι φίλα and ὦ φίλ' Ἄπολλον (154, 159). The concern that the gods do or are to show is matched by the zeal with which the citizens offer sacrifices to them: φιλοθύτων...πόλεος ὀργίων μνήστορες ἔστε μοι (179-80). The gods are asked to protect Thebes because of the specific claim the city has on their loyalty: Ares and Aphrodite are the ancestors of Thebes (105, 136, 140-142), Hera has the cult epithet πότνια and Apollo Λύκειος (153, 145), and Athena is Ὄγκα (164), whose temple stands near one of the city's gates and makes her in Eteocles' word, ἀγχίπτολις (486-7, 501). In the stasimon, however, the gods are asked to defend the city—its name is mentioned once—on more general grounds, either because the gods could not find any better land (304-5), or because it is pitiable for so ancient a city to be destroyed (321-2). The stasimon could almost apply to any city under attack, the parodos can refer only to Thebes: the Argives are in the parodos an ἑτερόφωνος στρατός (170, cf. Schütz, 1076). A consequence of this difference is that, as we have seen, Ares in the parodos is the Theban Ares and in the stasimon the god of war.

Two traits, then, distinguish the stasimon from the parodos. It is more "psychological" in tone and more general in content. Could there be a connection between these two aspects? Does the Chorus' turning inward effect a corresponding loss of distinctness? Does the anonymity of the gods point to an area where the gods have less and human beings more control over their destiny? The Chorus ask at first, τί γενήσεται ἡμῖν; ποῖ δ' ἔτι τέλος ἐπάγει θεός; (156-7), but later they only ask, τί γένωμαι; (297),[2] and the gods' purpose is lost from view. Is it too much to say that the shift from a future to a subjunctive mood—there are no deliberative subjunctives in the parodos— reflects the double shift we have described—a turning inward and a less certain reliance on the gods (cf. 217-8)? It is plain, I think, that to answer this question would help answer the question that has exercised so much recent scholarship. Does Eteocles decide his own fate, or is his fate determined by the curse of Oedipus?[3] The possibilities are not as clear-cut as they would seem, but as intertwined as Ares in his dual aspect. Only if one could show that the Ares in ὧν Ἄρης ἐφείσατο (412) is utterly distinct from the Ares of ἔργον δ' ἐν κύβοις Ἄρης κρινεῖ (414), and that only typographical consistency endows the second with a capital letter, would one be justified in posing that alternative; for between these two Ares lies a third, the Ares the spy ascribes to Hippomedon: ἔνθεος δ' Ἄρει/ βακχᾷ πρὸς ἀλκήν, θυιὰς ὤν (497-8). The way in which this triad is understood ultimately determines the way in which Eteocles' decision can be understood. Ares as 1) a willing, acting, anthropomorphic god, 2) a personification of war, and 3) a certain state of the soul, presents in himself the difficulty of understanding Eteocles.[4]

Something else marks the difference between the parodos and stasimon, but its import is not easy to discern. In the parodos but not in the stasimon goddesses are thrice distinguished from gods: θεοὶ θεαί τ' (87), τίς ἄρ' ἐπαρκέσει θεῶν ἢ θεᾶν (93-4), ἰὼ τέλειοι τέλειαί τε γᾶς πυργοφύλακες (167-8). Sexual differentiation disappears in the stasimon along with the names of the gods. What prompts the disappearance of sex among the gods might be Eteocles' outburst against women (181-202), which is so violent that

---

[2]Schütz nicely observes on 156-7: variatio haec temporum, praesentis et futuri, bene exprimit animum calamitatibus futuris tamquam praesentibus intentum.

[3]It is needless to give the full bibliography but only add the latest: L. Golden, CPh 59, 1964, 79-89; H. Erbse, Hermes 92, 1964, 1-9.

[4]How much the problem of the threefold Ares is connected with that of Eteocles is shown by considering together 709-711 ἐξέζεσεν γὰρ Οἰδίπου κατεύγματα· ἄγαν δ' ἀληθεῖς ἐνυπνίων φαντασμάτων ὄψεις, πατρῴων χρημάτων δατήριοι and 944-946 πικρὸς δὲ χρημάτων ἴσος δατητὰς Ἄρης (cf. 907-910). Note, further, how Scythian iron—κτεάνων χρηατοδαίτας πικρός —shares equally with the Erinys the responsibility for the war (720-733), for Herodotus tells us that an iron sword was the image of Ares among the Scythians (IV, 62, 2; cf. 59, 2; also Septem 529-532: Ch. 160-163 (uncertainly restored).

he divides his subjects into male, female, and the in-between (197)—as though the very walls of the city must obey him, but whose effect is to minimize the differences in gender and embrace everything in the city under a neutral term (something like, "the citizen body").[5] Eteocles, shortly thereafter, does not mention the names of major gods in the prayer that he wishes the Chorus to copy, but he subordinates their separate existence to their collective function, the city-protecting gods who preside over field and market-place (271–2, cf. Ag. 88–90, Fraenkel, ad loc.); whereas before the entrance of the Chorus, he had appealed to Zeus, Earth, and his father's Curse as well as to the city-protecting gods (69–70). Eteocles seems to have suppressed the sexuality of the gods in revulsion against the Chorus' excessive femininity. Indeed, he goes so far as to invent a genealogy that is meant to replace the images to which the Chorus are so stubbornly attached (258); and in order to do so he has to wrench the Greek language and replace the expected feminine with a masculine noun. Obedience, he says, is the mother of Success and the wife of Safety (224–5, σωτήρ instead of σωτηρία, cf. Wilamowitz).[6] Eteocles means no more than that success results from obedience joined with safety (cf. 494), and he is hardly conscious that his expression taken literally does not square with his contempt for women. He probably regards it as a concession to the Chorus. That the goddesses finally prove just as potent as the gods—κάρτα δ' ἀληθῆ...πότνι' Ἐρινὺς ἐπέκρανεν (886–7)—suggests that Eteocles now speaks more truly than he knows, even as the play's concluding with Antigone indicates Eteocles' mistaken estimation of women.[7] By disregarding women at the beginning, he cannot listen to them at the end (712). The Chorus, whom he had addressed as θρέμματ' οὐκ ἀνασχετά (181), are addressed after his death as παῖδες μητέρων τεθραμμέναι (792).[8]

If we now go back to examine the gods the Chorus name in the parodos, we find that there are as many female as male: Athena, Aphrodite, Artemis,

---

[5]Cf. S. Benardete, RhM 107, 1964, 138 n. 28.

[6]The formulaic ὧδ' ἔχει λόγος that here concludes his speech may mean as well, "So reason (as opposed to your unreasoning behavior) holds"; cf. Ag. 1661; Ch. 521.

[7]870–1 of Antigone and Ismene, πασῶν ὁπόσαι στρόφον ἐσθῆσιν περιβάλλονται are not more "grotesque" (Fraenkel's word) than Eteocles' μεταίχμιον, and they point to the same question: γυναῖκες take over from the Chorus of παρθένοι; cf. 864, 928. See Fraenkel, Ag. vol. I, 321 n. 1; Museum Helveticum 21, 1964, 58–9; H. Lloyd-Jones, CQ 53, 1959, 102–104.

[8]μήτηρ, on the first three occasions Eteocles uses the word, is what we would call metaphoric 16, 225, 416, 664; cf. 584–5.

and Hera; Zeus, Poseidon, Ares and Apollo. Aphrodite and Ares are the parents of Harmonia, who as Cadmus' wife founded with him the present generation of Thebans. But Aphrodite and Ares are only one source, the serpent's teeth that Cadmus sowed are another.[9] Thebes, then, has a sexual (divine and human) root and a nonsexual (sub-human) root, and according to Eteocles it is the latter in which the city must especially put its trust. The first and third Theban defenders are Spartoi (412–417, 474), and of the first Eteocles says that "consanguine justice" impels him to defend the "mother who gave him birth". Every able Theban is to aid "mother earth, their dearest nurse," who nurtured the inhabitants to be reliable soldiers in time of need (10–20). Eteocles presents the earth as the sole progenitor of the Thebans, regardless of whether their ancestry warrants it or not; for in listing what has to be defended—city, altars of native gods, children, and earth—he does not mention human parents. One has only to recall Nestor's plea to the Achaeans—ἐπὶ δὲ μνήσασθε ἕκαστος/ παίδων ἠδ᾽ ἀλόχων καὶ κτήσιος ἠδὲ τοκήων (Ο 662–63)— or, closer still, the cry of the Greeks at Salamis—ἐλευθεροῦτε πατρίδ᾽, ἐλευθεροῦτε δέ/ παῖδας γυναῖκας θεῶν τε πατρῴων ἕδη/ θήκας τε προγόνων (Pers. 403–405)—to realize how much weight must here be given to Eteocles' silence about women and human ancestors. Such a silence implies, I think, an unqualified devotion to the country, and not so nicely calculated a balance between country and family as one finds in Cicero: *Sic, quoniam plura*

---

[9]The first two words of line 1, Κάδμου πολῖται, point to a peculiarity of the Septem as a whole. They seem to have been deliberately chosen to avoid mentioning Thebes, for Thebes, as Tucker observed, never occurs in the play but only, we might add, in its title (compare the apparently similar case of the Eumenides, Fraenkel, Ag. vol. III, 547 n. 2). The Thebans throughout are called Cadmeans, and their city the city of Cadmus (17 times in all). One might try to account for this silence by appealing, as Tucker did, to the Athenians' supposed hatred of contemporary Thebes, but Aeschylus by that reasoning would have been equally forbidden even to write the Persians, and, besides, his silence on the name could hardly have blotted out his audience's awareness that, after all, the Cadmean city was Thebes. The periphrases for Thebes and Thebans, then, were chosen for their own sake: to keep on calling our attention to the foundations and founder of Thebes. They would be the first hint that the present siege was not an ordinary one, but that its character somehow throws light on the origins of Thebes, and hence, by implication, on the origins of any city. Aeschylus' failure to mention Cadmus' Phoenician origin could be thus explained, for it would have turned Thebes' origin into a derivative and no longer a primary phenomenon; cf. U. v. Wilamowitz, Interpretationen, 98 n. 1; also 92 n. 1.

beneficia continet patria, et est antiquior parens quam is qui creavit, maior ei profecto quam parenti debetur gratia (de re publ. I, fr. 1a Ziegler). The devotion can remain unqualified because Eteocles has made the "fatherland" into a literal mother, who needs no help in generation from the family. Eteocles understands, in short, the Ares who spared the Spartoi but not the Ares who married Aphrodite, a goddess as alien to him as to Hippolytus. He tries to ignore the family and regard it as a sub-political (and hence insignificant) element in the city; as though he did not know that Laius' sexual passion—his φίλοι ἀβουλίαι as the Chorus delicately put it (750)[10]—was the ultimate cause of the present war. Apollo had told Laius to die without issue and save the city—γέννας ἄτερ σώζειν πόλιν (749)—and Eteocles, in extending autochthony to include all Thebans, glosses over the fatal doubleness of sexual and non-sexual generation with a single origin. In obedience to Apollo, as it were, he tries to save the city γέννας ἄτερ. A patriotism, whether genuine or assumed, blots out that fatal doubleness in the city that he and his family particularly reveal (cf. 753–756)[11]. Both the Chorus, then, as maidens and the goddesses they revere show up the weakness in Eteocles' apparently complete devotion to the city. Although Eteocles might insist on and obtain the Chorus' silence (232, 250, 252, 262–3), and though he might stop all mention of the gods as sexual beings—he himself later refers only to the virgin goddesses Artemis, Athena, and Dike (450, 501, 662)[12]—he cannot at all affect the principle for which they stand. His wish to live apart from the female race is indeed only a wish (187–8), and Antigone survives him to split the city exactly where he boldly assumed that it was whole (1069–1071). Not only perhaps does Eteocles disregard the later pleading of the Chorus to abstain from challenging Polynices because they are women, but because he has so equated his own concern with the city's that he has ceased to be aware of his own family. Who else is more just, he asks himself[13], to stand against Polynices: ἄρχοντί τ᾽ ἄρχων καὶ κασιγνήτῳ κάσις, ἐχθρὸς σὺν ἐχθρῷ (673–675)? The specious symmetry of ruler-brother-foe against ruler-brother-foe blinds him to the difference between ruler and brother, brother and foe. It is a blindness to which the Chorus, in the presence of male and female statues of the gods who form

---

[10]Cf. Wilamowitz, Interpretationen, 80 n. 1.

[11]Cf. S. Benardete, "Sophocles' Oedipus Tyrannus" in: Ancients and Moderns (Basic Books, New York, 1964); also in: Ancients and Moderns (Basic Books, New York, 1964), 9–10.

[12]The spy calls the Dike on Polynices' shield γυνή (645), Eteocles παρθένος; he apparently changed the spy's σωφρόνως into an adjective.

[13]Cf. E. Fraenkel, "Die sieben Redepaare im Thebanerdrama des Aischylos," S. Ber. Bayer. Akad. Wiss., Phil.-hist. Kl. 1957, Heft 3, 56.

the family of Zeus, could never wholly succumb.[14]

---

[14]One should consider the difference between the parodos and the stasimon in light of Iliad VIII, where Zeus is an assembly of the gods distinguishes between gods and goddesses (5, 7, 20), threatens them all if they interfere in the war, and widens the distance between heaven and earth (16, 427–431). The goddesses Athena and Hera are prevented from helping the Achaeans except by counsel (35–6, 218), while Zeus helps the Trojans and comforts the Achaeans with signs (245–252), as Diomedes is mocked as a woman (163), the Trojans fight by compulsion for their women and children (57), and Hector boasts to be the husband of Andromache (190). Zeus here reveals his plan (473–477). He is presented for the most part as the god of thunder and lightning (75, 133, 170, 405, 455)—οὐρανός is thrice as frequent here as in any other book (15 times), wholly indifferent to Hera and cold to Athena (370, 407–8, 477–483). Zeus shows himself as almost asexual, beyond the distinction between male and female, while the heroes become more conscious of their weakness (271, 306); we learn of the fatal weakspot in horse and man (84, 326).

Two Notes on Aeschylus' Septem

(2nd Part)

II. Eteocles' Interpretations of the Shields

The spy tells Eteocles that Tydeus carries a shield whose insigne is the sky blazing with stars, and a full moon, the "eye of night," gleams in their midst (388–390). There are no words on the shield, for there is no one who could properly be thought to speak them, but Tydeus was heard to castigate the soothsayer Amphiaraus and reproach him for cowardice, since, Amphiaraus claimed, the sacrifices were still unpropitious (377–383). Eteocles, in his reply, offers an interpretation of the shield that is meant to allay the fears of the Chorus, as he apparently considers that women who are ready to fall down before statues of gods would be prey to false imaginings. He declares himself to be immune to anything of the kind (397–399). He tries to show that Tydeus, who despises soothsaying, carries a sign that might itself be a prediction (400–406). He puts the stress, accordingly, on the night and not on the sky: νύκτα...οὐρανοῦ replaces οὐρανόν...νυκτός and he says the night, not the sky, is ablaze with stars. If Tydeus is killed, the night would fall upon his eyes, a Homeric phrase that turns upside down the spy's "eye of night." The night of Tydeus' shield is literal and the eye metaphoric, while the night in Eteocles' interpretation is metaphoric and the eyes literal. "Eye of night" is not a literal account of what the spy saw; it too is an interpretation. It might therefore be completely unmetaphoric, if the moon were regarded as a sentient being. Eteocles seems, however, to have divorced the phrase from its reference to the moon, applied it to Tydeus, and played with it as though it were simply a periphrasis for night (cf. Pers. 428, Eur. IT 110). Eteocles, in any case, has been forced to find a meaning in Tydeus' shield which in itself it may not bear. Even the spy's phrase ὑπέρφρον σῆμα (387, cf. 391) goes beyond the representation, which contains nothing to inspire fear or reveal a presumptuous pride (cf. (Θ 555–559)[1] Only the bells attached to the shield are meant to ter-

---

[1] How easily one can be seduced into agreeing with the spy's or Eteocles'

rorize (356), and Tydeus' presumption is more in what he says than in what he shows. Eteocles, then, is guilty of over-interpretation. He imposes a 'reading' on what perhaps cannot be read.

The shield of Capaneus, however, is the man. It shows an unprotected or naked man with a blazing torch, and golden letters proclaim, "I shall burn the city" (432-434). Eteocles finds it easy to connect Capaneus' insigne with his boast that not even the "strife of Zeus" could check him in his course.[2] These words lead Eteocles to apply the description of the insigne to the lightning that Capaneus thinks so harmless: ἄνδρα πυρφόρον becomes τὸν πυρφόρον κεραυνόν (444/45). Whereas in the case of Tydeus, the shield's image is silent and Tydeus' words without a direct bearing on it, Capaneus' words, through the resemblance of man-made fire to lightning, allow or rather prompt the union of an image no longer silent with a boast that implicitly ranks fire higher than lightning. Eteocles' hermeneutics, on his second try, has improved. He now transforms an image of something into something else without appealing to any metaphor: οὐδὲν ἐξηκασμένον (445).[3] Tydeus had shown an image of the night sky which had to be forced to bear on what he said; but Capaneus' words refer to the Zeus of the sky and his insigne to the present siege of Thebes. Tydeus had not mentioned gods, Capaneus threatens them. The shield

---

interpretation is shown by Fraenkel's comment on ὑπέρφρον σῆμα: "Die Überheblichkeit des Symbols ('ich Tydeus der volle Mond, die anderen nur Sterne') war wohl jedem Griechen ohne weiteres verständlich"; ib., 9 n. 18.

[2]Cf. Fraenkel, ib., 17-19.

[3]446 may have to be deleted with Verrall, Tucker, and Fraenkel, ib., 22-23; Ag. III. 575 n. 1; but Fraenkel's arguments do not show it. He asserts that Eteocles never mixes together what the shield-bearer says with his interpretation of the shield; but Eteoclus, Hippomedon, and Polynices do not say anything, and Amphiaraus does not have a device, and three cases are hardly enough to insist on such consistency. Eteocles, moreover, clearly borrowed ἐξηκασμένον from what Capaneus said, just as he transferred the fact that Tydeus spoke to a μάντις to his interpretation of Tydeus' shield. Lobel's observation, that Eteocles always varies the expressions he hears from the spy, applies here as well; for Eteocles means not only that it is not an image that will strike Capaneus, but that it cannot possibly be likened to the sun. Eteocles denigrates the sun with the same words that Capaneus used to denigrate lightning. The meaning changes even though the words almost remain the same, for the addition of τοῖς ἡλίου reminds us, inevitably after the moon has been called νυκτὸς ὄμμα, that the sun πάντ᾽ ἐφορᾷ καὶ πάντ᾽ ἐπακούει. The cosmic gods appear only to be disregarded, for they are not by themselves punitive gods; cf. μ 377-388.

of Tydeus is partly bright and partly dark with nothing but cosmic gods: man and man-shaped gods have there no place. The shield of Capaneus, on the other hand, is the world of unarmed, post-Promethean man, who challenges the sun and Zeus as ineffectual (cf. Eur. Phoen. 1122). We seem to be presented, then, with two stages of, or two layers in, men's understanding of the sky that overarches them, and each layer is in turn subject to a double interpretation. The first is the sky at night with a full moon which looks on men but seems indifferent to them; but the moon wanes and disappears, and the night becomes understood as the blackness of death: Night gave birth by herself to Death (Hes. Th. 211–213). The first interpretation can be imitated, the second can only be talked about; but, for the second layer, the view that regards lightning as harmless can only be talked about in likenesses, and only unprotected man can be shown: Capaneus' threats seem to be only talk. Eteocles, in his interpretation of this second layer, trusts that unprotected man will prove to be exposed to the just ($\xi\grave{\upsilon}\nu$ $\delta\acute{\iota}\kappa\eta$) punishment of heaven. Thebes' champion against Tydeus with his cosmic device was one of the Spartoi, whom "consanguine justice," the justice of defending his own mother, the earth (cf. 477), will exhort (cf. Wilamowitz, 415). Eteocles, then, has transferred his trust from earth to heaven, even as Tydeus' reliance on the sky has yielded to Capaneus' reliance on himself. Eteocles indicates this change when he presents the first confrontation as a matter of chance even if Ares presides over the throw of the dice, and the second confrontation between Capaneus and Polyphontes as entirely in Thebes' favor, since the good-will of Artemis and other gods seconds Polyphontes (449–450).

Eteoclus, the third Argive attacker, has a shield that shows a hoplite approaching with a scaling ladder the walls of a city, and he proclaims, "Not even Ares would cast me from the ramparts" (466–469). Eteocles' reply of nine lines is the shortest of his interpretations (the next shortest is the fifth with twelve), but it is no less significant than the others. He seems again, as he did with Tydeus and Melanippus, to regard the issue between Eteoclus and another Spartos Megareus as a toss-up, for he concedes that Megareus might be killed; but if he is not, "he will adorn his father's house with booty," when he seizes "two men and the city on the shield" (477–480). Eteoclus himself does not make any boast, he leaves it to his emblem to speak for him; and what the shield shows is literally true: Ares cannot cast this image from the ramparts. This absorption of Eteoclus, as it were, into his image is echoed by Eteocles, who almost puts the image of the hoplite and the hoplite himself on the same level, even as the image of a city, if captured, is almost as glorious a deed as the capture of Thebes. In the first interpretation of Eteocles, the literal and the metaphoric in the image were inverted; in the second, the image suggested something else that was not an image; but now an image becomes the equivalent of that of which it is an image. This closing of the gap between the image and the imaged is subtly presented as the merging of the spy with the Argive leaders. Eteocles ends by saying, κόμπαϛ' ἐπ' ἄλλῳ (480), on which Schütz acutely observes: ...etsi nuntius non id agebat, ut ipse hostium robur aut ferociam iactaret aut exaggeraret, tamen eius narratio sensim sic incalescebat, ut ipse quasi in societatem ostentationis venire videretur. ita qui in sole ambulant, etiamsi id non agant, tamen vel inviti colorantur; et qui de magnarum rerum altitudine dicunt, ipsi inter loquendum caeco impetu attollunt sese, et in digitos eriguntur (cf. Wilamowitz, 500). If Schütz had only added that Eteocles himself can be equally charged with confounding the reporter with the report, just as he has doubled Eteoclus, whose name is almost the double of his own, then Schütz would have, I think, accurately described the result of the third confrontation.

It was impossible to confuse the armored Capaneus with his device of an unprotected man, but it seems a smaller step to treat the image of a hoplite as a hoplite, especially since the hoplite Eteoclus is silent and the image of a hoplite speaks. The silence of the central Argive, Hippomedon, is even greater and produces greater consequences; for though he shouts, his shouts are meaningless: αὐτὸς δ' ἐπηλάλαξεν...βακχᾷ πρὸς ἀλκήν (497/98). His shield, moreover, contains no letters. It pictures Typhon breathing soot-laden fire through his mouth (493/94). This is the only image whose artfulness the spy mentions, as its bearer is the only one who strikes terror in him (490–492), for it is the first image of a god on the shields. The spy, in fact, becomes so filled with the scene he describes that two other gods beside Typhon are said to be present. Hippomedon is ἔνθεος Ἄρει, and his terrifying glance (φόβον βλέπων) induces the spy to declare that Φόβος now glories at the city's gates (498, 500). Eteocles is forced to meet Hippomedon on his own grounds. He first says that Onka Athena, whose temple stands nearby, will keep the serpent from the nestlings (501–503). He takes the simile of the serpent from the snakes that are coiled round the rim of Hippomedon's shield (495/96); and for the first and last time he assigns an emblematic shield to the Theban champion. Hermes, the god of interpretation, brings them reasonably (εὐλόγως) together (508). Hyperbius will bear the likeness of Zeus as the hurler of lightning, and since Zeus conquered Typhon, it is likely (εἰκός) that Hyperbius will conquer Hippomedon (510–520). Both men yield in importance to the images each displays, for the outcome of their contest should be in proportion (πρὸς λόγον) to their signs. Eteocles had taken the image of Eteoclus' shield as possessed of a certain weight in the world, but it did not prevail over its bearer, for image and image-bearer were still two. Now, however, the image of Typhon appears so powerful that only another image can match it. Hyperbius and Hippomedon are each subordinate to their tutelary devices. The devices, moreover, are almost separate from what they imitate: Zeus upon the shield, Eteocles implies, might prove to be Zeus Sotêr (520). The Chorus reinforce this implication when they sing the antistrophe (521–525). They trust that the bearer of Zeus' adversary, which is at once the malign body (δέμας) of a chthonic god and an image (εἴκασμα) hateful to gods and men, will lose his life before the gates. It is Typhon's image that gods and men abhor, it is his body that Hippomedon carries before him. Only in the Septem is δέμας applied to an image (again at 542), for its adverbial and periphrastic use is quite different, neither of which Aeschylus in fact employs.[4] What confirms that the Chorus, like Eteocles, are gradually endowing the images with a life of their own, is the way in which the spy refers to Hippomedon. He is Ἱππομέδοντος σχῆμα καὶ μέγας τύπος (488), which, context aside, could literally be "the tall figure and statue of Hippomedon". Hippomedon loses a reality that Typhon gains. None of these turns of phrase by itself is conclusive, but their cumulative effect points to their literal meaning as overshadowing their less precise and figurative sense.

The third and fourth devices, along with the men who bear them, seem to form as close a unit as the first and second had. Eteoclus' hoplite is clearly opposed to Capaneus' unprotected man, and we no longer have to do with interpretations of the cosmos but with the city, for the city now first appears in an image, whereas before it was only present in words (πρήσω πόλιν). The city replaces the sky, just as Eteoclus' boast about Ares replaces Capaneus' boast about Zeus.[5] The gods, however, are still in speech and not until the central episode are they manifest. They then show themselves as of two kinds, chthonic and Olympian. What was a contest between naked man and the sky (Capaneus) becomes a contest between the old and the new gods. Both Tydeus and Zeus are armed with fire, but only Zeus is of human shape, for Typhon had a hundred snake heads (Hes. Th. 824/25; cf. P. V. 353). We do not know what shape, if any, Capaneus and Eteocles would have before attributed to Zeus, as neither mentions any human or non-human trait.[6] Eteocles then trusted that the "fire-bearing lightning" would strike Capaneus, but now it is a Zeus who sits erect (σταδαῖος ἧσται) that makes a missile flash in his hand

---

[4]Eum. 84 is not, as the whole scene makes plain, a periphrasis. Cf. Eur. Alc. 348/49 for a contrast between δέμας and εἴκασμα: σοφῇ δὲ χειρὶ τεκτόνων δέμας τὸ σὸν εἰκασθέν; also 1063.

[5]ἅλω δὲ πολλήν, ἀσπίδος κύκλον λέγω (488) shows how much what Tydeus' insigne depicted has been suppressed. ἅλως strictly means the disk of sun or moon (Hesych. s. v), and the genitive substantive with κύκλος elsewhere in Aeschylus is the sun (PV 91, Pers. 504), as it usually is in Herodotus, Sophocles, and Euripides (or some other celestial phenomenon).

[6]On the total identification of Zeus with lightning, see H. Usener, RhM 60, 1905, 1–30 (= Kl. Schriften, IV, 471–497).

(διὰ χερὸς βέλος φλέγων). Function and being are now distinct: Zeus is no longer expected to hurl the thunderbolt.[7] The emergence of Zeus as an anthropomorphic god accompanies the "psychologization" of Ares, who now is embodied in Hippomedon (497), that is, Ares too has become anthropomorphic. Ares' incarnation was anticipated by Eteoclus' boast that not even Ares could cast him from the ramparts, as though Ares were a soldier on the side of Thebes. Ares still remains a soldier when he appears as Hippomedon, but he never again is a Theban (910, 945). He becomes impartial and universal as he becomes "human". We had seen before, in comparing the parodos with the first stasimon, that the Chorus, once forbidden to adore the statues of the gods, cease to pray to them by name, and their fear, apparently because of this, becomes more deeply settled within them. Now, however, we have a counter movement. Ares and Zeus are once more visible, Ares in the guise of Hippomedon, Zeus in a human image, and even fear is drawn out of the heart and becomes, at least in speech, visible as well (500). What further distinguishes the third and fourth layers from the first and second is the greater agreement between Argives and Thebans. The first two layers could bear a double interpretation, the third and fourth seem to point to a single meaning. Not only does Eteocles have to resist Hippomedon's emblem with another one, but he has to resist it on its own terms. He no longer indulges in transformations of the literal into the metaphoric and vice-versa, nor has he transferred an adjective from the enemy's device to his own hopes (πυρφόρος). He now admits that the area of conflict is the city and its gods. The gods of the city are either of the earth or of the sky, either Gê, to whom Eteocles originally prayed (70), or Athena and Zeus. Eteocles had at first trusted Earth and her descendants (Melanippus and Megareus) to be the main bulwark against the Argive invaders; but Hippomedon's image of Typhon, whose snake-heads inevitably remind us of the serpent's teeth from which the Spartoi sprang, forces Eteocles to abandon Earth to the enemy—Capaneus is a Giant (424)—and rely solely on the Olympian gods. Eteocles purifies as he restricts the basis on which the city stands. Thus the war which began as a war between two cities becomes a war within a single city between its two principles. These two principles, which first appear as far apart as Typhon and Zeus, turn out in the end to be related. Eteocles and Polynices, the offspring of an incestuous union between mother and son, mutually destroy themselves.

Parthenopaeus carries the image of the Sphinx, the solution to whose riddle was man, Parthenopaeus who swears by his spear, in which he reverentially puts more trust than in any god, that he will sack Thebes in spite of Zeus (529–532). All seven attackers had jointly sworn by Ares, Enyô, and Phobos

---

[7]Cf. Wilamowitz, Herakles, vol. I, 371.

either to sack the city of the Cadmeans despite the Cadmeans or to die in the attempt (45–48); but now Parthenopaeus drops the alternative of possible defeat, swears by his own power, and extends the war to include the gods. The war becomes more openly theological—Hippomedon had been silent—as it comes closer to being fratricidal. Amphiaraus will soon predict his own conversion into a Theban oracle (587/88), and Parthenopaeus now carries an image which, though inimical to the Thebans, is not alien, as Typhon was, to them. The body (δέμας) of the Sphinx in high relief (ἔκκρουστον) tramples a Theban underfoot, "so that most spears are cast against this man" (539–544). ἐπ' ἀνδρὶ τῷδε is more simply related to the sculpted Theban than to Parthenopaeus, as if the image were the more important to the defense of Thebes. Perhaps, however, the ambiguity is deliberate, and ἐπ' ἀνδρὶ τῷδε means either image or image-bearer depending on the interpreter. Eteocles, at any rate, sees the greater threat in the Sphinx. Aktor, he says, will not allow this beast to enter ἔξωθεν εἴσω—a phrase exactly describing the internalization of the war (cf. 200/01)—, but the Sphinx, overwhelmed by blows beneath the city's walls, will reproach her bearer (556–561, with 559 deleted).[8] The Sphinx lives. She tries to enter the city under her own power and, when foiled, will speak. The Sphinx is in such high relief that she seems to be not wholly nailed down.[9] If the images of Typhon and Zeus overshadowed their bearers, they still had not yet become so animate that they moved and spoke (cf. 556/57). Eteocles considers the Sphinx to constitute a present danger to Thebes. He does not argue that as Zeus conquered Typhon, so Oedipus conquered the Sphinx, and hence the emblem augurs as well for Aktor as Hippomedon's emblem did for Aktor's brother Hyperbius (555). The Sphinx has to be destroyed again. Her destruction by a mere mortal no longer suffices. Whether the mention of Oedipus would have reminded Eteocles of his father's curse, or the Sphinx as an image has lost none of its terror (cf. 563–565)—the satyr-play was devoted to her—, Eteocles has so far entered into the world of signs that from now on signs alone will seem real to him. The image finally usurps the place of the thing imaged.[10]

---

[8]Cf. Fraenkel, op. cit., 40–1; Erbse, op. cit., 13–15.

[9]Cf. Eustath. Comment. ad Hom. Il. 1160, 49–50, cited by Hermann.

[10]Something similar occurs in Agamemnon. The Chorus in the parodos describe the omen that occurred to the Achaeans at Aulis, Calchas' interpretation of it, and Agamemnon's sacrifice of his daughter, but they omit Agamemnon's transgression. They slide from the sign of the transgression to its consequence, and hence suppress the justice of Agamemnon's punishment: Artemis is ἁ καλά, not ἁ δικαία (140). The sign entirely replaces that of which it is a sign and seems a sufficient cause in itself to compel Agamemnon's sacrifice. The theme of the Oresteia, therefore, is the bringing out into

After the appearance of the anthropomorphic Zeus, the spy tells Eteocles that the fifth attacker is the beautiful Parthenopaeus, whose savage spirit belies his name (536/37). Neither his beauty nor his name reveals the truth about him. Appearances are deceptive, and their meaning cannot be directly read. Parthenopaeus undermines the basis of Eteocles' previous interpretations, for if seeming is unconnected with being, there is no way of knowing the true significance of the shields. Parthenopaeus thus prepares for the soothsayer Amphiaraus as the sixth attacker, whose shield bears no device, οὐ γὰρ δοκεῖν ἄριστος, ἀλλ᾽ εἶναι θέλει (592). It might seem, then, that Amphiaraus' refusal to carry a device would have the effect of shifting the play from δοκεῖν to εἶναι. We should now be done with illusion once the bare truth has been revealed. But Amphiaraus' truth in fact confirms the assimilation of δοκεῖν to εἶναι, so that the two become indistinguishable. δόκος δ᾽ ἐπὶ πᾶσι τέτυκται. Eteocles had begun with a contrast, though he seems unaware of it, between the soothsayer Tiresias and himself. He must manage the tiller (οἴακα νωμῶν) of the ship of state with his eyes open and awake (βλέφαρα μὴ κοιμῶν ὕπνῳ, 3), but the blind Tiresias manages with his ears and wits (ἐν ὠσὶ νωμῶν καὶ φρεσίν) birds of augury (25/26). The conclusions of each seem appropriate to their trust in either sight or hearing. Tiresias, in spite of Eteocles' elaborate praise (24–27), can only report that the Argives have held a nocturnal council and will attack the city (28/29); while Eteocles has sent out scouts and spies (36–39), one of whom soon returns to report on the exact dispositions of the enemy. And yet Eteocles ends up by accepting as true the visions that came to him when asleep (709–711). What prepared the way for his acceptance has been the insignia of the enemy and his interpretation of them, which paradoxically find their culmination in Amphiaraus' empty shield. Amphiaraus inter-

---

the open of τὸ δίκαιον, which must remain latent as long as Zeus is Ζεὺς ὅστις ποτ᾽ ἐστίν (160). This progressive revelation of justice is indicated by the use of δίκην (meaning, "just like"), which occurs some 24 times in the trilogy, but in its last occurrence appears close to οἱ δίκαιοι (Eum. 911/12). Another example of the coalescence of the sign and the thing signified is in Choephoroe, where Orestes begins a prayer to Zeus by comparing Electra and himself to eaglets abandoned by their father, and then turns the metaphor of eagles into the implied proportion: as the race of eagles, once destroyed, will no longer send signs to mortals, so Zeus will no longer be appeased with sacrifices, if he destroys Orestes and Electra (246–261). It is through the comparison that Orestes tries to make himself and his sister indispensable to Zeus; cf. Wilamowitz, Orestie (Berlin, 1896), 179–180. What makes perhaps this merging of sign and thing signified more understandable is the manner in which Electra has just recognized Orestes.

prets Polynices' name to mean exactly what it says (576–578, cf. 658). The counter example of Parthenopaeus has no weight for either him or Eteocles. Seeming is being and being seeming, for Amphiaraus, in predicting his own death and the failure of the expedition as a whole (580–589, 609–619), testifies to the truth of Eteocles' interpretations. What up to now had been only likely become inevitable meanings. Signs have become fates. The arbitrary order in which the attackers appeared—they obtained their posts by lot (55, 126)—became necessary once Eteocles decided to match the Theban champions in light of his own interpretations of the Argive shields; and whatever degree of freedom he had in matching them before Hippomedon, disappears as soon as he believes it fitting that the image of Typhon should be opposed to that of Zeus.[11] That confrontation thrusts Eteocles into a world where gods as the representatives of men impose a compulsion on them (cf. 719), and which, confirmed by Amphiaraus as true (cf. 562), prevents Eteocles from later distinguishing his own will from the gods'. Amphiaraus' acceptance of his prophesied death becomes the model for Eteocles' own acceptance. What the Chorus call his ἔρως and ἵμερος, he calls a god and a father's curse (686–697). Not that what he says is false and what the Chorus say true, but that anthropomorphic gods "are" as much inside (ἔνθεος Ἄρει) as outside a man (Ζεὺς σταδαῖος ἧσται). They are as much to be seen in statues as sensed in the heart (592–594). They are as much of the body as of the soul.[12]

---

[11]I have tried to formulate this in such a way that it includes both those Thebans who already have their posts and those Eteocles assigns on the spot; for Eteocles himself does not make a distinction, as far as the suitability of the matching goes, between the two cases; cf. 472/3; Wilamowitz, Interpretationen, 76/7; Fraenkel, op. cit., 30–32; Erbse, op. cit., 1–9. τύχη and its compounds occur 13 times, all between 333 and 633, i.e., mostly in the interval of the seven pairs of speeches. The Septem is the only play of Aeschylus where ἀνάγκη never occurs, though βία in all senses is most frequent (cf. 1033, 1042); consider the unique χάρις at 703.

[12]Cf. K. Reinhardt, Aischylos als Regisseur und Theologe (Bonn, 1949), 123. After the Chorus' mention of the heart in the first stasimon, neither it nor θυμός, λῆ6μα, νοῦς, ὀργή, φρήν, and ψυχή (plus their positive compounds) occur again until 448 where Eteocles uses λῆμα to describe Polyphontes, 484 where the Chorus use the phrase μαινομένα φρήν just before the description of Hippomedon, and 507 where Eteocles uses θυμός to describe Hyperbius; but they occur often from Amphiaraus on (some 24 times), reaching their culmination in Antigone's address to her own soul at 1034 (unique in the play, through ἀψυχία and ἄψυχος occur thrice, 192, 259, 383); but see Lloyd-Jones, op. cit., 109–110. Connected perhaps with this in the absence of θεός between 772 and 1016, the lamentations of Antigone, Ismene, and the Chorus,

Eteocles and the Argive champions between them have reestablished the presence of the gods that Eteocles had at the start ordered the Chorus to forsake; but their reappearance is no longer solely as statues. They are now vividly present as defenders and attackers (Zeus and Typhon), who only have to move and speak to become the principals in the war. It is the work of Polynices' shield.[13] His emblem is twofold: a woman soberly leads an armed warrior, "and she claims to be Dikê, as the letters say: 'I shall bring back this man from exile, and he shall occupy his ancestral city and home'" (644-648; cf. Her. I. 60. 3-5). For the first time we have a god who speaks and moves. Eteocles had to attribute motion and speech to the Sphinx, which by itself needed its bearer to approach the city; but now the scene is so complete in itself that ἄνδρα τόνδε refers at once to Polynices and his double on the shield. The phrase is not ambiguous as it was on Parthenopaeus' shield (549), whose interpretation depended on the interpreter. Here it means the same person regardless of whether the image or the imaged is meant. On Tydeus' shield there was no man, on Capaneus' a man who could not be Capaneus, but on Eteoclus' shield Eteoclus himself was shown, though he still remained distinct from his image. On Hippomedon's shield, in turn, a god was shown, whose relation to his bearer had to be supplied; and on Parthenopaeus' shield, though its meaning is unmistakable, Parthenopaeus himself does not appear—only the image and not the image-bearer belongs to Thebes; but now god and man come together in a single image, and their relation to the city is completely spelled out. The ultimate manifestation of the gods among men is the ἐνέργεια, the being-at-work, of the anthropomorphic goddess Justice. And Eteocles accepts it as it shows itself. He does not have to discover or bring out a latent meaning in it. "If the daughter of Zeus, the maiden Dikê," he says, "were present in his deeds and wits, then perhaps this [what the letters say] would be" (662/63). He does not distinguish between the image of Dikê and Dikê herself, but only claims that if Dikê backs Polynices, she is falsely named (671/72); but that of course does not differ from Polynices' claim. It is no longer two gods of different principles but one and the same god whom both sides lay claim to. The dual origin of the city is nothing but the duality of justice and the city, whose coincidence Eteocles affirms, Polynices denies, and Antigone

---

though it occurs some 62 times before the lamentations and four times after them. Curiously enough, δαίμων occurs in that gap five out of its 13 occurrences (six times before 236); and δυσδαίμων, δαιμονάω, δαιμόνιος are only to be found there. Ares, in all of Aeschylus, is the only Olympian god called a δαίμων, Septem, 106; cf. W. Kranz, Stasimon, 48, 279 n. to bottom of 47.

[13]Cf. T. G. Rosenmeyer, The Masks of Tragedy (Austin, Texas, 1963), 37.

questions: πόλις ἄλλως ἄλλοτ' ἐπαινεῖ τὰ δίκαια (1070/71).[14] It is this
duality which Antigone calls ὑστάτη θεῶν (1051).

The action in these seven pairs of speeches consists in the interaction
between the effect each shield has on Eteocles' interpretation and the effect
each interpretation of Eteocles has on the succeeding shield. Eteocles' interpretations are so evocative that they transform the discrete series of: the first
shield, its interpretation, and Theban champion: the second shield, its interpretation, and Theban champion: and so on, into an unbroken succession of:
the first shield and hence its interpretation and hence Theban champion and
hence the next shield and hence the next interpretation and hence the next
Theban champion, and so on. Eteocles becomes so gripped by the images he
hears about and so much enters into their spirit that he seems capable of sum-
moning the next image through his interpretation of the previous image. He no
sooner opposes Zeus to Typhon than Parthenopaeus challenges Zeus. Eteocles
is a citizen of Plato's cave, whose chained inhabitants compete for prizes in
divining the sequence of shadows cast on the wall. It is the consistency of
image and interpretation when put together and in order that constitutes the
compulsion in Eteocles' choice. His serendipity proves to be his fate.

---

[14]Earth, which at first is identified with the city (16, 74), is gradually
made more and more distinct from the city (cf. 522), until it simply becomes
the earth on which Eteocles and Polynices shed their blood and in which they
will be buried (939, 950, 1002, cf. 585–588), only to be reidentified with the
city at the end (1007, 1008, 1015). Antigone, in her exchange with the herald,
though she mentions burial often enough, never mentions earth or dust; cf.
Lloyd-Jones, op. cit., on 1039, 97–99.